Approaches to
Old Testament Interpretation

Apollos

The first edition of this book was dedicated
'to Ann, Steven, and Mark, who described what kind of day
it had been, cleaned out hamsters, and ate cheese
sandwiches all around me without putting me off (much),
and who make home a place that is neither boring nor
without love'. The hamster-owner is now a systems
analyst (and anyway the hamster eventually got terminally
lost), the sandwich-maker now makes pizzas within
delivery area of the publisher's book warehouse
in Nottingham, and even my wife claims that she doesn't
describe what kind of day it has been (and, indeed,
never did). The book is still dedicated to them all, with love.

I am also glad to re-express my gratitude
to colleagues and friends whose comments have contributed
insights to this book or eliminated howlers from it, and
in particular for the friendship of my Old Testament
colleagues at St John's College, Nottingham, Edward Ball and
Gillian Muddiman; to the staff of the college library,
of the University of Nottingham library, and of the college
bookshop, for going out of their way to obtain material
for me; to Janet Gillard, Ros Harding, Joyce Tomkinson,
Sue Elkins, and Karin Thut, for their typing skills; and to Eric
Clapton, Van Morrison, and Bruce Springsteen, for
helping me wind down to a good night's sleep after an
evening's cerebration for APOLLOS, the new Inter-Varsity
Press imprint in England.

APPROACHES
TO
OLD TESTAMENT
INTERPRETATION

John Goldingay

Inter-Varsity Press
Downers Grove, Illinois, U.S.A.

InterVarsity Press
P.O. Box 1400, Downers Grove, Illinois 60515, U.S.A.

Published in the United States of America by InterVarsity Press, Downers Grove,
Illinois, with permission from Universities and Colleges Christian Fellowship,
Leicester, England.

InterVarsity Press is the book-publishing division of InterVarsity Christian Fellowship, a student movement active on campus at hundreds of universities, colleges and
schools of nursing in the United States of America, and a member movement of the
International Fellowship of Evangelical Students. For information about local and
regional activities, write Public Relations Dept., InterVarsity Christian Fellowship,
6400 Schroeder Rd., P.O. Box 7895, Madison, WI 53707-7895.

Distributed in Canada through InterVarsity Press, 860 Denison St., Unit 3, Mark-
ham, Ontario L3R 4H1, Canada.

ISBN 0-8308-1303-9

Printed in Great Britain

Library of Congress Cataloging-in-Publication Data
Goldingay, John
    Approaches to Old Testament interpretation/John Goldingay.—Rev. ed.
    p.   cm.
    Includes bibliographical references and index.
    ISBN 0-8308-1303-9
    1. Bible. O.T.—Criticism, interpretation, etc.—History—20th century. 2. Bible.
O.T.—Theology—History—20th century. 3 Bible. O.T.—Hermeneutics. 4. Bible.
O.T.—Criticism, interpretation, etc.—Bibliography. 5. Bible. O.T.—Theology—
Bibliography. 6. Bible. O.T.—Hermeneutics—Bibliography.
I. Title.
BS1160.G58   1990
221.6'01—dc20
                                                                    90-37126
                                                                        CIP

15 14 13 12 11 10 9 8 7 6 5 4 3 2 1
99 98 97 96 95 94 93 92 91 90

Preface

This book began life as a contribution to a series studying 'Issues in Contemporary Theology'; for this new edition I am grateful for the opportunity to write an extra chapter covering developments during the past decade (and to correct a few slips). I have tried to take some of the issues further in *Theological Diversity and the Authority of the Old Testament* (Grand Rapids: Eerdmans, 1987), but I am glad to be able here to bring the survey itself up to date.

It seems entirely appropriate that it now appears under the 'Apollos' imprint in England. Apollos was a man who brought together a knowledge of the Hebrew scriptures, a background in the foremost centre of intellectual learning in the Mediterranean world, and in due course a commitment to Jesus as the Christ. If this survey of approaches to the interpretation of those Hebrew scriptures helps people to bring together their own immersion in the 'First Testament', their study of the scholarship of our own day, and their personal knowledge of Christ, I shall be more than satisfied.

Contents

References

The main bibliography is on pages 156 to 188; the supplementary bibliography, on pages 200 to 204, lists those books referred to in the Postscript by the symbol †.

The footnotes to each page give only abbreviated bibliographical information. Some more important books are referred to by the author's name plus an asterisk (*e.g.* *Anderson), other books by a short title (*e.g.* Banks, *Jesus and the Law*), *Festschriften etc.* by the person to whom the volume is dedicated (*e.g.* G. E. Wright volume), articles by the number and date of the issue (*e.g. JTS* 25 [1974]); in the bibliography the item will be found under the name of the author of the article or book. Where a volume has appeared in several editions, I have used the most recent British one listed.

The abbreviations used for reference works and journals are as follows:

ALUOS	*Annual of the Leeds University Oriental Society*
ASTI	*Annual of the Swedish Theological Institute*
ATR	*Anglican Theological Review*
AUSS	*Andrews University Seminary Studies*
BA	*Biblical Archaeologist*
Bib	*Biblica*
BibRes	*Biblical Research*
BJRL	*Bulletin of the John Rylands Library*
BKAT	*Biblischer Kommentar Altes Testament* (Neukirchen: Neukirchener Verlag)
BSOAS	*Bulletin of the School of Oriental and African Studies*
BTB	*Biblical Theology Bulletin*
BZAW	*Beiheft, Zeitschrift für die alttestamentliche Wissenschaft*
CBQ	*Catholic Biblical Quarterly*

CHB 1	*The Cambridge History of the Bible* 1 (ed. P. R. Ackroyd and C. F. Evans; Cambridge/New York: CUP, 1970)
cf.	compare
CTJ	*Calvin Theological Journal*
DBS	*Dictionnaire de la Bible*, Supplement, 1928–
EQ	*Evangelical Quarterly*
ET	English translation
EvT	*Evangelische Theologie*
ExpT	*Expository Times*
HBT	*Horizons in Biblical Theology*
HJ	*Hibbert Journal*
HTR	*Harvard Theological Review*
HUCA	*Hebrew Union College Annual*
IDB	G. A. Buttrick *et al.* (eds.), *The Interpreter's Dictionary of the Bible*, 4 vols., 1962
IDBS	*IDB*, Supplementary vol., 1976
Int	*Interpretation*
JBL	*Journal of Biblical Literature*
JBR	*Journal of Bible and Religion*
JJS	*Journal of Jewish Studies*
JR	*Journal of Religion*
JSJ	*Journal for the Study of Judaism*
JSOT	*Journal for the Study of the Old Testament*
JSS	*Journal of Semitic Studies*
JTS	*Journal of Theological Studies*
KD	*Kerygma und Dogma*
LQHR	*London Quarterly and Holborn Review*
LT	*Literature and Theology*
NovT	*Novum Testamentum*
NTS	*New Testament Studies*
OBT	Overtures to Biblical Theology (Philadelphia: Fortress)
OTS	*Oudtestamentische Studiën*
RB	*Revue biblique*
RelS	*Religious Studies*
RHPR	*Revue d'histoire et de philosophie religieuses*
RHR	*Revue de l'histoire des religions*
RQ	*Revue de Qumran*
RTP	*Revue de théologie et de philosophie*
SJT	*Scottish Journal of Theology*
ST	*Studia Theologica*

TDNT	G. Kittel and G. Friedrich (ed.), *Theologisches Wörter-buch zum Neuen Testament*, 1932–74; ET *Theological Dictionary of the New Testament*, ed. G. W. Bromiley, 10 vols., 1964–76
TDOT	G. J. Botterweck and H. Ringgren (ed.), *Theologisches Wörterbuch zum Alten Testament*, 1970– ; ET *Theological Dictionary of the Old Testament*, trans. by J. T. Willis, 1974–
ThL	*Theologische Literaturzeitung*
TR	*Theologische Rundschau*
TSFB	*Theological Students' Fellowship Bulletin*
TynB	*Tyndale Bulletin*
TZ	*Theologische Zeitschrift*
VT	*Vetus Testamentum*
VT Supp.	*Vetus Testamentum*, Supplementary vol.
WD	*Wort und Dogma*
WTJ	*Westminster Theological Journal*
ZAW	*Zeitschrift für die alttestamentliche Wissenschaft*
ZNW	*Zeitschrift für die neutestamentliche Wissenschaft*
ZTK	*Zeitschrift für Theologie und Kirche*

Introduction

This book is concerned with how we are to understand and appropriate the significance of the OT within the Christian Church in the modern world. Its aim is not so much to propound a particular approach to interpreting the OT as to survey the various approaches that have jostled with each other in the world of western scholarship over the past twenty or thirty years.

When I was asked to write a volume on this subject, I was tempted to wonder whether the interpretation of the OT, absorbing though I find it myself, was now an 'issue in contemporary theology' in the way it had been at the beginning of this period. But whether consciously seen to be so or not, it remains a key theological question. Indeed, *A. H. J. Gunneweg opens his survey of the subject by claiming that 'it would be no exaggeration to understand the hermeneutical problem of the Old Testament as *the* problem of Christian theology, . . . seeing that all the other questions of theology are affected in one way or another by its resolution'.[1]

The chapters that follow interweave consideration of the OT's status with consideration of how the OT is to be interpreted. The two questions are interrelated, and different answers to the second question often reflect different approaches to the first.[2] The issues involved in this first question are encapsulated in the title Christians give to this collection of Jewish writings. It is the 'Old Testament'. That title presupposes the conviction, shared with Jews, that these

---

[1]*Gunneweg, p. 2. *Cf.* *van Ruler, p. 10: our whole understanding of the Christian faith is determined by our attitude to the OT. This is vividly illustrated by the OT's use in recent political and liberation theology: I have discussed these issues in 'The hermeneutics of liberation theology', *HBT* 4/2 (1982), pp. 133–161.

[2]*Cf.* Gunneweg, pp. 1–3, 20; Rössler, von Rad volume, on the ways these various approaches then affect preaching.

Jewish writings belong together and are to be set off over against others from the pre-Christian period as having canonical status. They count as Scripture.

But why should we assume that they have this status? In his book on *Marcion*, Adolf von Harnack remarked in words that are often quoted, 'discarding the Old Testament in the second century [as Marcion did] was an error which the Church rightly rejected. Holding on to it in the sixteenth century was a fate which the Reformation could not yet escape. But still preserving it as a canonical document within Protestantism after the nineteenth century is the result of religious and ecclesiastical paralysis.'[3]

Harnack was no doubt right that the force of ecclesiastical tradition would not have allowed the formal abandonment of the OT, no matter how nominal the church's commitment to it had become. What, however, led to its becoming part of the equipment that has accompanied the church on its journey? The answer is not that social and political factors of the period long after Christ caused the Church to drift in this direction, as happened in the development of the church's structure of ministry. The OT (or, as it was then, simply 'the scriptures') belonged to Christianity from the beginning. The Jewish scriptures had an integral place in the faith of Jesus and of the Christians of the early church.

Now early Christianity is not a book religion in the sense that contemporary Judaism was. Significantly, the early Christian writings include no consecutive biblical (*i.e.* OT) commentary work such as other Jews were producing in Jerusalem, in Alexandria, at Qumran, and elsewhere. The agenda for early Christian theology centred on Christ himself. This was in keeping with his own explicit claims. He was not like the scribes, who dared not think an original thought and confined themselves to discussing the possible contemporary ramifications of the given law. He spoke 'with authority', manifesting a startling originality, freshness, and freedom. His life and deeds ultimately challenged people to acknowledge *him* as the revelation of God. He 'set himself above' the Jewish scriptures.[4]

Neither Jesus nor the NT writers regarded these scriptures as God's last word. Sometimes the commands of Christ are more searching than those of the OT, sometimes the OT laws are set aside in the NT.

[3] ET from *Marcion*, p. 217.
[4] J. W. Wenham, *Christ and the Bible*, p. 32.

But they still accepted the scriptures as God's first word as whole-heartedly as other Jews did. Commenting on one of his own OT quotations, Paul declares that 'whatever was written in former days was written for our instruction, that by steadfastness and by the encouragement of the scriptures we might have hope' (Rom. 15:4). The NT as a whole reflects that conviction. It would be an exaggeration to say that there are direct allusions to the scriptures on every page of the NT, but it would not be a gross exaggeration. Actual citations[5] are only the tip of the iceberg of the OT's influence on the NT; the latter's interests, themes, questions, and presuppositions are determined or influenced by the former on a much broader scale than mere quotation or concrete allusion indicates. While Jesus is the key to understanding the scriptures, they provide the context and concepts for understanding him.[6]

This feature of the NT also corresponds to Jesus' own attitude. While Matthew particularly emphasizes the way Jesus' life and teaching reflect the scriptures, this theme features throughout the gospels and appears clearly in what is usually regarded as the oldest material, in Mark and Q. Thus at his baptism (Mk. 1:11) the voice from heaven describes his role in terms that come from the Psalms and Isaiah. In the wilderness, he responds to temptation with words from Deuteronomy: 'It is written . . . ' (Mt. 4:1–11). Asked a question by some Jews, he invites them to discuss the matter on the basis of the Torah (Mk. 10:2–9). Challenged by John the Baptist regarding his status, he offers a catena of Isaianic phrases to describe the role of the coming one (Mt. 11:2–6). Looking forward, he finds the pattern for his calling, including the cross, in the scriptures (Mk. 8:31; 9:30–31). On the cross, he expresses his anguish in the words of a psalm (Mk. 15:34). But the influence of the Jewish scriptures extended far beyond specific quotations, as is the case with the rest of the NT. They 'constituted Jesus' frame of reference

---

[5] According to Shires (*Finding the OT in the New*, p. 15), there are 1604 of these in the NT.

[6] *Cf.* Borgen, *NTS* 23 (1976–7), pp. 70, 71–73. Bultmann (in *Anderson, p. 34) suggests that the OT is used only when it is natural to the proclaimer and the hearers (*cf.* Harnack, *Sitzungsberichte der Preussischen Akademie 1928*; Braun, *ZTK* 59 [1962]). But only a handful of short NT documents make little reference to the OT. Bultmann includes John in this category (*cf.* *Gunneweg, p. 143), whereas *Amsler's comment (p. 34) that John is steeped in Scripture seems more accurate. *Amsler (pp. 9–10) notes that the OT's influence includes Luke, a Gentile writing to Gentiles.

as well as being a source for direct reference':[7] they provide the overall shape of his faith.

It is difficult to give appropriate emphasis both to the importance within the NT of the gospel as the proclaimed word of God and of Jesus as the incarnate word of God, and to that of the scriptures as the written word of God handed down from the past.[8] The NT itself holds these together with less unease than has often been felt since. Aware of standing in a new era of God's activity in Jesus Christ, it yet assumes that 'we receive the Old Testament from the hands of Jesus Christ' and interpret it by him and him by it.[9]

Admittedly to speak of receiving the 'Old Testament' from Christ is an anachronistic way to make the point. The title 'the Old Testament' presupposes the existence of a New Testament and was devised well after Christ.[10] Thus it is not one that Christians share with Jews, who refer to their scriptures as 'the Torah, the Prophets, and the Writings'. The Christian title reminds us that the producing of these two collections is separated by what Christians regard as that climactic event of all history through which the old covenant/testament was replaced by a new one.

So how do Christians interpret the OT after the coming of Christ? What significance do the canonical Hebrew scriptures have the other side of this event? It has long been a temptation to look for one central category that will express the relationship of OT and NT, and for one hermeneutical approach that will enable us to interpret the OT. But the NT writers had various ways of relating the OT to themselves. Their own example suggests that we ourselves would be mistaken to look for one key to Christian interpretation of the OT.[11]

In this book I have categorized these approaches in five ways. Each has seemed in some circle *the* way to understand the OT. Each is certainly *a* way.

1. The OT may be seen as a faith: a set of beliefs about God and man. These actual beliefs are less explicit in the narrative books than they are in the prophets, psalms, or wisdom books. Nowhere are

[7] Borgen, p. 74.

[8] In *NTS* 23 (1976–7) Borgen emphasizes the latter, Lindars the former. See further the discussion in *von Campenhausen and *Hanson.

[9] Von Rad, *Genesis*, p. 41/[3] p. 43; *cf.* *von Rad II, p. 329; *G. A. F. Knight, p. 7.

[10] Further, the Hebrew canon may not have been precisely fixed by Jesus' day; see section 5c below.

[11] *Cf.* *Westermann, p. 11; *Barr, p. 134.

they expressed as analytically or systematically as we may wish to express them, but they are there. So how are these beliefs to be investigated, and how do they relate to those expressed in the NT?

2. The OT may be seen as a way of life: a corpus of guidance concerned with right behaviour. This concern is prominent in the laws, the prophets, and the wisdom writings. It may also be present elsewhere; for our way of life is not merely influenced by the commands we hear, but also by the stories we read, the beliefs we hold, and so on. But what is the significance of the OT's guidance, given that in Christ the people of God 'are not under law but under grace' (Rom. 6:14), and given the specificness, the diversity, and the limitations of the OT's guidance?

3. Half the OT comprises the story of God's dealings with Israel (and with the world and with individuals). What is the significance of this story? What is its relationship to the story the NT tells? What is its relationship to history as the historian investigates it?

4. The OT looks forward to events still to come, as well as back to events of the past. If the OT story comes to its climax in Christ, how far is there a hidden forward reference in the actual events of OT times? If there is, what difference does this make to the way we interpret these events? And when OT prophecy is explicitly forward-looking, what is it referring to?

5. One thing true of the whole OT is simply that it is a written text; that is the most basic feature of Scripture. Even in OT times there began to be references back to earlier writings, and then there is substantial interpretative work from the NT period. But when did the OT become 'canon' and what difference does this make to its interpretation? Can we take up the NT's methods in interpreting OT texts?

All the approaches we shall consider are at least as old as the church itself. All of them have more recently been examined closely in the light of a modern instinct for a historical approach to Scripture. All of them (in my view) have a place in contemporary interpretation of the OT as we seek to answer the question, 'What does the Old Testament text in its historical meaning say to mankind living in the eschaton of Jesus Christ?'[12]

---

[12] Wolff in *Westermann, p. 190 (Wolff describes this as typology's specific concern).

Chapter One

The Old Testament as a faith

*I, I am Yahweh, and besides
me there is no saviour.*
                    (Is. 43:11)

*In many varied ways God
spoke to our fathers by the
prophets, but in these last
days he has spoken to us by
a Son.*   (Heb. 1:1–2)

We have noted in the introduction that the first Christians appropriated the Jewish Bible in the conviction that their faith was one
with its faith. This conviction they held to despite, or perhaps because of, their additional belief that Jesus was the messiah. Thus
these scriptures substantially shaped their idea of God, of man and
of how he related to God, and of the position and calling of the
people of God. The NT presupposes that OT and NT faith is fundamentally one, and that a NT faith is inevitably also an OT faith. OT
beliefs are not merely background to the NT (like the beliefs of
Qumran or those of the rabbis). They are part of what the NT itself
treats as theologically normative. We are thus affirming the attitude
the NT took when we ourselves appropriate the OT and make its
beliefs our own.[1]

One aid to our doing this is the study of OT theology. As it seeks
to re-conceptualize the OT's theological message, it can help us to
allow the OT to contribute effectively to our understanding of the
Christian faith. But how is it to go about this task?

Modern study of OT theology is but the most recent stage of a
discipline that has been active for some centuries, and the history of

---

[1] See, for instance, *Gunneweg, pp. 223–232; *Bright, pp. 112, 126–136;
*Eichrodt I, pp. 25–35; *Herberg, pp. 44–48.

this investigation has been frequently chronicled.[2] Two closely related questions that have concerned many scholars will be examined here. In section 1a we consider the aims and approach of the OT theologian: is his task objective, scientific, descriptive, or may he (even, should he) allow his personal involvement with the subject to influence his approach and aim?[3] The other question (see section 1b) concerns the unity of the OT. Its books come from various authors who lived in many different periods and have many different viewpoints. How can these be seen as one theology?

There are, of course, differences between OT and NT faith. The way the NT itself views the matter suggests that such differences have to be seen within the context of broad similarity, rather than vice versa,[4] but we have to acknowledge the differences and consider how we understand them theologically (see section 1c).

a. Old Testament theology: aims and approach

First, should study of OT theology aim to be objective and presuppositionless? This was the general ideal of scholarly study of the OT in the nineteenth and early twentieth centuries. It wanted to be strictly scientific and historical in approach. This led to advances in our understanding of the OT's origins and meaning, but it excluded the writing of OT theology because that seemed a subjective enterprise; scholars wrote histories of Israelite religion instead.[5]

Although OT study held to the ideal of being objective and free of presuppositions, in practice it was inevitably affected by the presuppositions of its day. Romanticism's idealizing of the unspoilt primitive, allied to an antipathy to cultic religion, appears in the negative attitude to cultic material, and to the later OT period and early

---

[2] E.g. by *Childs, *Dentan, *Harrington, *Harrison, *Hasel, *Kraeling, *Kraus, Porteous in OT and Modern Study, Reventlow in TZ 17 (1961) and JSOT 11 (1979), and Würthwein in TR 36 (1971).

[3] Cf. earlier Goldingay, TynB 26 (1975).

[4] Cf. Jacob, RHPR 46 (1966), p. 126; G. E. Wright in *Anderson, p. 178.

[5] Even in 1926 Eissfeldt (ZAW 44) urged that OT theology, as a subjective exercise based on faith's response to what it saw as God's revelation, had to be distinguished clearly from scientific study. Cf. Wernberg-Møller, HJ 59 (1960–1), p. 27.

Judaism, in some OT theologies.[6] Evolutionary views affected how scholars portrayed the 'unfolding development' of OT faith.[7] Rationalism encourages us to 'demythologize' statements, not because the text offers grounds for interpreting them symbolically, but because our worldview excludes the possibility of taking them literally.[8]

It is actually impossible to study without have one's own beliefs and framework of thinking, and being influenced by them. Indeed, we need some such framework if we are to make coherent sense of the data we examine. What is important is to be open to recognizing our presuppositions, and then to be prepared for the material we are studying to challenge them and to modify the perspective with which we approached it.[9]

It is, of course, always easier to see someone else's perspective vitiate his interpretation than to see the same process at work in one's own efforts. Thus one important reason for studying the work of those who start from a different perspective is to see whether there are elements in the material to which they are doing justice in a way one is not oneself.

For instance, one generation can sometimes see aspects of the truth of which another generation is unaware, and the study of biblical interpretation in earlier centuries can thus re-open our eyes to perspectives we would otherwise miss.[10] Jewish theology reminds us of the OT emphasis on the law as God's revelation and on Israel as God's people.[11] Contemporary political, economic, and social questions have drawn our attention to OT themes such as liberation

---

[6] *E.g.* *Köhler, p. 7; *cf.* the comments on *Eichrodt by Barr (*RTP* III.18 [1968]) and Gottwald (*ExpT* 74 [1962–3]). Gottwald (*JBL* 93 [1974], p. 594) also finds a 'personalistic idealism' behind *Fohrer's work, which is also negative in attitude to the law and the world of worship (and to the notion of a special relationship between Yahweh and Israel). See also R. J. Thompson's discussion of the presuppositions of Graf and Wellhausen in *VTSupp* 19, pp. 35–49.

[7] *Cf.* Rowley, *Re-discovery of the OT*, pp. 14, 18.

[8] *Cf.* *Smart's discussion (pp. 133–136) of the pillar of cloud and fire.

[9] *Cf.* Wildberger, *EvT* 19 (1959), pp. 73–80; *Smart's comments (pp. 97–98) on Bright; and Reventlow's (*JSOT* 11 [1979]), pp. 12–14) on Bultmann.

[10] *Cf.* *Childs, pp. 139–147, and his other works; *Clements, pp. 186–191; *G. A. F. Knight, p. 7, noting that his work is thus only '*a* theology of the Old Testament. *The* theology of the Old Testament will never be written. Each generation sees new vistas within the scriptures of which earlier generations were unaware'.

[11] See Borowitz, *HUCA* 40 (1969–70); also Neusner's works.

or the land.[12] A more phenomenological approach to worship in the ancient world led to a clearer positive theological appreciation of worship within the OT.[13] Critical study – namely, the investigation of OT tradition development – was what made von Rad aware of the theological importance of history in the OT.

All these approaches to the OT can help us to break out of the limitations imposed by presuppositions of which we are only half aware, and to find new points of entry into an appreciation of the theology of the OT.

What of the specifically Christian presuppositions of many OT theologians? If OT and NT are in fact one in faith, and the coming of Jesus is the climax of the purpose Yahweh was concerned with in OT times, it will not be unscientific to allow this link between the two Testaments to affect the way one presents the OT material.[14] Indeed, this may enable one to see what someone else might miss.[15] On the other hand, the fact that the emphases of OT and NT are not identical means that a Christian's investigation of OT theology may be in danger of underplaying distinctive OT themes such as the law, Israel, the land, and worship. There is thus a case even for Christian theologians trying to write 'as if the New Testament did not exist',[16] in order to do justice to the OT's theology as a whole.

Nineteenth century scholarship also sought to be objective in the sense of avoiding personal involvement in the subject. It was concerned with facts, not feelings, experiences or interpretation. Now OT faith is based on facts, and these need investigating objectively. But the faith itself is more than cold facts, and there is a limit to how far we can understand it by distancing ourselves from it. In any discipline the method of study must match the object of study. In order to understand a religious faith we have to cultivate an empathy with it that is willing to breathe its atmosphere and stand in the place

[12] Cf. Goldingay, TymB 27 (1976) and works cited there; Brueggemann, Land, pp. xii, 1–3 (on this theme see also Davies, Gospel and Land); Dumas, Political Theology.
[13] Cf. Mowinckel, Psalms I, p.15.
[14] See *Eichrodt, ch. 1 (also ZAW 47 [1929]); *Jacob, p. 12; *G. A. F. Knight, p. 7.
[15] Cf. *Porteous, p. 45; Seebass, WD 8 (1965), pp. 26–30.
[16] *McKenzie, p. 319; cf. *Fohrer, p. 29. *Zimmerli seems to have the same ideal.

of its adherents.[17] One strength of the 'diachronic'[18] or historical approach to OT theology is that it helps one to be empathetically involved in the moments of meeting between Yahweh and Israel which the theologian seeks to understand.

Does this mean that we can really understand OT faith only if we share in it ourselves?[19] Clearly we have a new form of understanding if we actually experience something, as is the case with understanding marriage or understanding depression. But if theology involves the kind of understanding which is impossible for those who do not share the faith they are studying, no Christian (nor, indeed, a modern Jew) can understand OT faith. In actual fact, one very valuable form of understanding is open to an empathetic student who suspends questions about the truth of what he is investigating. Faith goes beyond this kind of study, not as a further 'instrument of knowledge' but as 'the acceptance and existential appropriation of what has been understood'.[20]

But a believer does not pretend to be a non-believer when he studies the OT scientifically, and further a whole response to the OT cannot stop at uncommitted empathy. The material itself draws us on and asks us to commit ourselves to the God it presents. This takes us to a further sense in which we have to determine how far objectivity can be our goal in studying OT theology. Is the discipline to be confined to describing what OT faith was, or should it seek to prescribe what faith today should be?

If we accept the first of these alternatives as right, then OT theology has a close relationship to the study of Israelite religion. Both are descriptive tasks. The former studies what the OT implies should have been believed; the latter examines what Israelites actually did believe, and how they expressed their beliefs in worship.

On the other hand, given this understanding, the distinction between biblical and dogmatic theology is quite clear. Biblical theology

---

[17] Cf. *H. W. Robinson, pp. 281–282; *Dentan, pp. 114–116; Watson, ExpT 73 (1961–2), p. 200.

[18] Cf. Harvey, BTB 1 (1971); works such as *von Rad, *Voegelin, and Zimmerli's Man and His Hope in the OT illustrate the point made here.

[19] So *Porteous, pp. 23, 44–45; *G. A. F. Knight, p. 19/ [2] p. 20; cf. Childs, Int 18 (1964).

[20] *Gunneweg, p. 93. Crenshaw's Samson provides a recent example of the fruitfulness of 'suspending disbelief' and 'believing the story', as a means of understanding Judges 13–16 (see pp. 21–22).

aims to express the content of the biblical faith, its structure and its component parts in their dynamic interrelationship, in the Bible's own terms and according to its priorities. It is a descriptive study like Buddhist theology or Jewish theology. Dogmatic theology then has the task of going on to re-express the biblical faith in contemporary categories and of seeing how it interacts with the approaches, concerns, and assumptions of the contemporary world. It is dogmatic theology that expresses the theologian's own faith and seeks to help people appropriate the reality to which it refers.

The main argument for this approach is the slightly paradoxical one that only when the theologian is *not* concerned about the contemporary relevance of his study is he likely to do justice to the Bible itself. Otherwise, he will tend to read modern categories and interests back into the biblical material. Dogmatic theology has often imposed its own concerns on biblical study and hindered the Bible's own concerns and categories from emerging. Every theologian who has sought to assimilate biblical and dogmatic, or historical and theological, study (*e.g.* Aquinas, Barth, Bultmann) offers evidence of this point. Kept independent of systematics, biblical theology may be enabled to listen to the whole Bible.[21]

There are, however, problems involved in separating the two disciplines in this way. There is the risk that systematics, even if it wants to be Bible-based, may lose contact with scientific biblical study and thus with the Bible's own historical meaning, simply because the disciplines work independently.[22] There is also the complication that a concern to express what something means today can in fact contribute to a fuller historical understanding of it.[23]

But many OT theologians who argue for and practise the descrip-

[21] Cf. Stendahl, *IDB* 1, p. 421, also *Bible in Modern Scholarship*, pp. 205–207; *Nineham's comments on Barth, p. 263 (also *BJRL* 52 [1969], pp. 190–191); Morgan's discussion of Bultmann, *Nature of NT Theology*, pp. 33–62, and Wrede's own discussion of NT theology in Morgan, pp. 69, 75–84; de Vaux's (not critical) citing of Aquinas, *Bible and Ancient Near East*, pp. 61–62. It is this belief in distinguishing the disciplines that in part explains the odd fact that *von Rad, though seeing the OT as the story of what God has done and not the story of man's faith, actually writes a history of the human response to God rather than retelling God's story himself; while *Zimmerli, though seeing the OT as 'address', simply describes its contents instead of himself addressing the reader on God's behalf (*cf.* Reventlow, *JSOT* 11 [1979], p. 3).

[22] So *Childs, p. 79; contrast *Hasel, pp. 15–18/ [2] pp. 39–42.

[23] So *Ebeling, p. 330, and *Childs' observation (p. 96) that Barth's rediscovery of Romans arose out of his work as a pastor.

tive approach are actually concerned that their study should ultimately affect what we believe today. Their interest is not just scientific curiosity: they want to influence dogmatics. They have a dogmatic commitment, even if they are overtly scientific and historical.[24] The very fact that they concentrate on the books in the OT canon and pay much less attention to other pre-Christian Jewish writings reflects their dogmatic commitment.[25]

This shows that there may be a middle ground between the descriptive and the normative; the theologian's description of OT faith may be reckoned to be normative for today, though still needing re-statement in the light of NT insights and contemporary needs. As he seeks to enter sympathetically into the faith of an OT believer, the theologian may himself believe that the God this believer speaks of is also his God; or he may come to this belief as a result of his work. In the midst of it, then, he makes a response of faith in this God and associates himself with the stance of OT Israel. If he does this, his theology is still descriptive: he is seeking to appreciate what the faith was, not to re-state what might be its contemporary equivalent. Yet it is in another sense normative, since he is affirming that this was the true faith, which is thus the one that demands re-expressing today.[26]

Although this is a popular position, it has inherent problems. First, it may sacrifice the advantages of the purely descriptive position (namely, that the scholar is committed to distancing himself from the text) without securing the advantages of the normative approach (namely, that when he has written his OT theology we know what he thinks we should believe today on the basis of it).[27] If we regard the forms of OT faith as superseded (though then God-given), can we claim to have made a response of commitment to OT faith without having yet thought through its meaning for today?

Secondly, there are grounds for doubting whether the word 'theology' can really be applied to the contents of the OT. Admittedly it

[24] Cf. *Ebeling's comments, p. 89.
[25] Cf. Wrede's observations on NT theology, pp. 70–73, 101–103.
[26] This seems to be the position of writers such as *Bright (pp. 112–115, 141–143), *Vriezen (pp. 121–123/ ² pp. 147–150), *G. A. F. Knight (p. 7), *Jacob (p. 31 and elsewhere), *Porteous (p. 44), and Avery Dulles (Bible in Modern Scholarship, pp. 210–211, responding to Stendahl).
[27] Cf. Barr, Semantics, pp. 273–275.

is full of material which from our point of view invites explicating in the careful and clear way that theology adopts; and admittedly within the OT period Israelite faith becomes less a religion of rites and symbols and more a religion of a book, more amenable, therefore, to theological treatment. Nevertheless, precisely by explicating, articulating, and defining, the OT theologian is not merely describing OT faith; he is creating new concepts of God and the world through the interaction between what the OT actually says and what we bring to it.[28] So OT theology cannot be a purely descriptive discipline – it inherently involves the contemporary explication of the biblical material!

But the major grounds for maintaining that OT theology must prescribe what should be believed today, and not merely describe what was believed in the past, goes beyond this. It is that nothing short of the normative task really deserves the title theology. 'It is in the very nature of theology to concern itself with living faith, rather than with the history of ideas'. So the task of OT theology is to mediate between the religion of the OT and the religion we believe and practise today.[29]

Admittedly, distinctions such as those between descriptive and normative OT theology, like those between OT theology and the study of Israelite religion, may seem clearer in theory than they are in practice.[30] OT theologians profess a variety of standpoints,[31] but such theoretical differences do not seem in themselves to lead to markedly different results. All the approaches to study that we have been considering have their valid place, and usefully counter-balance each other. Objectivity, distancing and concentrating on the descriptive may help us to avoid imposing our present beliefs, interests, and questions on the text. But faith, involvement, and commitment may open us to other aspects of the text's own concerns and enable

---

[28] Cf. *Clements, pp. 2–3, 23, 155, 191; Kaufman, Essay on Theological Method, p. 33 (he instances Mary Douglas's Purity and Danger, with its treatment of Levitical law, as an example of explication of what is hardly perceived by the original writer); *Ebeling, pp. 93–94; Johnstone, SJT 22 (1969), pp. 206–207, on *Bright.

[29] *Clements, p. 20, also pp. 10, 155; cf. *Porteous, p. 37; Otto, Kairos 19 (1977), pp. 53, 67; Reventlow, JSOT 11 (1979), pp. 3–4. Childs in his various writings has worked particularly hard at the task of combining historical study with contemporary reflection, though more in seeking to interpret specific OT books or texts than in seeking to explicate themes of OT theology.

[30] Cf. Barr, JTS 25 (1974), pp. 275–278.

[31] E.g. *Eichrodt, *Vriezen, *McKenzie, *Clements.

us to avoid the barrenness of a cold 'objectivity'.

b. The form of an Old Testament theology

OT theology has traditionally worked with the same structure and framework as that commonly utilized by systematic theology: theology (Who is God?), anthropology (What is man?), and soteriology (How is the gulf between God and man bridged?).[32] This reflects biblical theology's origin as a handmaid to systematics.

But most recent OT theology has looked for a structure inherent in the biblical material itself, rather than one brought to it from elsewhere which might misconstrue its overall shape or miss aspects of it. Walther Eichrodt's work is the best known example. He took over an outline suggested by Otto Procksch, 'God and the people', 'God and the world', 'God and man'. He superimposed on this framework the motif of covenant, as enshrining Israel's most fundamental conviction, its sense of a unique relationship with God.[33] Furthermore, he attempted a thoroughgoing integration of theology and history, treating the different aspects of OT faith historically within his overall covenant scheme.[34]

Eichrodt's use of covenant as the key to organizing OT theology is open to various criticisms.[35] The covenant idea is not present throughout the OT (arguably it is mainly a Deuteronomistic interest).[36] Indeed in Eichrodt's own work it is really the framework only for Volume I. Nor is it very prominent in the NT,[37] even though it was central enough for the two parts of the Bible to take their name from it![38] Further, it is a term of various meanings. It has even been questioned whether Hebrew $b^c r\hat{\imath}\underline{t}$ (or Greek $diath\bar{e}k\bar{e}$) really means

---

[32] Cf. *Sellin; *Köhler, who defends it (p. 7) on the grounds that the OT has no scheme of its own and that this traditional one is simple enough not to 'obtrude'; *van Imschoot, p. 5; Jacob, Coppens volume, pp. 266–267.

[33] See *Eichrodt, especially I pp. 11–45; cf. the writings of Beauchamp, Fensham, Jocz, and Payne.

[34] Contrast *Sellin, who treats history and theology in separate volumes; cf. Eissfeldt's comments, ZAW 44 (1926).

[35] See especially *Spriggs.

[36] So Perlitt, *Bundestheologie*; response by McCarthy, *Biblica* 53 (1972); cf. Weinfeld, *Biblica* 56 (1975).

[37] Cf. Barr, *Weerwoord*, pp. 16–17.

[38] Cf. Clements, Torrance volume, p. 1.

'covenant',[39] though this English word is less open to objection than the equivalent German word *Bund* which rather suggests a mutual contract.[40]

Eichrodt forestalls some of this criticism by explaining that he does not always mean by covenant the relationship that Israel herself describes as a $b^e r\hat{\imath}\underline{t}$. Covenant is a general term for the relationship between Yahweh and Israel established by God's free act in history which makes Israel his unique people.[41] But the problem with the word covenant draws our attention to a difficulty which has received insufficient attention in OT study. As an analytic, formal discipline, OT theology needs to define terms clearly and relate these terms to each other. But when the OT writers themselves used terms such as covenant or kingdom, or spoke of God being one, or of Israel being Yahweh's people, they were using images or symbols, whose resonances and associations are as important as their defined meaning. They were not technical terms which could be brought into a system, and we need to be wary of misunderstanding them in this way. We can explicate them in these terms, though not without losing some of their significance.[42]

Since Eichrodt, OT theologians have tried various ways of arranging the material so as to allow its own internal dynamic to emerge rather than be submerged in an alien scheme. *Otto Procksch (1949) built his own work on the outline adopted from him by Eichrodt. *T. C. Vriezen (1950), too, began from the divine-human relationship, seen as one of intimate communion; the theme of the relationship between God and his people is more systematically central in the revised edition (1966). Shorter works were subsequently produced by *Edmond Jacob (1955) and *G. A. F. Knight (1959). Both are structured round aspects of God's character and his activity in creation, history, and Israel, with final sections on redemption and

---

[39] *Cf.* Kutsch, *BZAW* 131 and *ZTK* 74 (1977), maintaining that the words mean obligation, undertaken by God or imposed on man – but not essentially a mutual matter. Response by Eichrodt, *Int* 20 (1966) and *TZ* 30 (1974); mediating position by Weinfeld, *Biblica* 56 (1975) and *TDOT* 2; McCarthy, *VTSupp* 23; discussion in Brekelmans, *Questions Disputées d'AT*, pp. 71–164.

[40] *Cf.* Barr, Zimmerli volume.

[41] *Eichrodt I, p. 18. *Vriezen uses 'communion' similarly (p. 142/ ² pp. 169, 351); *cf.* Gottwald, *ExpT* 74 (1962–3), p. 210, and Carroll's observation (*When Prophecy Failed*, pp. 14–16) that covenant is a less personal term.

[42] *Cf.* *Porteous, pp. 25–27; Clements, *LQHR* 190 (1965), pp. 12–13; Perrin, *Jesus and the Language of the Kingdom*.

hope. Knight's work is best known for its explicitly Christian perspective, but this does not issue in a distinctive arrangement of the material.

*Rudolf Smend was able to fill a small book with the various suggestions that have been made regarding what central concept lies at the heart of OT faith and provides the right vantage point from which the material as a whole can be viewed. Nevertheless these suggestions can be categorized fairly clearly. A number locate the OT's theological centre in some aspect of God himself: God as the holy one, God as the Lord, God's presence and activity in history, God's reign, God revealing himself, God as the sole deity to be acknowledged, the name of Yahweh by which he both reveals and yet conceals himself, the promise of Yahweh, the presence of Yahweh and so on.[43] Perhaps it is simplest to say simply that God is the centre of the OT.[44] But this may seem a truism that is only the beginning of the real discussion.[45]

The major alternative to the view that God is in some way the centre of the OT is the suggestion that God's relationship with mankind (specifically with Israel) is the midpoint of OT faith from which all other aspects of it should be examined. This view is exemplified by those who focus on God's covenant with Israel, the communion relationship between Yahweh and Israel, God's election of Israel, the twin concepts of the rule of God and communion between God and men, the speaking and responding of 'I am Yahweh', 'You are Yahweh', or the dual relationship of Yahweh as the God of Israel and Israel as the people of Yahweh.[46] An advantage of this approach is that it enables one to acknowledge not only the priority of God's words and acts, but also the theological significance of the human

[43] See respectively *Sellin II, p. 19; *Köhler, pp. 30–35; *Jacob, pp. 32–33; Seebass, WD 8 (1965); Reventlow, TZ 17 (1961), pp. 96–98; Schmidt, Das erste Gebot, pp. 10–11, 49; Zimmerli, in various writings; *Baumgärtel, also *Kaiser; *Terrien.
[44] *Hasel, pp. 62–63/² pp. 99–103 and references; *Kraus, pp. 383–385; *Deissler.
[45] *Von Rad II, p. 415; cf. pp. 362–363.
[46] See respectively *Eichrodt; *Vriezen; Wildberger, EvT 19 (1959), pp. 77–78; *Fohrer; *Zimmerli; *Smend, following Wellhausen and Duhm (and for this view cf. Jacob, Théologie de l'AT, p. xii; *Clements, pp. 53–103; though note Schmidt's critique, op. cit., pp. 51–53).

response to God by means of which he also worked.[47]

In one sense, the search for the right structure of an OT theology, and for the right central concept from which to view OT faith as a whole, has been fruitless (or over-fruitful!). *Gerhard von Rad believes that there is no such structure or central concept; to look for one and to try to systematize the OT's thinking by means of it is to continue to let systematic theology's approach have an excessive influence on OT study.[48] 'The Old Testament writings confine themselves to representing Jahweh's relationship to Israel and the world in one respect only, namely as a continuing divine activity in history', and it is these testimonies that should be the subject of an OT theology.[49] Now it would be quite possible to make the theme of God's activity in history the focus of a thematic OT theology,[50] but von Rad rather concentrates on treating these successive testimonies in chronological order, first mainly the histories and then the prophets.

Von Rad thus introduced a further level at which a theological interest in the OT may operate. Other theologians have examined symbols such as covenant or kingdom, by means of which OT authors expressed themselves. They have looked at the beliefs expressed by these symbols, which we seek to analyse more conceptually: for instance, the conviction that Yahweh is the only God who matters, or that the relationship between God and his people is one in which he has the initiative, acting by grace, but that he expects a response. Or they have concerned themselves with the assumptions which

[47] See *Porteous, pp. 15–19, 38–39; Johnstone, *SJT* 22 (1969), pp. 200–202; contrast Reventlow's comments in *TZ* 17 (1961), pp. 96–98, which seem to imply that only the purported divine revelation within the OT counts as the divine message; psalms, history, and wisdom, and so on are (merely) the human response to this revelation.

[48] See also von Rad in *Westermann, pp. 24–25. Von Rad sees this kind of OT theology as rationalist – in the pre-Kantian sense of over-emphasizing the human mind's systematizing of truth; *Eichrodt (I, pp. 12, 17) dissociates himself from (post-Kantian) rationalism's excluding of what cannot be proved by reason. Barr comments, if Eichrodt is a rationalist, von Rad is a romanticist (*JTS* 25 [1974], p. 269)! Baumgärtel defends OT theology's attempt to think issues through in a way that enables one to relate its findings to systematics (*ThL* 86 [1961], columns 903–904); but von Rad sees this as still yielding too much to systematics' way of doing theology.

[49] I, p. 106; see further pp. 105–128.

[50] *Cf.* G. E. Wright's outline, Vriezen volume, pp. 381–388; also Stauffer's *NT Theology*. *Fohrer (p. 95) suggests that von Rad covertly regards Yahweh's self-revelation in history as the focal-point for OT theology; this observation applies more to Wright or Stauffer.

underlie these convictions but which hardly ever become matters of controversy and thus of conscious formulation – assumptions such as theism and aspects of attitudes to topics such as anthropology or cosmology. Von Rad urges theological interest in the OT to concentrate on another aim, the elucidation of the messages that particular writers explicitly sought to convey to the specific situations in which they lived.

At one point, it seemed that OT theology could never be the same after von Rad. Whereas a spate of works had been written or translated during the 1950s, no new ones were published in the 1960s. Then in the 1970s it seemed that reflection was again succeeded by activity. The German volumes of the 1970s[51] dispute von Rad's views that the OT focuses on God's activity in history and that a thematic treatment of it is inappropriate. Like Eichrodt, they do not ignore historical diversity and the historical events on which the faith is based, but they take more account than von Rad does of other ways in which the OT speaks.[52] Recent American and English work on OT theology is less circumscribed by the parameters of the Eichrodt/von Rad approaches, though like von Rad it is wary of the baneful influence of systematics. It has, however, been less concerned about questions of focus or structure than about questions of aim. The tendency has been to underline the theological nature of the discipline (see section 1a), and in various ways to emphasize questions about the canon in their relation to OT theology (see sections 5bcd).[53]

Despite the intense discussion of method and the prolific production of works of substance, OT theology still lacks a generally accepted understanding of its principles and structure.[54] But if we have not yet discovered the single correct key to producing a satisfactory synthesis of OT faith, this suggests that there is no such key. Understanding the OT resembles understanding a battle or a person, or appreciating a landscape,[55] rather than understanding the layout

---

[51] *Deissler, *Zimmerli, *Fohrer, Westermann's *What Does the OT Say about God?*

[52] See *Zimmerli, p. 11, and Westermann, *op. cit.*, pp. 11–12 for the awareness of being in dialogue with von Rad over these questions.

[53] *McKenzie (see especially pp. 15–29), *Clements, Childs in various works; also Barr, *JTS* 25 (1974) and elsewhere.

[54] *Cf.* *McKenzie, p. 15; Westermann, *EvT* 34 (1974), pp. 111–112; Osswald, *ThL* 99 (1974), column 654.

[55] For these similes, see *McKenzie, pp. 20–27; Barr, *JTS* 25 (1974), p. 272.

of an architect-planned new town. We can appreciate a landscape by starting from its roads, its contours or its water supplies, or by taking as its centre a hill, a church, an inn or a bus stop; each perspective will lead us to a different aspect of its understanding. Similarly, many starting-points, structures and foci can illuminate the OT's landscape. No one solution to the problem of structuring an OT theology will illuminate the whole; a multiplicity of approaches will lead to a multiplicity of insights.

c. The difference between Old and New Testament faiths

Although OT and NT faiths are fundamentally similar, their diversity also needs to be acknowledged.

Their understanding of God is not identical. The emphasis of the OT is that Yahweh, the God of Israel, is the one God to be acknowledged, and his character is summed up in the words 'Lord' and 'holy'. In the NT the focus is as much on Jesus as it is on God. His claims and his followers' claims for him complicate the key Jewish insight into the oneness of God, and God's character is summed up in the words 'Father' and 'love'. And whereas the OT emphasizes Yahweh's special relationship with and commitment to Israel, the NT emphasizes God's concern for the whole world.

Again, in the NT God's activity centres on the life of his people and that of the individual believer, and his chief blessing is forgiveness and spiritual renewal. The OT God is involved in this world, in politics and war, and his blessings are this-worldly. He is Lord of Sheol, but does not really relate to men after death. The hope of the messiah and of God's final dwelling with his people envisages a presence in space-time institutions rather than merely in a world to come or in a primarily spiritual realm.[56]

There is a corresponding difference in the portrayal of God's people in the two Testaments.[57] In the OT there is a close relationship between the religious community and the political and cultic group. The covenant, God's kingdom and God's people are meant to be realities of this world, even though the OT itself comes to realize that they cannot be. These concepts reappear in the NT, but with marked

[56] Cf. Kaiser, *Isaiah*, pp. 169–170; *McKenzie, p. 323.
[57] For what follows, see Baumgärtel in *Westermann, p. 146–147; Bultmann in *Anderson, pp. 29–31 and in *Westermann, pp. 59–75.

29

differences in meaning. Further, in the OT the focus is on this relationship between God and his people corporately. It is as a member of Israel, in the worship of Israel, that the individual finds access to God. The NT puts more emphasis on the individual believer's relationship with God; cultic ceremonies have a less prominent place. In the NT, faith generally implies an asssured knowledge of one's relationship with God on the basis of the achievement of Christ and the indwelling of the Spirit. In the OT, men more often struggle, doubt, rage, and protest.

In the light of these differences, there have always been Christians who have insisted that Christianity should abandon the OT, as 'the document of an alien religion'.[58] A particularly systematic exposition of the view that the OT really has nothing to do with Christianity is *Friedrich Delitzsch's Die grosse Täuschung. 'The great deception' is that the OT purports to be the word of God, but is not. Because the God of the Jews is so particularist and bloodthirsty, because the Jewish people themselves are so self-centred, because their worship is so pre-occupied with externals, because their vision is so this-worldly, and so on, we must conclude that links between the God of the Jews and the Jewish people on one hand, and Jesus and his church on the other, can be made only by means of a spiritualizing allegory.[59]

Yet although it has been a weakness of some more conservative works that they have underplayed the differences between the Testaments, Delitzsch's view oversimplifies the OT in the opposite direction. He underestimates the extent to which the Testaments are at one in their understanding of God, of man, and of the relationship between them. Further, the faults he finds with OT faith may often be based on misunderstanding.

For instance, does the OT really maintain that salvation comes from mere physical membership of the nation Israel? Rather, there is no comfort in belonging to Israel unless you are a man of faith.[60] Nor are the psalms' prayers about one's enemies necessarily emo-

[58] See *Gunneweg, ch. 5; also *Kraeling, ch. 10, 14, 15; cf. Baumgärtel, EvT 14 (1954), p. 312.

[59] E.g. I, pp. 70–71, 79–80; II, pp. 18–19, 38–42. *Kraeling (p. 162) comments that at least Delitzsch's work dissolved the 'pious daze' in which people often read the OT. Cf. *Gunneweg, pp. 144–147, 161.

[60] Cf. Vischer, in *Anderson, pp. 95–96.

tional and vindictive outbursts; their attitude may not be so very different from the approach to God's merciful justice in Genesis 18, which compares with Jesus' own attitude rather than with that of his disciples who wanted to call down fire on their enemies.[61] Similarly, the universalism of the NT offer of salvation has as its background the universalism of Genesis 1–11.[62] Sometimes it seems that the OT cannot win: either it is reckoned too 'worldly', or it is seen as too keen on withdrawal from the world into the realm of the cult.[63]

There is another aspect to this oversimplification.[64] The coming of Jesus indeed brought a new form to Israel's faith. But this had already happened several times within the OT itself. The three pentateuchal covenants, for instance, imply a formal recognition of three stages in Israel's religion. Thus, when the coming of Christ leads to some aspects of OT faith being pushed into the background (the stress on nation, institution, and cult), the features that replaced them in prominence (notably the immediacy of the God-man relationship) are themselves aspects of OT faith that now come (again?) into the foreground.

Further, it is an oversimplification to suggest that the OT indicates the 'question' to which Jesus is the 'answer', or reveals the 'need' which could then not be met till Jesus came. The NT itself 'directs people continually to the OT. There they find manifold examples of what it means in Jesus Christ to be loved by God and to love him, to become guilty before him, to be judged and yet to be sustained by him.'[65] The OT does not merely reflect human life BC. It does reveal clearly man's need of a saviour, but it also reveals that Yahweh is that saviour.[66]

The view that the OT is the antithesis to Christianity also oversimplifies the NT. *Delitzsch[67] notes that even references in the OT to God's concern with the nations (Is. 56:7; Am. 3:2; Zc. 8:23) remain

---

[61] Cf. *Gunneweg, p. 165; *Vischer, p. 126.

[62] Cf. Westermann, OT and Jesus Christ, pp. 55–56.

[63] Cf. J. G. Davies, Every Day God, ch. 3. Davies then sees the NT not as abandoning worldliness but as secularizing the idea of holiness (p. 53).

[64] For what follows, see *Vriezen, ²pp. 109–110.

[65] Vischer, in *Anderson, p. 99.

[66] McKenzie, in *Anderson, pp. 110–112; cf. Achtemeier, Myers volume; *Hanson, p. 250, commenting on Michalson's essay in *Anderson.

[67] II, p. 19.

Israel-centred. But the NT is similarly exclusive in claiming that salvation (for eternity) belongs only to those who acknowledge Jesus and join the church. Again, as the OT actually demands personal faith and not merely outward membership of Israel, so the NT emphasises the corporate dimension to the believer's relationship to God. In the NT, too, God's special relationship with Israel remains a topic of theological significance (e.g. Rom. 9–11).[68]

The coming of Christ might seem to imply that the believer's cry for vindication is now over.[69] Yet in the NT that cry is still being uttered (e.g. Lk. 18:1–8; Rev. 6:9–11). Indeed, the NT emphasizes the judging activity of God as clearly, if not as frequently, as the OT (Mt. 24:51; Rom. 12:19; 1 Thes. 2:16; Heb. 12:25; Rev. 16:1–7; 19:1–3), and sees it at work in this world and in the life to come. The 'completeness' of the NT should not be exaggerated. Its hopes are unrealized, its world is not one in which justice yet reigns, its salvation history is unfinished. Jesus' approach to salvation/wholeness/healing also suggests that the 'other-worldliness' of its understanding of salvation should not be exaggerated.[70]

Further, to suggest that OT and NT faiths are antithetical ignores the Jewishness of Jesus and the NT;[71] or rather (in Delitzsch's case) it seeks to circumnavigate these. At the end of his work[72] Delitzsch expounds his understanding of the non-Jewish Jesus. He believes that, coming from Galilee, Jesus was not racially a Jew, nor are his attitudes those of a Jew. But this suggestion, by its very implausibility, again undermines the attempt to draw a sharp contrast between Jewish and Christian religions. Instead, we must see the OT as pre-Christian, but not anti-Christian. The differences between the Testaments are ones of emphasis. NT Christianity is a Jewish sect rather than an alien religion.[73]

How, then, are we to approach the differences between OT and NT faith? Recent OT study raises at least five questions. First, in accepting the theological value of an OT text, do we have to understand it in the same way as its author did? In the past, interpreters

[68] Cf. *van Ruler, pp. 95–98.
[69] So Baumgärtel, in *Westermann, p. 154.
[70] Brueggemann (Land, pp. 167–196) also believes that the NT is interested in the theme of the land, though its spiritualizing of this motif is more obvious.
[71] On this, see Sawyer, From Moses to Patmos, pp. 5–7.
[72] II, pp. 58–73.
[73] Cf. *Gunneweg, pp. 166–172; *Vriezen, [2] p. 109.

often gave formal allegiance to the whole of Scripture, but in practice avoided parts that did not fit their understanding of Christianity, by allegorizing them or by simply ignoring them. In recent study, scholars have suggested that we let ourselves be addressed by parts of Scripture which seem to be theologically questionable by regarding these as witnesses to man's sinfulness, with which we associate ourselves.[74] In my view, however, this preserves the form of OT authority without the reality; to accept the OT as a faith means accepting it for what it meant to its adherents in OT times.[75]

A second, related question is whether we are committed to accepting the OT as a whole, or whether we have to distinguish between theological insight and error within it. Is there a canon within the canon? This question is a confused one, because it is not always clear whether 'the canon within the canon' refers to the real heart or highpoint of OT faith (in which case the rest is also acknowledged – it is simply less central or less profound), to the parts of the OT which in practice seem particularly important to a particular era (in which case the rest is also acknowledged in theory, though it may exercise less authority in practice), or to the part of the OT which is really true (in which case the rest is not or may not be).[76] The belief implied by this third understanding of the canon within the canon is that we have to distinguish between what is God's word in the OT and what is not.

But in my view, for a Christian to interpret 'the OT' implies that he has a confessional stance in relation to it: although it is a collection of books by human authors, it is one book having scriptural status. He believes that its contents are coherent, and that the insights of one part are to be seen in the light of the whole and vice versa. To interpret the OT involves seeking to relate diverse approaches to each other, rather than to separate insight from error.[77]

Related, in turn, to this second question is a third: what is the

---

[74] Cf. Mowinckel's approach to Esther (OT as Word of God, p. 110); *Baumgärtel's approach to the OT's (mis)understanding of God's promise (pp. 27, 64–66; cf. Hesse, in *Westermann, pp. 299–313); and the common understanding of Ecclesiastes as pointing us to Christ in a negative way by its doubts (e.g. Lauha, Kohelet, pp. v, 24, 37, 60); more generally Porteous, ExpT 75 (1963–4), p. 72.

[75] Cf. *Bright, p. 91.

[76] Cf. *G. E. Wright, pp. 179–183; also *Vriezen, pp. 88–90/²pp. 111–113; *Ebeling, pp. 92–93; Morgan, Nature of NT Theology, pp. 39–46; *Fohrer, pp. 29–32.

[77] Cf. Childs, Int 18 (1964), pp. 438–440.

relative status of OT and NT? Those who seek to distinguish between acceptable and unacceptable aspects of the OT commonly assume that the NT provides the criteria for doing this.[78] But the NT leans, if at all, the opposite way: the question was not whether the OT was Christian but whether the NT was biblical.[79] In reaction to this approach, *Arnold van Ruler[80] speaks of the OT as the real Bible, the NT being its explanatory glossary.

In my view, it is better to give parallel status to both Testaments, as joint witnesses to the one God whose speaking in each helps us to understand the Christ who came between the Testaments.[81] The Old lays the theological foundations for the New and sometimes explicitly looks forward in a hope which the Christian sees confirmed or fulfilled in Christ. The New presupposes this foundation and looks back to Christ, concentrating on what needs to be said in the light of his coming, but encouraging rather than discouraging us to do this against the background of the OT's broader concerns. Faith in Christ with its background in the NT may provide the pre-understanding for our approach to the OT; but where we find the OT saying something in tension with that pre-understanding, our reaction will be to allow it to broaden the latter, not to accept only what conforms to what we know already. Christ helps us to understand the OT, but the OT helps us to understand Christ.[82]

If the two Testaments have a different range of concerns and insights, this does not mean that one Testament ought to be the basis for narrowing our interests in relation to those of the other; and if they have different emphases in relation to themes they have in common, these may be seen as complementary rather than as alternatives to each other. Thus Christian theology needs to be open to OT

---

[78] Cf. *Bright, pp. 200, 211–212; *Vriezen, pp. 121–122/²pp. 148–149; Baumgärtel, ThL 76 (1951), column 262, and elsewhere.

[79] Cf. Sanders, Wright volume, p. 552, also JR 39 (1959), pp. 233–235; Freedman, Theology Today 21 (1964–5), pp. 227–228; Wildberger, EvT 19 (1959), pp. 80–83; *Bright, pp. 95–109.

[80] See pp. 72, 74; cf. pp. 49–57 on the NT's 'one-sidedness'.

[81] Cf. *Kraus, pp. 320–321; von Rad in *Westermann, p. 39; *Barth, II, 1, pp. 71, 101, 103; Wolff, *EvT 12 (1952–3), p. 102; Jepsen, in *Westermann, p. 264; *Hasel, pp. 78–79/²pp. 118–119; Childs, Int 18 (1964), pp. 440–443; Wildberger, EvT 19 (1959), pp. 73–80.

[82] Mays, Wright volume, pp. 512–513; *Barr, pp. 139–140.

insights on the nature of God,[83] on the world and on everyday human life as God's gifts,[84] on the continuing theological significance of Israel,[85] on what it also means for the church to be the people of God,[86] and on how the individual believer relates to God.[87] OT and NT approaches to these questions are both to be seen within the context of Scripture as a whole, and both contribute freely to Christian theology.

Fourthly, how does the event which took place in between the writing of the two Testaments affect the OT, which was written earlier? That event has to be interpreted in the light of the Hebrew scriptures, but at the same time it gives these scriptures a new context. Only in its light do they become the *Old* Testament. The Father of Jesus Christ is the God of the Hebrew scriptures, but in Christ something decisively New takes place.[88] Things that were ambivalent and ambiguous become clear and sharply-focused.[89] In a sense, then, the OT has to be understood in the light of Christ (as the NT has, too).

[83] *E.g.* Jacob, *Grundfragen*, pp. 18–24; *Deissler, pp. 151–152; Barrett, *ExpT* 72 (1960–1), pp. 356–360; Schwarzwäller, *EvT* 39 (1979), pp. 303–304; *G. E. Wright; *Childs, pp. 216–219.

[84] Zimmerli, *OT and the World*; *Miskotte; *van Ruler, pp. 34–36, 88–93; *Fohrer, ch. 7; Westermann, *1000 Years and a Day*, pp. viii, 20–72; Ellul, *Politics of God*; Steck and Wallis on nature, *TZ* 34 (1978); Bonhoeffer, *Letters and Papers*, Collins Fontana edition pp. 93–95, 100, 112, 126–127; Rylaarsdam, *BibRes* 10 (1965), on sex; Brueggemann, *Land*; also *Lohfink, pp. 165–169, Vawter, *JBL* 91 (1972), pp. 170–171, and Rahner, *Theological Investigations* 16, pp. 186–187 on the importance of this life. But see *Gunneweg, pp. 166–172, on the danger of a concern with this world becoming an assertion of independence.

[85] *Van Ruler, p. 35; *cf.* Wolff's application of Joel 2:18–32 to modern Israel (*Joel and Amos*, p. 70) and Vischer's treatment of Esther (*EQ* 11 [1939]).

[86] *Cf.* the closing paragraphs of many sections of Wolff's commentaries on Amos and Hosea, of Kaiser on Isaiah 1–39, Elliger on Isaiah 40–55, and of Kraus on the Psalms; Brueggemann, *Tradition for Crisis*, pp. 124–144, on prophetic ministry in the church; *cf.* Goldingay, *Evangelical Fellowship for Missionary Studies Bulletin* 5 (1975). 'The Old Testament guards the Christian message from false individualizing' (Wolff in *Westermann, p. 196).

[87] *Cf.* von Rad, *Genesis*; *Biblical Interpretations in Preaching*; also, for a positive evaluation of OT man's doubts, struggles, and protests as creative features of positive commitment, Brueggemann, *Int* 33 (1979), p. 122; Davidson, *ASTI* 7 (1968–9); Holm-Neilsen, *ASTI* 10 (1975–6), pp. 48–51.

[88] Jepsen in *Westermann, p. 261; *Vriezen's comments on van Ruler, pp. 81–87, 98/²pp. 93–98, 121 (also in *Westermann, pp. 218–221); Nielsen, Zimmerli volume, p. 288.

[89] *Vriezen, p. 87 and n. 3/²p. 100 and n. 4; Mowinckel, *OT as Word of God*, pp. 56–59; Kaufman, *Int* 25 (1971), pp. 106–107; Ebeling, *Study of Theology*, p. 35.

In the incarnation, for instance, the divine self-revelation of which the OT speaks becomes completely personal. God indwells his people in a new way which makes material and sacral mediation henceforth unnecessary.[90] In the incarnation, the OT's this-worldliness is presupposed and vindicated. By the cross, however, it is also put into a revolutionary new context; the glory of the king of Israel is only reached this way.[91] It transpires that OT hopes of judgment, redemption, and reconciliation are fulfilled only via the cross, and that the enigma and the agony of human life which the OT recognizes become meaningful only via the cross.[92]

By Christ's resurrection, too, the OT's this-worldly perspective is again confirmed, as the hope of man's resurrection becomes central rather than marginal to faith; this hope further helps to resolve the enigma of incompleteness and inequality in this age which the OT recognizes.[93] Overall, it is Christ who is now the focus of the relationship between God and the world; it is to this one Israelite, then, that the nations will ultimately bow as the means of their redemption.[94]

Finally, are OT and NT theology to be studied in isolation from each other? For practical reasons and out of historical interest this may be appropriate, but theologically it seems questionable. The Bible as a whole is the normative context for interpreting any one of its parts; therefore to fence off one area (Old or New) and generalize about it in isolation seems likely to lead (and has led) to imbalance. Christian theology needs a biblical theology, rather than an OT theology which has difficulty in referring to Christ, or a NT theology which omits the NT's normative but unspoken theological background and context.[95]

---

[90] *von Rad II, p. 356.

[91] *Gunneweg, pp. 230–231; *Vriezen,²p. 98; Dumas, *Political Theology* pp. 65–66; Kraus, *Psalmen*, pp. 21–22, 329, 337–338.

[92] Seebass, *WD* 8 (1965), pp. 30–34; Wolff, *Joel and Amos*, pp. 15, 304; Dillenberger in *Anderson, pp. 166–167; Bonhoeffer on the 'vindicatory psalms', *Psalms*, pp. 56–60.

[93] Cf. Westermann, *OT and Jesus Christ*, p. 68 on the implications this insight offers for the vindicatory psalms.

[94] Whether gladly or grudgingly; Schmidt (*EvT* 35 [1975], pp. 138–139) notes that we must be wary of too easy an appeal to God's love which forgets this point.

[95] *Clements, pp. 7–8; Seebass, *WD* 8 (1965), p. 30; de Vaux, *ZAW* 68 (1956), p. 226; Jacob, Coppens volume, pp. 431–432; Siegwalt, *KD* 25 (1979); Wagner, *ThL* 103 (1978); and the recent essays of Gese, Haacker, and Stuhlmacher.

The life of Christ and the giving of the Spirit led to the development of a trinitarian understanding of God, and inevitably biblical theology will speak of Father, Son and Spirit. God could not speak in such terms in OT times (cf. Jn. 7:37), and this understanding is not to be read into the exegesis of OT passages. Again, although the OT witnesses to Christ, it does so indirectly; he is not explicitly named there, and overtly it is a witness to God, not to Christ, which links OT and NT.[96]

But while God's activity did not begin with Jesus, it came to its fulfilment in him. Thus God's activity in OT times must ultimately be understood Christologically, and one can agree with Luther that all experiences of grace, even those of OT times, are finally to be seen as experiences of Christ.[97] It is not that the coming of Christ gives us extra information on the meaning of OT passages, but that it gives us extra information on the realities that OT passages refer to. It would be a mistake to try to find a Christological meaning in the creation story in Genesis 1. It would, however, be legitimate (perhaps mandatory) to refer to Christ in discussing the contemporary implications of Genesis 1 as a passage from the Christian scriptures; for the creation event of which Genesis 1 speaks is ultimately to be understood in the light of Christ.

Indeed, for a Christian everything of which the OT speaks has to be seen in the light of Christ. But immediately one says that, one has to add again that everything in the NT has to be seen in the light of the OT. For the Christian view is that Jesus is the one on whom the faith of Israel ultimately came to focus. But faith can only be Christian if it is built on the faith of the Hebrew scriptures.

---

[96] *Barr, pp. 151–154; Wright, May volume, pp. 301–303; *Hasel, pp. 71–72/²pp. 111–112; Wildberger, EvT 19 (1959), pp. 80–81.

[97] Wagner, ThL 103 (1978), column 796, referring to Bornkamm, Luther and the OT.

Chapter Two

The Old Testament as a way of life

> You shall be careful to do
> therefore as Yahweh your God
> commanded you.   (Dt. 5:32)

> These things happened to them
> as a warning, but they were
> written down for our
> instruction.   (1 Cor. 10:11)

'Judaism is not a theology, and not a system of piety. God did not
reveal Himself in that way at the meeting [at Mount Sinai]. Judaism
is a task, an activity'.[1] In emphasizing that God is concerned with
his people's way of life, Judaism echoes one central strand running
through the Hebrew scriptures themselves. As Deuteronomy puts
it, you are to be faithful to 'the way in which Yahweh your God
commanded you to walk' (13:5). The life of an OT believer is a 'walk'
(*halakah* – the word used by Judaism in discussing questions of
behaviour) in the 'way' (*derek* – the Greek equivalent is used of
Christianity in passages such as Acts 9:2) following Yahweh's 'direction' (*torah* – the word which was used for the Mosaic laws and
the prophets' teaching and which eventually came to refer to the
pentateuch as a whole). So how should the scriptures direct this
walk?

a. The ways in which Scripture shapes our way of life

An ethicist might distinguish at least the following five aspects to
this matter.[2]

  1. The OT contains a great many *explicit commands*, predominantly

---

[1] Blue, *To Heaven, with Scribes and Pharisees*, p. 17.
[2] *Cf.* surveys in *Birch and Rasmussen; Gustafson, *Int* 24 (1970); Long, *Int* 19
(1965) and his *Survey*.

in the pentateuch, but also in the prophets and the wisdom books. Traditionally, the heart of biblical ethics has been found in these specific commands regarding the way of the Lord.[3]

Yet many OT commands are not binding today (e.g. much in Dt. 12; 13; 20). But if some commands do not bind the modern reader, on what grounds can we say that others do? Can these commands be universalized? How can they be related to each other, to those of the NT and to modern insights? How can they be applied to the questions raised by our own world, which is often so different from the biblical world? Many modern writers doubt whether this is a feasible or worthwhile exercise.[4] We will return in sections 2def to consider what principles might facilitate the application of OT commands to the Christian believer and the modern world.

2. The narrative books, in particular, provide many potential *examples of behaviour* to be imitated or avoided, and a story can form character at least as powerfully as a precept.[5] Christian preaching has long quarried this treasure and sought to edify believers out of the lives of Abraham or Joshua or David.

But stories of this kind raise the same questions as commands: can their lessons be universalized, and can they be related to other OT, NT, and later insights? They also raise their own questions. First, do they mean to offer us models of behaviour (positive or negative)? The major function of the OT story is to relate how God has acted, despite the acts of men as much as through them. Admittedly the OT is sometimes concerned with examples and warnings, and this concern sometimes appears in the NT's use of the OT.[6] But fundamentally the OT is *God's* story. To concentrate on the human deed, then, is often to miss the point of it.[7] Indeed, it is not merely to misuse it: it is to bring a message that is its opposite. The story declares that the crucial events are the acts of God. A 'moralizing' concern runs the risk of making the crucial events the acts of men.

[3] Murray, *Principles*, pp. 14, 24.

[4] *E.g.* Preston, *BJRL* 59 (1976), p. 173; Sleeper, *Int* 22 (1968), p. 451.

[5] Greenberg, Wright volume, p. 461.

[6] *E.g.* in Genesis some narratives both offer models or paradigms of what it means (or does not mean) to be a believer, and form part of the overarching story of the working out of God's promise and God's curse in history (as well as also explaining the origin of particular phenomena). See von Rad, *Genesis*, on Gn. 12; 13; 15; 18; 22; and Roth, *CBQ* 34 (1972), on Gn. 24. *Cf.* also the Joseph story.

[7] Noth, in *Westermann, p. 86.

It turns the OT into law.

A second problem about taking stories as moral examples is their specificness. The particular decisions that OT characters had to make were unique to them, as every man's decisions are, so their action cannot be directly relevant to another situation. Biblical stories cannot anticipate situations we may find ourselves in. Although human nature may not fundamentally change, nevertheless 'the problems and difficulties of one age are not those of another. When the modern church-goer is solemnly assured that he is in essentially the same situation as the Prophet Moses, or Nicodemus, or Cornelius, he ought to burst out laughing'.[8]

The problem is not only one of the pulpit. It arises particularly in discussion of the political application of the OT message. Can the exodus narrative be used as a paradigm (an exemplary model) for understanding divine action (and prescribing human action) in the contemporary world? How does one determine whether to see a modern power as a latter-day Pharaoh, needing God's judgment, or as a latter-day Assyria, the rod of God's judgment? On what basis are technology, happiness, the state, money or communism identified as the 'modern Sennacheribs' which trouble us as Israel was once troubled, as opposed to other candidates for this equation?[9]

There is a difficulty, then, about determining with whom we can identify ourselves or others in a story, a difficulty about applying the lessons of biblical narrative to our own day. But behind this is the further problem of identifying the meaning of the biblical narrative itself. Who and what in the story has the narrative's own approval? OT stories are certainly evidence for Israelite ethics (that is, for how Israelites actually behaved), but it is more difficult to infer what they tell us about OT ethics (that is, about how Israelites ought to have behaved).[10] Indeed, it is possible to question how far we can really understand biblical narratives (or other forms of biblical literature) at all. *Dennis Nineham observes that once we appreciate the huge differences between cultures, ways of thinking, and all manner of little things that can be taken for granted within a group,

---

[8] Barr, *Bible in Modern World*, p. 47; *cf.* Noth, p. 87; Sleeper, p. 451.

[9] See Gutiérrez, *Theology of Liberation*, and Goldingay in *TynB* 1976; Gustafson, *Int* 24 (1970), pp. 442–444; Ellul, *Politics of God*, and Brueggemann in *JBL* 92 (1973).

[10] Murray, *Principles*, pp. 13–14; McKeating, *JSOT* 11 (1979), p. 70; Barton, *JSOT* 9 (1978), p. 56.

but which stand out when one compares societies separated by geography, language, race or time, we become aware of the possibility that all our attempts to understand the Bible may be radical failures. And the trouble is, there is no way of knowing whether this is the case.

In the 'hard' form in which Nineham first propounds this culture-relativist thesis it is an exaggeration. Nineham implies this himself. Having expounded it and thus warned against the Bible's abuse, he comes to the positive exposition of his own approach, and can only assume that in its radical form the theory is wrong. Otherwise it would be pointless to try to use the Bible at all (and arguably pointless to try to write a book about it, because the problem of communication today might be just as great). Indeed, common sense suggests that the theory is an exaggeration, for people are continually having the experience of being confronted by the message of some alien, ancient text, often one that disturbs and challenges rather than merely reflects and reassures.

Nevertheless, Nineham's work reminds us that the task of interpretation (particularly of narrative) is a complex one which is never finally completed. Aspects of a text may get through to me now, but they are probably only aspects; others escape me. Elements in my so-called understanding actually stem from my imposing meaning on the text. I have to cultivate both a sensitivity and a critical discipline if I am to perceive where a narrative is setting an example before me and what that example is, and thus to go on to work out what significance that example has within the Bible as a whole and for the modern world.

3. The OT in general can be a source for an understanding of the kind of *values or principles* that should be embodied in our way of life. When one becomes aware of the hazards involved in directly applying OT commands or in rightly interpreting OT narratives, then it may be attractive to look rather to the underlying principles, which often point to more radical requirements than do overt commands.

The OT's ethical values are particularly explicit in the prophetic books, which often refer to principles such as holiness, justice, faithfulness, mercy, and steadfast-love. But they also appear in the psalms, the wisdom books, and the laws (especially Deuteronomy). Values or ideals of other kinds also appear: *shalom* ('peace'), brotherhood, and stewardship, for instance. But the Bible has no one key

41

value, and its diversity has to be taken into account rather than evaded (see sections 1bc). In particular, OT and NT emphases need to be brought into relation. The OT is often reckoned to emphasize justice, the NT love, but both sides of this contrast have been exaggerated. In the prophets, love and justice are interrelated, the two sides of the same coin. Both are embodiments of holiness; justice complements love.[11]

4. But we can respond in a different way when we realize the difficulty of applying OT commands and narratives directly. We can emphasize instead how one's way of life is influenced by one's *overall view of reality*, one's perspective on life or personal construct. To put this in Jewish terms, *haggadah* (or theology) is as relevant to behaviour as *halakah* (teaching on the right way of life) itself is, because *haggadah* provides the reasons, the background, and the motivation for *halakah*.[12]

A key element in this total perspective which so affects how we live is that the OT sees life as lived before God. It means responding to God's deeds, reflecting God's nature, serving as a people under God's rule, obeying God's demand, living within God's covenant.[13] Our way of life is thus our acknowledgement of God: the prophets frequently refer to 'knowing God' (that is, recognizing him in the way one lives one's life) as a key aspect to behaviour (cf. Ho. 4:1, 6; Je. 22:16).

OT ethics thus comprise a response to the activity of the redeemer God. But they are also a response to the creator God, embody a conformity to the pattern of natural order, and apply as much outside

[11] Cf. Wolff, *Anthropology of OT*, pp. 190–191; Eichrodt, *Int* 20 (1966), p. 318; Maguire, *ATR* 61 (1979), pp. 57–59.

[12] Preston, p. 173; Lindars, *Theology* 76 (1973), p. 189; Janzen, *Int* 27 (1973), p. 346; *Eichrodt II, pp. 349–379, on goods and motives of moral conduct; Gustafson, *Religion*, pp. 316–320. Cf. Ackroyd's observation (*ExpT* 74 [1962–3], p. 164) that Esther is not concerned to set forward its human characters as examples to follow or shun, but to embody the conviction that right does triumph and wrong meet its downfall – a message of great relevance to the way its readers cope with the pressures they face.

[13] See Fletcher, *SJT* 24 (1971); Davidson, *SJT* 12 (1959); Barton, *JSOT* 9 (1978), pp. 57–61; Gustafson, *Theology and Christian Ethics*, pp. 147–148; Miranda, *Marx and the Bible*, pp. 137–160, on the laws' embodiment of God's justice as shown in the exodus; Stamm and Andrew, *Ten Commandments*, pp. 74–75, suggesting that what distinguishes Israel's laws is less their content than their context, in a relationship (the covenant); Amsler, Zimmerli volume, suggesting that most of Deuteronomy's ethical motivation is covenantal.

as inside Israel. There are standards that everyone has to acknowledge, standards on whose basis even God himself can be appealed to.[14] Thus one's doctrine of creation will comprise an important aspect of the basic orientation which determines the framework of one's approach to ethical questions. Specific importance will attach to one's theological understanding of topics such as man, sexuality and other human relationships, land, the state, and the outworking of human history in general.[15]

5. Finally, we may note that how we act is substantially determined by who we are and what we consequently see. Thus the Bible profoundly influences a person's manner of life by the way its stories, images, paradigms, and beliefs *shape character*.[16] How this comes about is a subtle affair; a character may be formed as profoundly by the stories in the Bible affecting one subliminally, like the parables, as it is consciously by the direct commands in the Bible, by its statements, or by its theology. In this sense we note again that the whole OT is *torah* or *halakah*. It is all designed to affect the way people live.

On the other hand, current stress on the ethical importance of principles such as justice or brotherhood, of one's total understanding of life, and of the formation of one's character ought not to be allowed to obscure the prominence in the Bible of explicit instructions regarding behaviour, which have been the traditional focus of the study of biblical ethics. The Bible does not assume that right behaviour will automatically issue from right theology and character. *Halakah* is made explicit, not left implicit, in *haggadah*.[17] The right way of dealing with the explicitly halakic material will be a focus of our study of the OT as a way of life in this chapter.

[14] *Eichrodt II, pp. 317–319; Barton *JSOT* 9 (1978) and *JTS* 30 (1979); Rodd, *ExpT* 83 (1971–2), pp. 137–139. Andrew (p. 75) notes that this approach is implicit in the laws, with their pre-covenantal background in everyday life, as well as in the prophets (e.g. Am. 1 – 2), the wisdom books, and the creation story.

[15] See Zimmerli, *OT and World*; Jacob, *VTSupp* 7, pp. 47–51; Turner, *ATR* 61 (1979), pp. 38–53; Ebeling, *Study of Theology*, pp. 149–150; Gustafson, *Int* 24 (1970), pp. 445–449; Field, *Homosexuality*, pp. 13–19; Brueggemann, *Land*; O'Donovan, *Christian View of War*, p. 8, contrasting with Ellul's 'tortured despair about the realities of political power' in his *Violence*. See further section 1c.

[16] *Birch and Rasmussen, pp. 88, 104; Preston, *BJRL* 59 (1976), p. 173; Gustafson, *Theology and Christian Ethics*, pp. 147–159; Bonhoeffer, *Ethics*, pp. 17–25; Lindars, *Theology* 76 (1973), pp. 188–189; *Porteous, p. 167; Greenberg, Wright volume, pp. 461–462.

[17] Davidson, *SJT* 12 (1959), p. 381; *Birch and Rasmussen, pp. 23–24, 33–35.

b. Law in the Old Testament

One of the most familiar designations of the OT is as the law. The NT follows contemporary custom in using this term to refer to narrative as well as legal material in the pentateuch (*e.g.* Gal. 4:21–22), and also to refer to passages from the prophets (*e.g.* 1 Cor. 14:21) and from the writings (*e.g.* John 10:34). So the Hebrew scriptures are the law; and the law is annulled in Christ (Rom. 7:1–6; 10:4; Gal. 3 – 4).

Of course Paul does not mean that the Hebrew scriptures are annulled. Indeed, his argument that the law is annulled appeals to these scriptures. But he does assert that they are no longer binding as law. So does the law have any function for the Christian believer?

In an influential work on 'The laws in the pentateuch', Martin Noth suggested that the OT's own theology of the law is quite different from the one set forth and then demolished by Paul. Indeed the OT's attitude is itself rather complex. But the starting-point for understanding it is that the law belongs to the covenant relationship between Yahweh and Israel (essentially Israel as the people of God: the law is not state-law). Further, the order of these two concepts is significant: the covenant relationship existed first, established on the initiative of Yahweh. The giving of the law followed Yahweh's establishing of his relationship with Israel; it was designed to demonstrate and safeguard the distinctiveness of Israel as Yahweh's covenant people. Put theologically, grace is prior to law in the OT.[18]

But, continued Noth, the exile signified that this covenant relationship had been brought to an end. The basis of the law's validity was thereby also removed. Some of the prophets hoped for the establishment of a new covenant, but the reorganization of the community under Persian patronage recorded in Ezra and Nehemiah hardly constituted that. The covenant had been the basis of Israel's

---

[18] See *Noth, pp. 1–60; Knight, *Law and Grace*, p. 25; Murray, *Principles*, pp. 181–201; *J. A. Sanders, p. 4, noting that the pentateuch (or better hexateuch, as the story finds its natural conclusion in Joshua) is really a narrative in which laws are set, rather than a lawbook; *von Rad I, pp. 192–194; II, pp. 390–395, though von Rad also relates the giving of the law more integrally to Israel's election by describing the proclamation of the law embodying Yahweh's will over her as a means of putting her election into effect. *Cf.* *Barth II, 2, p. 509: the law is 'the form of the Gospel', that is 'the sanctification which comes to man through the electing God' (pp. 561–564 apply this to Deuteronomy in particular).

community life in relation to God, which had in turn been the basis of the validity of Israel's laws. Now, in contrast, it was the acknowledgement of the law by Israel which constituted the basis of the covenant relationship between God and people.

Eventually, as Noth sees it, the law comes to have a status of its own, independent of the covenant, and emphasis swings completely from divine activity to individual human behaviour. Instead of God taking the initiative and man responding, now man's conduct is decisive and God only reacts to this behaviour according to the standard laid down by the law. Noth draws attention to the stress on the individual's attitude to the law in Psalms 1, 19 and 119, and sees this development bearing fruit in the legalism against which Paul polemicizes.[19] By implication, Christians are ill-advised to try to involve themselves with OT laws, lest they repeat Israel's mistakes and end up in legalism.[20]

Many specific features of Noth's scheme have been questioned.

1. Since the early creative work of Eichrodt and Noth, emphasis on the covenant's importance has swung right into fashion but then, partly through its being used uncritically, right out of fashion (see section 1b). Theologically, the content of the laws can be connected with the doctrine of creation as well as with the covenant; there is an OT 'natural theology' (see section 2a).

2. Noth believed that the original covenant community to which the laws belonged was the 'sacral confederacy of the twelve tribes of Israel' or 'amphictyony'. The theory that Israel's earliest structure was that of such an amphictyony is now widely questioned.[21]

3. Walther Zimmerli[22] has pointed out that in the prophets God's commands are recalled not merely in connection with exhorting his people to keep their side of the covenant, but also as a means of warning them of the danger they are in through ignoring those commands. The covenant itself also warns of the consequences of

---

[19] See *Noth, pp. 60–107.

[20] The classic Lutheran position; see e.g. Luther's own sermon 'How Christians should regard Moses', Luther's Works 35, pp. 155–174; also his 'Prefaces to the Old Testament' in the same volume.

[21] See Mayes, Israel; De Geus, Tribes; Smend, EvT 31 (1971); Fohrer, ThL 91 (1966). But perhaps even if the amphictyony approach has to be abandoned, something rather like it has to appear in its place (so *Gunneweg, pp. 100–104).

[22] ThL 85 (1960); Law and Prophets, pp. 46–92, especially p. 60; cf. *von Rad II, pp. 395–402; *Ebeling, pp. 265–266; *Gunneweg, pp. 134–140.

ignoring Yahweh's stipulations. Not that the prophets are finally negative about Israel's future; the other side of judgment there will be renewal. But God's commands and God's judgment are connected, and thus Paul's connection of law and condemnation is by no means foreign to the OT.

4. *R. E. Clements[23] has noted that the law-centred approach to the OT was not imposed on it, as something alien, by post-biblical Judaism. The pentateuch is, after all, dominated by law, despite its narrative framework, and the pentateuch as the law provides the concept which co-ordinates the whole canon. Indeed, the very concept of canon (normative rule) presupposes a quasi-legal approach to the role of the scriptures. Thus in the NT, as elsewhere in Judaism, even narrative is appealed to in a quasi-legal way (cf. Mk. 2:23–26).

5. H.-J. Kraus has pointed out that Psalms 1, 19, and 119, do not *have* to be read in a 'legalistic way'. At most they are ambivalent.[24] On a broader front, *E. P. Sanders has demonstrated that the picture of Judaism's law-centred piety as legalistic and guilt-ridden is neither that given by Judaism nor that implied by Paul. Paul and Judaism agree on the relationship between grace and works. What distinguished them is the embodiment of grace which they respond to, and the character of the works responsive to it which they emphasize. For ordinary Jews it is the making of the Sinai covenant, and the response of keeping its laws. For the Christian Jew it is God's power manifested in Jesus as Lord, and the response of faith in him. Thus for Paul, 'what is wrong with [the law] is not that it implied petty obedience and minimization of important matters, not that it results in the tabulation of merit points before God, but *that it is not worth anything in comparison with being in Christ* (Phil. 3.4–11)'.[25] It is not the Torah which is to be identified with the eternal Wisdom or Word, as happens in Ben Sira and the rabbis; it is Christ.

Although Noth's work is thus subject to modification, his essay and these other studies make it clear that the law fulfils many theological functions within Scripture.[26] It provides a basis for the declaration of judgment, the key to avoiding judgment, and the

[23] Pp. 104–120; also Torrance volume. Cf. *Gunneweg, pp. 96–105, questioning whether there is so much difference between the degree of emphasis given to law in the early period and in Judaism.

[24] *EvT* 10 (1950–1); cf. *Psalmen*; also *Gunneweg, pp. 130–131.

[25] P. 550.

[26] Cf. Hübner, *KD* 22 (1976); Stuhlmacher, *ZTK* 75 (1978).

explanation for the experience of judgment. As such it prepares the way for a proclamation of God's forgiveness which can only come from beyond the boundaries of its own perspective. But it functions in connection with judgment in these ways because it first expresses the will of God, the creator, which he expects his creatures to obey because they are his creatures, and the will of God the redeemer, which he expects his people to obey because they are his people. Israel's hope of salvation is of a day when the law will be obeyed (cf. Je. 31:31–34), perhaps of a day when a new law will be given,[27] but not of a day without law.

From an OT perspective, then, it seems quite natural for an examination of OT interpretation to include consideration of how the law ought to influence behaviour. But is this possible from a NT perspective?

c. Law in the New Testament

Paul can see, in the light of his Christian experience, that the old covenant and the old law were not finally satisfactory. Indeed, they were only ever intended as a temporary measure; they have fulfilled their function (Gal. 3:24). Insofar as the law puts him in a state of anxiety because he does not fulfil it, the gospel releases the believer from this anxiety.[28] The man who believes in Christ is freed from the law (Rom. 7:6). It no longer has a hold on Jews and ought not to be allowed to gain any hold on Gentiles. It is replaced at the heart of the believer's relationship with God by Christ himself, and the demand of Christianity is concentrated in him.[29] Even (especially?) for the believer the law is unable to engender true obedience. On the contrary, it leads to death (Rom. 7). Only the Spirit of Christ can give new life to him, and that same Spirit then leads the believer in the way of God (Rom. 8:1–14). Thus in Paul 'ethics are connected above all to receiving the Spirit'; he utilizes OT ethical teaching when it coheres with Christian insights, but this does not constitute a tacit

---

[27] So Davies, *Torah*; *Setting*, ch. 3 – 4; but the evidence is thin.
[28] Barth, *God, Grace and Gospel*, p. 26.
[29] Davies, *Paul and Rabbinic Judaism*; *Torah*; Stinespring volume, pp. 314–315; *Concilium* 7/8.10 (1974).

endorsement of the continuing validity of the law as a whole.[30]

There are, however, other more positive aspects to Paul's attitude to the law. He can describe it as 'holy, just, and good' (Rom. 7:12), God's gift in connection with the old covenant (Rom. 9:4–5). He does not doubt that it truly expressed God's expectation of his people.[31] Under the new covenant, as under the old, a certain way of life is expected of the believer, who is thus 'under the law of Christ' (1 Cor. 9:21, cf. Gal. 6:2 – though the precise significance of this phrase is debated). In theory, perhaps, a Christian needs nothing but to be told to follow the Spirit's leading, and is better off without further explicit guidance, lest he fall back into legalism. Yet, 'a glance at the Corinthian church is sufficient to show that not all Christians know by inspiration what things they ought to do, and that even when they know them they do not necessarily do them'.[32] Although they belong to the age to come, they have to cope with belonging to this age, too. Although AD men, there remains something BC about them.

Consequently Paul (and other NT writers) give considerable attention to teaching the nature of the response to God's grace which Christian discipleship requires. Christ is the end of the law but not the end of commandment, and under the new covenant as under the old disobedience brings disaster.[33] Paul believes, moreover, that obedience to Christ means meeting the law's own fundamental concerns – so that 'love is the fulfilling of the law' (Rom. 13:8–10). The fundamental principles of Christ's law cover those of Moses' law. Consequently it is not surprising to find that Paul sometimes gives expression to his Christian teaching by reminding his hearers of particular biblical laws (Eph. 6:2–3).[34] C. E. B. Cranfield[35] goes as far as to say that Paul sees the law as now established through Christ

---

[30] *E. P. Sanders, p. 513 and pp. 474–515 generally; cf. Bruce, Paul, pp. 192, 200–202; Jensen, NovT 20 (1978), p. 162; *von Campenhausen, pp. 29–37; D. F. Wright, Christian Graduate 29 (1976); Longenecker, Paul; Kaye, Law, Morality and Grace, pp. 76–79; *Amsler, pp. 49–52. The NT's teaching relies heavily on other sources as well as OT law – Christ's authority, apostolic authority, apostolic tradition, nature, conscience (cf. Meier, CBQ 40 [1978]).

[31] Zimmerli, ThL 85 (1960), column 491, against Hesse. Cf. *von Campenhausen, pp. 26–27, on Paul's attitude to Scripture generally.

[32] Barrett, 1 Corinthians, p. 214.

[33] Eichrodt, Int 20 (1966); cf. Longenecker, Paul, p. 175.

[34] *Amsler, pp. 51–52; Furnish, Theology and Ethics in Paul, pp. 29–34.

[35] SJT 17 (1964); Romans, p. 384; cf. Ridderbos, Paul, pp. 278–288.

in the sense that the believer can now fulfil its concerns.

It is tempting to emphasize one side or other of Paul's complex attitude to the law, which has been described as 'the most intricate doctrinal issue in his theology'.[36] Indeed, other NT writers sometimes stress one aspect or the other. A comparable attitude to its more negative aspect appears also in Luke and in John. The second, more positive side to Paul's attitude appears especially in Matthew, and also in James. Matthew will have nothing to do with 'legalism' but his real enemy is antinomianism, and he pictures Jesus as revealing the true meaning of the Torah and calling his disciples to put it into practice.[37]

Jesus' attitude to the law also has complex strands to it, investigation of which is complicated by scholarly disagreement as to how far we can distinguish his own words from the development of the gospel tradition and the work of the evangelists. Clearly one aspect of Jesus' attitude is to treat the law as far from the final word regarding God's expectation of people, and to add his own teaching to it. The antitheses in Matthew ('You have heard that it was said . . . But I say to you . . .', Mt. 5:21–48) express this aspect very clearly. Some of these antitheses can be seen as a protest against the way the law has been interpreted and supplemented, or as a sharpening of the Torah, but some (see verses 31–42) explicitly contrast with biblical laws.[38]

On the other hand, here Jesus also shows that he, too, is concerned

---

[36] Cranfield, *SJT* 17 (1964), p. 44, quoting Schoeps.

[37] *Cf.* *von Campenhausen, pp. 1–61; on Matthew, also G. Barth in *Tradition and Interpretation in Matthew*. Käsemann sees these differences as reflecting a degeneration (though an inevitable and legitimate one) from the radical insights of earliest Christianity to the incipient catholicism of later NT documents (*NT Questions*, ch. 12). But Drane (*Paul*; also *NovT* 16 [1974]) points out that the dialectic between salvation by grace and commitment to the standards to which the law also testified is present in Paul himself, and Hübner (*KD* 22 [1976]) suggests that the complexity of NT attitudes reflects the variety of misunderstandings of the law which the writers had to correct.

[38] It is a matter of scholarly debate whether Jesus' teaching should be seen as an exposition of the law, or a penetration to its implicit inner principles, or a radicalizing of it, or a replacement of it for the new age, or an independent revelation of God's will which does not relate very directly to the law's concerns. See works such as G. Bornkamm and G. Barth, *Tradition and Interpretation in Matthew*; Davies, *Christian Origins*, pp. 31–66, and other works; Packer, *Our Lord's Understanding of the Law of God*; Banks, *Jesus and the Law*; Westerholm, *Jesus and Scribal Authority*; Jackson, *JJS* 30 (1979); D. Wenham, *Themelios* 4 (1979); McEleney, *CBQ* 41 (1979); Meier, *Law and History in Matthew*.

to be prescriptive about the behaviour of those who want to follow him. The Sermon on the Mount, like Paul's teaching later, is not merely a description of a disciple, but a set of commands in the imperative.[39] And Jesus can speak very positively of the law. He determines his own conduct by what 'is written', berates the Pharisees for ignoring God's commandments concerning one's attitude to one's parents, discusses the propriety of divorce on the basis of texts from the Torah, and willingly teaches concerning what are the most fundamental commandments within the law (Mt. 4:1–11; Mk. 7:9–13; 10:2–9; 12:28–31).

It seems to me that we have to accept a dialectical 'yes-and-no' to the law, as we have to say yes-and-no to the question of whether man's commitment to God's ways is important to his relationship with God (and as God has to say yes and no to man: see Ho. 11). This tension over the relationship between grace or salvation and behaviour has been usefully examined by Edward Leroy Long in analysing the Reformers' understanding of the function of the law. In the Bible and in the Reformers he finds two approaches. Both assume a soteriology of grace, but one (characteristic of Paul and Luther) then works with an ethic of contexts, and avoids the trap of legalism. The other (characteristic of the Old Testament, Calvin, and the Puritans) then works with an ethic of norms, and is concerned that the man who belongs to God by grace does not fail to live responsibly before him. These two approaches need to be held in tension if neither is to fall into the other two positions (classicially antinomianism and legalism) which lie just beyond them.[40]

Those who emphasize contexts tend to suspect those who stress norms of being legalistic,[41] while those who emphasize norms tend to suspect those who stress contexts of being antinomian – despite the fact that even the most orthodox ethicists have recognized that nearly every rule has its exceptions.[42] (The first thing I remember learning as a student – from G. C. Stead's lectures on Aristotle's *Ethics* – is that there cannot be more than one prescription without

[39] O'Donovan, *TynB* 27 (1976), pp. 69–72; contrast Moule, *ExpT* 74 (1962–3), p. 371.

[40] *Norm and Context in Christian Ethics*, pp. 265–295; cf. Fischer, *CBQ* 40 (1978), also *E. P. Sanders' participationist, Spirit-led soteriology in Paul and covenantal nomism in the OT (pp. 511–515).

[41] Cf. Long's own criticism (p. 273) of Murray, *Principles*.

[42] Cf. Owen, *Theology* 76 (1973), pp. 18–19, with reference to Aquinas and Kirk.

any exception, because once you have two prescriptions you have the possibility of a context in which they clash.) In practice, everyone allows for both norms and contexts.[43] The difference lies in where one sees the need for emphasis to lie. Is the danger antinomianism and the need for a stress on norms (as was the case for James)? Or is the danger legalism and the need for a stress on freedom and contexts (as it was for Paul in Galatians)?

Thus it may be true that 'Christians do not need to read in Exodus that they should not kill or steal or commit adultery'.[44] Yet the NT does remind them of these demands, and sometimes quotes Exodus in doing so (Eph. 4:28; Jas. 2:11). So while the Christian ethicist is not going to take the OT law as God's last word on behaviour, it seems equally clear that it would be odd for him simply to ignore it as a possible source of guidance for decision-making over the way of life God expects of his people.

d. The specificness of Old Testament commands

If in principle it is appropriate for Christianity to utilize the laws and other material concerning behaviour in the OT in seeking to identify the way of life that God approves, how is it to do this in practice?

One complex of problems involved in applying OT commands today relates to their specificness or particularity. They are not so much universal absolutes, designed to be applicable in any circumstances, as specific enactments made in particular historical, social, and cultural situations, and designed to function in those particular situations.

One consequence of this specificness appears in the fact that they seem largely independent of each other. In the laws and in the wisdom books, command follows command with little discernible pattern or inter-relationship, and they do not make clear what unified fundamental attitude they are concerned with. Further, the very nature of a bare command is to demand only subservient acquiescence to an alien law, not a response of the whole person to the inherent goodness of the will of God.[45]

[43] Cf. Gustafson, HTR 58 (1965).
[44] D. F. Wright, Christian Graduate 29 (1976), p. 104.
[45] *Eichrodt II, pp. 325–326, 346; *Vriezen, pp. 340–342/²pp. 402–404.

A second consequence of this specificness is that these commands, like the stories we considered in section 2a, directly address a historical and cultural situation which is very different from that of most modern readers. The problem here is not that the enactments were not the right laws, God-given indeed, in the contexts to which they belong.[46] It is that precisely insofar as they speak appropriately in those contexts, they may not be applicable in others. Indeed, it may be difficult to understand the point of them. 'You are not to boil a kid in its mother's milk': the command is important enough to appear three times in the pentateuch (Ex. 23:19; 34:26; Dt. 14:21). The linguistic meaning of the words in this command is clear enough, but we can only guess at its significance and at the reason for its importance to OT Israel.[47] In consequence of this we can gain no certain guidance from it for our own lives. The observant Jew avoids drinking white coffee after eating meat lest he infringe it, but it remains unclear whether this meets or misses the point of the law.[48]

This suggests a further difficulty. We ourselves live in a particular historical situation which raises for us sharp ethical questions which the Bible does not directly address. It does not envisage the questions of a technological society, of a world that is becoming overcrowded, and of life sciences which lay before men new possibilities of genetic decision-making.[49] The specificness of biblical commands to their context raises the question of what guidance we have for the specific issues we have to face.

Perhaps later irrelevance is the inevitable price of present specificity? *Karl Barth seems to turn this into a theological principle. To try to apply the specific commands of God to a situation or to people other than those to which they were addressed is not merely difficult or impossible in practice. It is methodologically misguided. They are either so specific that they do not apply to us, or so general (as in the case of the decalogue) that they only mark the boundaries of 'the area . . . in which concrete divine commandment and pro-

---

[46] Fischer (*CBQ* 40 [1978], p. 296) remarks, 'I take it that no one would posit that the Decalogue is directly revealed law'. Really?

[47] For recent examinations, see Carmichael, *HTR* 69 (1976); Haran, *JJS* 30 (1979).

[48] *Cf.* the Jehovah's Witnesses' prohibition of blood transfusions on the basis of Lv. 17:10.

[49] *Cf.* Houlden's comments on NT ethics, *Ethics and the NT*, pp. 115–118.

hibition take place'.[50]

It is opinions such as these that lie behind the hesitation over utilizing the prescriptive material in the OT, which we noted at the beginning of this chapter. Out of an awareness of them, scholars periodically warn against 'proof-text' ethics.[51] But to be against proof-texting is no more adventurous than to be against sin. The question is whether we are for or against an attempt at responsible interpretation of texts. One might respond to Barth, for instance, by suggesting that the fact that God's commands are specific to men in a particular historical context does not exclude the possibility that they are the concrete expression of some principle. It would be odd if they were simply disconnected, arbitrary imperatives, as seems to be presupposed by some writers, perhaps overreacting out of an (exaggerated?) fear of legalism.[52] Similarly it is possible to overreact as a result of an awareness that cultural change is real, and to forget that cultural continuity is also real. God remains consistent and the conditions of human life today are not totally discontinuous with those of the biblical cultures.[53]

Further, although biblical commands are rarely systematized, the books of law sometimes suggest priorities and ordering among their enactments. The decalogue, for instance, is implicitly set forth in Exodus as general principles which the subsequent laws embody concretely in paradigmatic precepts.[54] Leviticus commonly bases its laws on the holiness of Yahweh: they are a way of imitating that holiness (e.g. 11:44–45; 19:1–2). Deuteronomy places the whole of its legal demands (Dt. 12 – 26) within a covenantal framework, and prefaces them (Dt. 5 – 11) with an exposition of the moral and personal attitudes to God of which outward obedience is by impli-

[50] III, 4, p. 12; cf. II, 2, p. 684; also pp. 673–674 (illustrating the point from many passages in Exodus). Cf. even more sharply Bonhoeffer, No Rusty Swords, pp. 35–44 ('There are not and cannot be Christian norms and principles of a moral nature', p. 36). Jackson (JJS 24 [1973]) warns against seeking to identify principles from OT laws from a different perspective, that of a legal historian.

[51] Sleeper, Int 22 (1968), p. 451; Gustafson, Int 24 (1970), p. 448; more moderately, *Porteous, p. 159.

[52] O'Donovan, TSFB 67 (1973), p. 18; TynB 27 (1976), pp. 55–58. Recognized by Houlden, pp. 119, 123.

[53] Cf. Minear, Commands of Christ, pp. 18–19.

[54] *Eichrodt II, p. 320; Long, Int 19 (1965), pp. 154–158, noting that the 'laws' thus constitute examples of a quality and direction of action rather than a code of behaviour; cf. Calvin's Commentaries on Exodus to Deuteronomy which see the laws as applications of the ten commandments.

cation an expression.

The wider context of the canon offers further guidance on the interrelating of these commands. The prophets identify more clearly principles embodied in them such as justice and covenant-loyalty. Jesus later suggests that the whole law can be taken as an exposition of two fundamental commands (Mt. 22:40); he takes up a basic concern of Deuteronomy, with its stress on a love for God which is then embodied in keeping his laws, and a basic concern of Leviticus 19 – 26, with its twice repeated exhortation to love one's neighbour (Lv. 19:18, 34).[55]

Studying OT ethics is in fact quite similar to studying OT theology. The Bible presents us with various concrete observations concerning how things are and concerning how men should live. Theology and ethics take these as their raw material and look behind the concrete statements for principles and generalities, which sometimes are actually on or very near the surface, at other times are much less obvious.

So how do we identify them? The process involved is as difficult (sometimes) or as straightforward (at other times) as any other aspect of the task of interpretation. We look at a statement in the light of other comparable ones where principles may be more overt. We consider it in the light of parallel extra-biblical material. We examine it in the light of the overall biblical message, as we understand it, and of whatever we see as the 'key' to that (e.g. the love command or the motif of liberation or the idea of God's rule).[56]

It is in the theology which 'undergirds' or 'informs' the actual text that, in *John Bright's view,[57] the abiding normativeness and authority of the OT (and of the NT, for that matter) lies. And clearly, it is right that, given that biblical statements themselves often do not directly bind us, looking for principles behind these statements is a useful means to discover what are the equivalent statements for today and to check purported equivalent statements. Precisely insofar as the prescriptions of the laws were not actually put into practice and were perhaps never envisaged as being (as may have been the case

[55] *Eichrodt II, pp. 335–336. Cf. Meier, *Law and History*, ch. 3.

[56] Cf. Verhey, *Religious Studies Review* 4 (1978), pp. 32–33. We will also (consciously or unconsciously) consider it in the light of other ethical concerns and insights, e.g. Marxian ones (cf. Miranda, *Marx and the Bible*; Kirk, *Origin of Accumulated Wealth*).

[57] Pp. 140–160.

with the requirement of capital punishment for adultery and other offences), such prescriptions themselves point us to the ideals of behaviour that the laws propagate.[58] The emphasis placed by some ethicists on 'middle axioms', which are somewhere between a general commitment to an overall principle such as justice, and a specific, concrete policy decision,[59] parallels the biblical scholar's interest in principles which underlie the actual text.

But if we are concerned with interpreting the Bible itself, it is nevertheless not these hypothetical principles which are normative or canonical. The Bible itself remains the norm. The principles we find in it are part of our interpretation, not the object of our interpretation. They are limited by our blind-spots, and can be the means of missing aspects of the whole message of Scripture or of evading the meaning of the text itself, rather than of serving it.[60]

Further, what we ultimately need is not these general theological principles, but specific contemporary statements, embodying the principles that underlie the biblical text. These would be the equivalent for our day of the biblical injunctions in challenging us towards a concrete obedience which shows that we take biblical 'principles' seriously.

Thus either the Bible's statements tell us how to live, or (when they do not do this) these actual statements are the model for and the measure of our attempts to state how we are to live.[61] This means we do not ignore the particularity of biblical commands (and apply them to our own day as if they were timeless universals). Nor are we paralysed by their particularity (and thus unable to apply them to our day at all). We rejoice in their particularity because it shows us how the will of God was expressed in their context, and we take them as our paradigm for our own ethical construction.

[58] Cf. McKeating, JSOT 11 (1979), pp. 69–70. C. J. H. Wright's What Does the Lord Require offers an example, seeking to identify principles for social ethics and economics on the basis of a study of the jubilee law (Lv. 25) against its socio-economic, theological, literary, and historical background.

[59] Preston, BJRL 59 (1976), pp. 173–174, also Crucible 10 (1971); Gustafson, Religion, p. 331; Paradise, ATR 61 (1979), pp. 114–115.

[60] Cf. Clines, Social Responsibility in the OT, pp. 2–3; *Childs, pp. 132–134, 184–200; also Johnstone's comments on Bright, SJT 22 (1969), pp. 202–203.

[61] Cf. O'Donovan, TynB 27 (1976), pp. 74–75; also Cook's outline structure of approach to specific texts, Are Women People Too?, p. 19.

e. The diversity of Old Testament standards

Investigating the specificness of biblical commands, however, enables another complex of questions to emerge. Within the OT there is considerable diversity over ethical matters, as there is over theological issues. For instance, some of the laws are concerned for judicial impartiality, for the needs of the poor and under-privileged, and for immigrants in the community (Ex. 22:21; 23:6–9; Dt. 24:10–15). But what of the attitude expressed elsewhere to the deformed, the illegitimate, and the foreigner (Dt. 23:1–2, 20)? The Genesis picture of man made in God's image has implications for equal rights, and Amos's polemic repudiates slavery (Am. 2:6; 8:6). But what of the laws' acceptance of this institution (Ex. 21; Dt. 15)? Genesis 1 and 2 expresses a noble vision of the man-woman relationship, but what of the acceptance elsewhere of male domination, polygamy, divorce, levirate marriage, and so on? The books of Kings gave an (apparently approving) account of the bloody revolution Jehu brought about at Elisha's behest (2 Ki. 9 – 10), but Hosea declares that Yahweh will punish Jehu's house for the blood of Jezreel (Hos. 1:4). Deuteronomy tells us that God prospers those who honour him, but the psalmist believes that God is on the side of the poor (Dt. 28:11; Ps. 86:1).

A related problem is the fact that, while some OT commands are entirely in keeping with the teaching of Christ, others seem to conflict with it and to reflect sub-Christian moral standards. As we noted in section 1c, the most trenchant exposition of this point appears in Friedrich Delitzsch's two-volume attack on the OT, *Die grosse Täuschung*. Perhaps ironically for a German of his day, Delitzsch is particularly offended by the carnage of books such as Joshua and by the nationalism that runs through the prophets and the psalms.[62] But he also notes the unethical nature of some of God's commands and the low standards of behaviour on the part of Israel and her heroes, which various documents reveal and apparently accept.[63]

There is a further aspect to this problem which, at the same time as being an apparent difficulty, nevertheless points the way towards an important aspect of the solution. It is that OT Israel is both people

[62] Carnage, I, pp. 8–52; nationalism, I, pp. 80–89; II, pp. 18–21, 38–39.
[63] Commands, I, pp. 75–79; stories, I, pp. 43–45; II, pp. 40–48.

of God and political state, whereas people of God and state are now separate entities. It may then be questioned whether the OT's approach now applies at all, whether to the secular state or to the church.[64]

In my view, however, it seems in principle entirely appropriate to investigate Yahweh's ways with Israel and to ask at various points whether his word or his acts are what he might say to or do with any nation. Even if law is covenant-law, this does not exclude its being at the same time the expression of universal principle. Indeed, the OT's understanding of the relationship between Israel and the nations perhaps directly suggests that Yahweh's way with Israel models his way (or what could be his way) with the nations (cf. Gn. 12:1–3; Jonah). If so, then here lies a basis for the Reformers' assumption that one of the law's functions is societal, the 'civil use of the law'.[65]

But there is an objection to this suggestion. B. N. Kaye notes that the characteristic OT structures which are the context of its ethical statements (land, nation, kingdom, temple) become in the NT ways of speaking about Christ and what he achieved. He adds that 'when the Christian uses the Bible in ethical discussion and decision-making he must read the Old Testament from the standpoint of the New Testament'. He also notes, however, that 'the New Testament is least helpful in what may be called the structural questions of social ethics'. It is precisely here that the OT can be a considerable resource. But Kaye's understanding of the relationship between the Testaments prevents it from being so.[66]

Kaye assumes that the NT's re-interpretation of the OT exclusively determines the lines along which a Christian today uses the OT. Indeed we cannot use the OT as if Christ had not yet come. But if we are to see *how* the NT's use of the OT is instructive for us, we need to note the particular aim of that reinterpretation. The NT is centrally concerned with the question, in what way does the OT cast light on the significance of Jesus and his achievement? It is not concerned with the interpretation of the OT in itself, but with how

---

[64] Preston, *BJRL* 59 (1976), p. 185; Kaye, *Using the Bible in Ethics*, pp. 5–9.

[65] Long, in *Norm and Context* (pp. 267–268) suggests that this assumption deserves extensive new thinking; cf. Søe's essay in the same volume, also Greenberg, Wright volume, pp. 460–461, from a Jewish perspective.

[66] *Using the Bible in Ethics*, pp. 12–15, 20; cf. Kaye, *Law, Morality and the Bible*, ch. 5.

it applies to Christ. Now it seems an arbitrary restriction to make that the only valid question a Christian can ask regarding the OT, and it is difficult to reconcile with the NT's own belief that the OT is meant to be 'profitable' in as many ways as possible (2 Tim. 3:15–16).[67] It seems more appropriate to let the OT set some of the agenda for our interpretation of it; and its concern with living in society is an obvious item for this agenda.

But what of the differences within the OT and between it and NT? Probably the commonest way of understanding these is to think in developmental terms. The OT may then be granted to begin with rather primitive standards, but it gradually reaches higher ones.[68] It is true that there are aspects of ethics that become clearer as time passes. Polygamy may characterize primarily Israel's earlier period. The theology of violence is being seen in fuller perspective in connection with the experience of exile, and Hosea's disapproval of Jehu is later than Elisha's involvement with him – though earlier than Kings' apparently approving narrative of the event! And clearly Jesus' ethical teaching has a new profundity.

The developmental approach, however, has various problems. From a practical viewpoint, its implications are unfortunate, since it presumably suggests that we simply ignore the earlier material. Nor is it generally the case that God's ideal standards become progressively dominant in OT times. Many readers find a narrowing of the ethical vision in the increasing particularism of the post-exilic community. Conversely, the highpoints of OT ethics come as often near the beginning of OT times as near their end. On most theories, Genesis 2 with its ideal of marriage is one of the earlier chapters of the OT. The pentateuch itself implies that a lowering of standards came as a result of man's rebellion against God. This in turn means that when Israel became Yahweh's people, she was as sinful as any other earthly people. The OT frequently accepts rather low moral standards as a consequence of the fact that when God chose Israel to be his people he took her as she actually was as a historical entity (cf. Dt. 9:6–29). He then had to wrestle with her as she was and seek

---

[67] Cf. the comparable restriction which says that the creation narrative can be read only in the light of the story of Israel's redemption (Wright, What Does the Lord Require, pp. 5–6).

[68] See classically Fosdick's Guide to Understanding the Bible.

to pull her towards his ultimate will.[69] OT ethics, too, thus manifests a tension between the 'already' and the 'not yet'. Although Israel is redeemed from the power of Egypt, she is not yet redeemed from the power of sin.

The insight that OT ethics in large part are for an ordinary people living in this world suggests one reason for the diversity in its attitudes, and for the contrast between some of these and those of the NT. The OT's commands often express a lower standard than the ones the OT itself implies in its understanding of creation. Thus Genesis itself describes God modifying his creation commission to man, when that commission is reissued after the flood (Gn. 1:28; 9:1–6). In the OT God's standards are applied to fallen man in a fallen world.[70]

This is particularly clear in the OT laws. Legislation by its very nature is a compromise between what may be ethically desirable and what is actually feasible given the relativities of social and political life.[71] Its aim is to control aspects of these areas in as moral a way as possible, not to describe or prescribe theoretical ideals. For instance, the realities of power, economics, and so on, produce facts such as slavery and war. The aim of the OT law on slavery may then be seen as seeking to make slavery work with as little injustice as is possible. War, too, becomes something Yahweh is Lord of, something he can be positively involved in as a means of achieving a (relatively) just purpose. It is not, then, that the OT simply accepts human sin. In seeking to bring the whole of life under Yahweh's lordship,[72] including realities such as slavery and war, it aims to draw society back towards God's ideal.[73]

To view the OT as concerned with how God's standards can be at work in the real world thus suggests it can be an important resource for a theology for the nations. Yet there are at least two dangers about utilizing the principle of condescension as a hermeneutical key

[69] *Eichrodt II, pp. 323–325; cf. P. D. Hanson in *Coats and Long.

[70] Cf. Thielicke, Theological Ethics I, p. 148, citing Gal. 3:19. Thus 'morality is of the order of the fall', resulting from the presence of sin in the world; but also 'morality is of the order of necessity', to restrain sin (Ellul, To Will and to Do, pp. 39–72; he compares *Barth II, 2, p. 517).

[71] O'Donovan, TynB 27 (1976), p. 66.

[72] Zimmerli, EvT 35 (1975), pp. 103–104; *Eichrodt I, p. 308.

[73] Kidner, Hard Sayings, pp. 32–35, 40–45; Wolff, Anthropology of OT, ch. 21, 22 (including an analogous approach to the monarchy); van der Ploeg, VTSupp 22, p. 87.

to OT ethics. One is that the condescending standard may then be dismissed, because it does not express God's ideal. It ceases to be part of Scripture. Against this possibility, one has to assert that it is part of God's condescension to man, and helps us to see how to keep society as near as possible to God's ideals without being unrealistically idealistic.

The other danger is a contrary one. If God gives a lower standard, do we really have to bother with the ideal one? Does God himself, then, not encourage a lowering of standards? Against this possibility, one has to assert that the lower standard is a condescension to hardness of heart. When we are seeking to identify God's ultimate standards, we need to see any particular OT passage in the context of the canon as a whole.[74]

It is the primal ideal or the radical prophetic aspect to the OT understanding of God's will, contrasting with the legal minimum, which is taken up by Jesus.[75] He himself sees the diversity within the Torah's attitude to marriage and divorce in this light, as his discussion about divorce (Mk. 10:1–12) shows. There is a difference between how God intended marriage to be, and the human practice that the law has to deal with, taking account of people's 'hardness of hearts'.[76]

One new thing about NT ethics, then, is that God now reasserts his ultimate demands to people who are expected to face them seriously because of what God has done for them in Christ. If OT laws are God's standards for a fallen world, the Sermon on the Mount is the law of the new age. If the creation ethic is modified because of men's hardness of hearts, as the Second Adam, Christ reaffirms it.[77] Indeed he takes it further. In what can be said by his

---

[74] Examples in *Childs, pp. 132–138 (sex ethics); *Birch and Rasmussen, pp. 175–184 (attitudes to the poor).

[75] Cf. Meier, Law and History, pp. 71–73; he refers to A. Sand, Das Gesetz und die Propheten (Regensburg: Pustet, 1974).

[76] *Von Campenhausen (pp. 8–9) offers a different understanding of this phrase, but the point about the difference between God's primal will and his condescension is not affected. H. Anderson (Stinespring volume, p. 304) says that Jesus 'virtually overthrows Moses' here in assuming 'supreme freedom . . . over against the Scripture'. But Jesus' method of comparing texts here is not novel (cf. Dahl, Studies in Paul, pp. 159–177). Gn. 1 – 2 is as much part of the Torah as Dt. 24. His freedom is the creativity with which he relates these passages of Scripture to each other.

[77] Thielicke, Theological Ethics I, p. 349; Barclay, Law, Morality and the Bible, pp. 145–147.

death and on the basis of his death he brings something that the OT only hints at (in its treatment of the suffering of figures such as Jeremiah, Job, and the servant in Isaiah 40 – 55).[78]

Perhaps this is what is meant by Jesus 'fulfilling' the law (Mt. 5:17). The law constitutes a framework or a set of boundary markers, of which the teaching of Jesus can then be the substance or the positive content which 'fills the law full'.[79] But, like the evolutionary or development model, the idea of fulfilment can suggest that the newer replaces the older.[80] One can only emphasize the importance of right attitudes, however, if the nature of people's outward actions can be presupposed. In this sense the Sermon on the Mount certainly *builds on* the decalogue, and the model of building may be a more useful one for understanding the inter-relationships of the prescriptive material in Scripture. The lower courses of bricks remain essential to the stability of the total structure. We always need the negative boundary markers as well as the positive content.

f. The 'limitations' of Old Testament standards

When all allowance has been made, do we not have to admit that over some issues Scripture is simply wrong and that we are more enlightened, not necessarily because we are morally more sensitive but because we have more information available to us?[81]

Several distinct issues are raised by examples of where twentieth century ethics may seem more advanced than those of the Bible. First, many are instances of the Bible's not making explicit all the implications of its own theology.[82] We have noted the tension be-

[78] See further section 1c. Bonhoeffer's treatment of the imprecatory psalms again illustrates the point (*Psalms*, pp. 56–60).

[79] Fritzsche, *ThL* 98 (1973), columns 164–167; D. F. Wright, *Christian Graduate* 29 (1976), p. 103.

[80] D. F. Wright (*loc. cit.*) thus sees Jesus' stress on attitudes displacing commandments regarding actions such as adultery or theft. But the NT, like the OT, proscribes the action (Jn. 8:11; Eph. 4:28) as well as the attitude.

[81] So Gustafson (*Int* 24 [1970], p. 448), instancing its attitude to women, to slavery, and to capital punishment; Preston (*BJRL* 59 [1976], pp. 186–187), adding homosexuality.

[82] Recognized by Preston, *loc. cit.* One should perhaps view the lack of explicit condemnation of polygamy in the Bible (Hillmann, *Polygamy Reconsidered*; Cairncross, *After Polygamy was Made a Sin*) in this light. Many would take the same approach to the subordination of women; but contrast G. J. Wenham, *Churchman* 92 (1979), p. 314.

tween ideal and condescension in the OT. This also appears in the NT. It, too, accepts the institution of slavery, encouraging master, slave, and Christian congregation to work with this aspect of social structure, despite the fact that it seems in tension both with the theology of creation and with that of redemption.

The tension between ideal and condescension persists, in part because Christians have to live in a world in which Christ's redemption is still to have its effect – though we must be wary of an attitude which 'reduces the incentive to the rest of society to try to live the Christian life'.[83] But it is also because Christians themselves have to live with a tension between the two ages. They live in Christ, and are challenged to live the life of the Kingdom. But they are not yet finally delivered from 'this body of death', and sometimes need the condescensions God made in relating to man in a fallen world. The church as an institution, too, reveals itself as commonly little more able to cope with God's primal ideal than was OT Israel. Many 'social determinants' affect Christian theology and practice.[84] This is one reason why the same biblical material can be read in so many different ways by different people.[85]

Both Testaments, then, work within limitations imposed by their context in accepting some less-than-ideal practices. It is easy to think that we are more enlightened than they are in our attitude to such areas as the family, work, and international relations. But we, too, have to work within limitations imposed by our context. Thus their approach to authority and responsibility within family and society, for instance, can be particularly instructive for an age in which servile subordinationism is not a widespread problem, and the OT's stress on God's justice at work in international affairs is instructive for an age which values liberation and tolerance so highly. In a similar way the OT's undermining of the institutions of monarchy and slavery from the inside means that it offers scope for a less oppressive understanding of government and employment than some modern societies that emphasise democracy and freedom.[86]

In general, the points at which the Bible's attitudes differ from

---

[83] Lindars, *Theology* 76 (1973), p. 188.

[84] Gill, *Theology and Social Structure*, ch. 2.

[85] *E.g.* H. R. Niebuhr's five ways of relating *Christ and Culture*, all based on biblical material.

[86] So Wolff, *Anthropology of OT*, ch. 22; *cf.* the remarks on the OT and modern marriage customs on p. 169.

those of our own day are precisely the points at which we need to listen to it most carefully. Otherwise we may be using the Bible only to confirm ourselves in total submission to the attitudes of our own day – which are hardly likely to be totally correct. The modern age is tempted to treat its own understanding and attitudes as absolutes, while feeling free to regard those of previous ages as relative and time-conditioned.[87] We have to be wary of this temptation as we contemplate the 'limitations' of the OT.

Another limitation that has been found in the OT is that it does not clearly distinguish ethics as a uniquely important sphere of behaviour. The Torah mixes up ethics with three other modes of behaviour that are based on choice: custom (which can conceal, hinder, or develop morality), law (which draws boundaries, but relates only to what can be controlled) and religion (which relates morality to a worldview and to God, but can confuse the ethical with the merely cultic).[88] A book such as Deuteronomy vividly illustrates the intermingling of prescriptions regarding worship, religious loyalty, mourning practices, the administration of justice, the conduct of monarchy, and so on; indeed, the decalogue itself combines the religious and the moral. A consideration of a book such as Proverbs adds an extra mode of behaviour, practical wisdom in its various facets (from how to win friends and influence people, to how to succeed in business). All these are seen as aspects of the way of Yahweh. But much of this material is at best of only indirect value to the ethicist.[89]

Indeed, in some contexts the religious may seem to have priority over the ethical. To follow Yahweh's direction may take man to the very verge of the unethical (see Gn. 22). Israel's ideal heroes, who include Abraham the liar, Moses the murderer, and David the adulterer, are nevertheless heroes, because they followed in Yahweh's

---

[87] Cf. Berger, Rumour of Angels, ch. 2 on the consequent need to 'relativize the relativizers'.

[88] Cf. Ebeling, Study of Theology, pp. 141–142; *Eichrodt II, pp. 328–329. McKeating (JSOT 11 [1979], pp. 70–71) notes that, although religious or theological considerations lie behind many behavioural laws, these may only carry weight in forming society's patterns of behaviour when such considerations are backed by pragmatic ones. Standards of behaviour that seemed to have only religious and not pragmatic backing were less likely to be accepted by society in practice.

[89] Kaye, Using the Bible, p. 9. It is noticeable that religion and law are kept more separate in documents such as Hammurabi's Code, where the deity is referred to (fairly nominally?) in the introduction and conclusion.

way rather than accepting the direction of some other god.[90] The OT's attitude to war, and the particularism of Deuteronomy and of the post-exilic period (Dt. 23:1–2, 20; Ezra 9 – 10; Neh. 13), also seem to allow religious considerations to override narrowly ethical ones.[91]

The intermingling of the ethical and the religious is also characteristic of NT commands in such passages as the Sermon on the Mount and the teaching of Paul. Elsewhere in the NT, religious concerns seem to override strictly ethical ones (e.g. Jn. 13:34–35; Gal. 1:9; 5:12; and much of Rev.). Here, again, a different approach from our own can be instructive. The Bible as a whole believes that life as a whole is to be lived before God, and it does not seek to compartmentalize God's concerns or to declare that in principle 'ethics' is more important than worship. There is an insight here which we have to come to terms with, rather than a limitation we are now able to perceive. Ethics, like theology, is not really a biblical category!

A third related 'limitation' characteristic of some OT commands is that they are specifically expressive of the religion of Israel, whose forms are not binding on the Christian believer. A Christian is not obliged to be circumcised, to pay tithes, or to observe sabbaths, as an Israelite was.

The classic rationale for a distinction between commands' which are not binding on the Christian, and other commands which are, is the division of OT laws into the moral, the civil, and the ceremonial. But this division is an unsatisfactory instrument for analysing the laws. In one sense it is too blunt: there is a wider variety of law than

---

[90] Jacob, VTSupp 7, p. 42.

[91] Cf. Ellul's discussion of ḥerem (the 'ban'), To Will and to Do, pp. 205–229; Kidner, Hard Sayings, pp. 40–45; O'Donovan (in an unpublished paper 'OT ethics and moral change') describes this practice as a form of holiness or dedication without ethic; not an ultimate good, but a 'good' in this context as Yahweh turns a taboo into his command in the course of leading his people towards an understanding of the moral nature of his holiness. On particularism, *Vriezen (pp. 338–339/²pp. 400–401) suggests that the OT's less generous attitude to one's enemy than that of some Babylonian wisdom reflects the link of religion and ethics; polytheism and tolerance go naturally together. Conversely, acknowledgement of one God and intolerance go naturally together, and if pluralism is the secularized version of polytheism, it is not surprising if the contemporary world is more sympathetic with Babylonian tolerance than Israelite exclusiveness.

this division indicates.[92] In another sense, the division is too sharp an instrument, for moral, ceremonial, and civil cannot be distinguished as sharply as it implies. Even Calvin, while accepting the division, notes that ceremonial and civil laws embody moral principles.[93] While this may not be the case with circumcision, it is the case with the sabbath and with the payment of tithes.

It is easy for a distinction into 'moral, civil, and ceremonial' to lead to practical importance being attached only to the first category. We have seen already that in a carefree way the OT mingles various types of command, suggesting the view that all are to be seen as aspects of accepting the Lordship of the one Yahweh. *All* the commands of the OT are specific to their circumstances, *all* have to be seen in the light of Christ's coming, but *all* may be instructive today in the light of principles they embody.

Our discussion of the 'Old Testament as a way of life' has been problem-orientated, because much recent writing has emphasized the difficulties involved in using the OT (or the NT) for moral guidance. But two dangers threaten the person who is interested in the contemporary use of the Bible, in this area as in others. One is the danger of simplistic application. The other is that, once we are aware of the need to avoid being simplistic, we let the task seem to become so complex that it is hardly worth the effort. But it is appropriate to note here that, while interpreting OT commands is a subtle task, it is not ultimately a mysterious one. The OT can be a fruitful resource for ethical insight, as is shown by the writings of many of the scholars referred to in this chapter.

---

[92] Phillips categorizes law as criminal, civil, customary, family, and cultic (*Ancient Israel's Criminal Law*, p. 2; *cf.* C. J. H. Wright, *What Does the Lord Require*, ch. 2).
[93] *Institutes* IV. xx. 14; *cf.* D. F. Wright, *Christian Graduate* 29 (1976), p. 99.

Chapter Three

The Old Testament
as the story of salvation

*I am Yahweh your God, who
brought you out of the land
of Egypt.* (Ex. 20:2)

*He has made known to us in
all wisdom and insight the
mystery of his will, according
to his purpose which he set
forth in Christ for the fullness
of time.* (Eph. 1:9–10)

In section 1b we noted that *Gerhard von Rad questioned whether
the systematic approach to OT theology expounded with great insight
by scholars such as *Walther Eichrodt could nevertheless do justice
to the OT's own way of thinking. Von Rad and G. E. Wright saw
its dominant theme as the acts of God: Israel's faith is a theology of
history. So OT theology should consist in a proclamation of this
theme of salvation history (*Heilsgeschichte*)[1].

The theme of salvation history was not originated by modern OT
scholars; it is usually traced back to the mid-nineteenth century
'Erlangen school', especially J. C. K. von Hofmann.[2] It has also
been taken up by NT scholars, who have seen the Christ event as the
climax of God's saving acts in history.[3] It can then be seen as the
major link between the Testaments: they relate the beginning and
the conclusion of one story, Act I and Act II of the same drama.
The Christ event completes a story which would be otherwise trun-
cated; the OT gives the pre-history of an event which would other-

---

[1] *Von Rad, especially I, pp. 105–106; von Rad in *Westermann, pp. 24–32; Wright,
God Who Acts, pp. 11–13; Wright and Fuller, *Book of the Acts of God*, pp. 17–18;
*Bright, pp. 130–131.

[2] *Gunneweg, pp. 179–180; *Kraus, pp. 247–253. See also section 4d below.

[3] E.g. Stauffer, *NT Theology*; Cullmann, *Christ and Time*, p. 23; *Salvation in
History*; Goppelt, *Int* 21 (1967).

wise lack the context which makes it intelligible.[4]

Nor is an interest in a theology of history confined to biblical scholarship. In the nineteenth century historical study had seemed to alienate the OT from the NT, from Christianity, and from the modern world, indeed to threaten to undermine Christian faith altogether. Karl Barth and Rudolf Bultmann in different ways sought to evade the latter problem by doing without history as it is generally practised, but the stress on a theology of history instead took the offensive and appropriated history as a key category for understanding Scripture.[5] *Wolfhart Pannenberg, indeed, claimed that 'history is the most comprehensive horizon of Christian theology'.[6]

Even as this emphasis reached its high point in the 1960s, however, the idea that salvation history is the OT's major theme and its fundamental link with the NT was becoming the subject of a wide-ranging critique. Indeed, there is some danger of a reaction from an uncritical absorption with this theme to an equally uncritical (and perhaps embarrassed) rejection of it. In my judgment it is not 'time to say goodbye to *Heilsgeschichte*',[7] but the critique has certainly indicated points at which the idea needs clarifying and seeing in perspective.

a. How pervasive is God's activity in history?

Von Rad and Wright recognized that God's acts in history are not actually the OT's sole theme. The wisdom books are the obvious exception to any such overall claim,[8] but many psalms also lack any reference to salvation history. The prophetic polemic against Israel and against the nations, too, seldom refers to the exodus or the covenant, and seems to base itself on moral standards that should have been recognized by people whether they knew covenant law or not; it thus presupposes a natural theology rather than a *heilsges-*

---

[4] So *von Rad II, pp. 382–384; Wright, *God Who Acts*, p. 57; *Bright, pp. 138–140, 198–203.
[5] *Cf.* Wildberger, *EvT* 19 (1959), pp. 72–73; Jepson in *Westermann, pp. 246–249; Barr, *Int* 17 (1963), pp. 194–195.
[6] I p. 15; *cf.* the symposium *Revelation as History*; also Kaufman, *JR* 36 (1956), and his *Systematic Theology*; *Herberg; *Voegelin.
[7] *McKenzie (p. 325), following *Hesse; *cf.* the critiques in *Gunneweg and *Childs and the avoidance of the theme in *Clements.
[8] *Von Rad I, pp. 106, 453; Wright, *God Who Acts*, p. 103; *cf.* *Barr, pp. 72–76.

chichtliche theology.[9]

The wisdom tradition can be integrated into the salvation history approach. For instance, as law is connected with salvation history via Moses and the Sinai covenant, so wisdom can be so connected via Solomon and the Davidic covenant, following hints offered by the historical and the wisdom books in their portrayal of Solomon as the archetypal wise man. Or wisdom can be seen as the way of life that issues from God's original acts of grace and judgment in the primeval history. Or wisdom (and the psalms) can be seen as Israel's response to God's acts in history.[10] Arguably, however, the whole Bible can be understood as Israel's response to God.[11]

But why should wisdom (or other aspects of OT faith) be integrated into salvation history? The OT sees Yahweh as present and active in the regularities of nature as well as in the once-for-all events of history, in the blessings of everyday life as well as in salvation from periodic crises, in an overall lordship over the cosmos as well as in particular historical events, in the lives of all men as well as in the history of Israel; the former perspective is as important as the latter and provides an essential foundation for it.[12] 'Wisdom thinks resolutely within the framework of a theology of creation';[13] but we relate to creation not only historically, as the 'historical books' present the matter, but immediately and directly by living in the world whose being is continually maintained by the creator God, as many other parts of the OT often portray it.[14] So the OT invites us to a more dialectical understanding of the relationship between creation faith and redemption faith than the subordination of one to the other.[15]

The point may be broadened by noting the wide range of the means whereby Yahweh revealed himself to OT Israel. She experienced his presence and activity and heard his voice in the story of

---

[9] Cf. Barton, *JTS* 30 (1979); see further sections 2ab above.

[10] See respectively Prussner, *Transitions in Biblical Scholarship*; Zimmerli, *SJT* 17 (1964); *von Rad I, pp. 355–459 (cf. *Zimmerli, pp. 155–166).

[11] C. Barth, *EvT* 23 (1963), pp. 368–369; Murphy, *Int* 23 (1969), p. 290; Porteous, von Rad volume, p. 424.

[12] See von Rad's later *Wisdom in Israel*, with Pannenberg's comments in *Gerhard von Rad*, pp. 43–54; Westermann on *Blessing*; also Martin-Achard, *TZ* 35 (1979); Saggs, *Encounter with the Divine*, p. 52; Schmid, *ZTK* 70 (1973); Reventlow, *JSOT* 11 (1979), pp. 8–10.

[13] Zimmerli, *SJT* 17 (1964), p. 148.

[14] See Westermann, *Genesis*, pp. 89–92; Barr, *Weerwood*, p. 13.

[15] See further Goldingay, *EvQ* 51 (1979).

her past as a nation and she expected to experience it in her future. Thus she was aware of living in history. But she also experienced it in her present, in nature, in personal experience, in worship, in the theophany, in the hearing and uttering of the prophetic word, in her moral awareness, in the law, in her institutions and ordinances.[16] Here too the acts and voice of God were known, and the writings of prophets, psalmists, and wise men (and indeed the historical books themselves) echo it, making it clear that salvation history is not all there is to OT faith. Yet it remains true that the major overt emphasis of much of the OT is that Yahweh has acted, acts, and will act in Israel's history for her salvation. The importance of this emphasis should not be lost in the course of recognizing complementary features of OT faith.[17]

b. Did salvation history happen?

Salvation history, then, is a direct concern of some half of the OT (the narratives from Genesis to Ezra), and an indirect interest of other parts of it (much of the prophets, some of the psalms, and so on). These books believe that Yahweh has been active in events of Israel's history such as the exodus and the occupation of Palestine, and that this fact is of direct relevance to those to whom they speak and write.

If these events are to have that significance, they presumably need actually to have happened. But did they? As a critical historian, von Rad himself doubts whether the narratives can be taken as a reliable guide to the events of Israel's history. He suggests several reasons for this. One is that the narratives draw their picture by faith, embodying in the picture itself their understanding of an event's deep significance and permanent challenge; the picture is poetic rather than critical history. Another reason is that the narratives are written in the light of subsequent experience of Yahweh's acts on his people's behalf; that subsequent experience, as well as the original

---

[16] Cf. *McKenzie, pp. 31–34; *Fohrer, pp. 33–50, also *BZAW* 99, pp. 268–273, 285–288; Jacob, *Grundfragen*, pp. 35–37; Goldingay, *TynB* 23 (1972), pp. 58–78; also Knierim, von Rad volume, for a discussion of recent German study of revelation in the OT (see also *Zimmerli, pp. 17–21, *EvT* 22 (1962), and *Gottes Offenbarung*, pp 11–132).

[17] Cf. Jacob, *Grundfragen*, pp. 40–42; Smend, *Elemente alttestamentlichen Geschichtsdenkens*, pp. 36–37; Zimmerli, *ThL* 98 (1973), column 87.

event, is then reflected in the story. A third reason is that the story is told in the light of the ultimate purpose of God to which the events contribute, so that a story such as the conquest narrative anticipates that final purpose. And further, the story is told so as to speak to the situations of its readers. Like later haggadah, it explains, evaluates, and applies for their sake. It is a literary work with a message from an author to readers, not simply a chronicle.[18]

Von Rad does not believe 'that in these descriptions of her early period Israel may have lost contact with actual history. They are rather utterances . . . of a people obsessed with its actual history'.[19] He recognises, however, that the gap between the story the OT tells and the events as they actually happened raises problems for his approach to OT theology. If the history did not happen, how can it have been salvation history? Can the narratives retain theological value? *Prima facie*, they need to be fundamentally historical in order to make it possible for their readers to appropriate what they witness to – for what they witness to is a saving purpose of God at work in real history.[20]

The dimensions of the problem can perhaps be relaxed, however, by considering what kinds of narrative require to be fundamentally historical. R. Smend suggests a distinction between aetiological and paradigmatic narratives.[21] Paradigms, like parables, offer illustration of how things always are or should be, and their historicity may not be vital. Aetiologies explain how things came to be what they are,

---

[18] *Von Rad I, pp. 106–112; II, pp. 417–425; von Rad in *Westermann, pp. 32–35; cf. *Voegelin, pp. 121–122; Smend, pp. 26–31; *Amsler, pp. 200–209; Lonergan, *Method in History*, p. 185; Hesse, *ZAW* 81 (1969), p. 10.

[19] *II, p. 424. Von Rad has been accused of looking too much like an OT Bultmann by those who did not think he looked too much like an OT Cullmann (so *Eichrodt I, p. 515; Zimmerli, *VT* 13 (1963), p. 104; cf. Stoebe on Rendtorff, Hertzberg volume, pp. 203–204). But he is really an OT Barth, as his approach to saga in his *Genesis* shows (cf. *Barth, e.g. III, 1, pp. 76–90). Greig (*AUSS* 16 [1978], pp. 324–326) traces his attitude to poetic history to Dilthey.

[20] *Von Rad I, pp. 107–108; cf. the objections of Baumgärtel (e.g. *Verheissung*, pp. 120–122) and *Hesse, also *Hanson, pp. 229–233; cf. Nineham's comments about the gospel tradition in *JTS* 11 (1960), p. 264.

[21] *Elemente*, pp. 10–23; cf. Smend in *D. A. Knight, pp. 56–60. But Smend notes the complication that the OT does not keep the two separate (*Elemente*, pp. 23–28); cf. *Barr, pp. 68–70 (also *JR* 56 [1976], pp. 5–8) on the interweaving of historical and other material in OT narrative.

and they more clearly need to be historical.[22] Is the OT account of how Israel came to possess the land of Canaan, then, historically true (and therefore potentially theologically valid)?

Conservative scholars respond to this question with a clear 'yes', in the conviction that historical and archaeological study demonstrates the 'basic reliability of Biblical history'.[23] The danger of this view in principle, however, is that it may lead to an apologetic approach to the investigation of Israelite history which is, as such, always tempted to fudge the evidence. Furthermore, scholarship a generation later than G. E. Wright does not generally share his confidence in the Bible's basic reliability, at least as regards Israel's crucial early period.

R. Rendtorff and W. Pannenberg sought to coalesce the two histories by noting that the growth of Israel's understanding of God's activity in relation to her, which von Rad saw was reflected in the way she narrated her history, was as much part of her history as the outward events were. God's activity in Israel's history involved the inward event and the development of Israel's tradition, as well as the outward event.[24]

God's acts in history are thus rescued, but there is an impression of sleight-of-hand about the whole operation, since it involves tacitly re-defining salvation history. The concept was taken up on the grounds that the Bible itself gave prominence to God's involvement in national, public events such as the exodus, which comprise Israel's salvation history. Other events such as the growth of her self-understanding, expressed in her tradition, can be seen as reflecting

[22] H. D. Lewis, however, suggests that factual narrative is more compelling than fiction because we know it relates events that belong to the real world (*Freedom and History*, p. 164); thus even paradigmatic narratives gain from being factual. But on the positive possibilities of seeing OT narrative as fiction see Collins, *CBQ* 41 (1979); Ricoeur, *Semeia* 13 (1978); Buss, *Theology as History*, pp. 144–146; Thompson, *BZAW* 133, p. 329; though in their 'hard' form such suggestions seem to underestimate the OT's theological commitment to and dependence on the historicity of the acts of God in Israel's history.

[23] Wright, *God Who Acts*, p. 127; cf. de Vaux, *Bible and Ancient Near East*, pp. 59–60; Eichrodt in *Westermann, pp. 236–237; Soggin, *TZ* 17 (1961); *Gunneweg, p. 198 (despite his questioning of the salvation history concept). See the historical work of scholars such as Albright, Wright, and Bright.

[24] See their essays in the 1961 von Rad *Festschrift*, especially Rendtorff, pp. 89–93 (also *ZTK* 57 [1960], pp. 39–40, and his *Gesammelte Studien*) and Pannenberg, p. 135–138 (ET in *Pannenberg I, pp. 89–92); cf. Eichrodt, in *Westermann, p. 237; Noth, *Pentateuchal Traditions*, p. 252.

God's activity in her life,[25] but she did not understand these events in salvation history terms. It seems questionable to claim to follow Israel in interpreting the OT as salvation history, but to do this by re-defining salvation history. In the end, von Rad is retelling the history of the development of Israel's faith in God's acts in history (contrary to his overt intention), not retelling the acts of God.[26]

Von Rad's approach does allow for God being experienced as acting in national, public events and being pictured as such. Joshua 1 – 12 illustrates this: real experiences of a later period are here projected back into the story of the conquest.[27] But there is something unsatisfying about the suggestion that, while the saving events actually narrated did not occur, other saving events occurred of which the narrative does not directly tell us. It reminds one of the chestnut that if Moses did not exist we have to invent someone else to do his job.

W. Pannenberg is concerned to re-assert the 'original unity of facts and their meaning', questioned since Kant.[28] This suggests that the development of tradition should be seen as the developing grasp of the meaning of the events themselves, rather than the developing of new, extrinsic insights which are projected back on to these events. Not that we should cease to distinguish fact and meaning, and imply that only interpreted facts are real facts, for this involves abandoning the attempt to be objective about history.[29] Fact and meaning are to be linked, but distinguished; the latter will continue to emerge with time, and will be fully apparent only in the context of the whole of history.

But if the OT is really interested in history, why does investigating that history yield such unsatisfying results? In part this is a problem about the historical method, not merely about Israel's traditions. The historical-critical way of writing history is itself a moulding of the past in the light of present beliefs. It has its own biases, particu-

---

[25] Cf. Barr's observation (RTP III.18 [1968], pp. 209–212) that the development of Israel's ideas in the post-exilic period can be seen as part of her salvation history even though it involved her thinking less in terms of salvation history herself.

[26] Porteous, von Rad volume, p. 423; Zimmerli, VT 13 (1963), p. 104.

[27] See Weippert, Settlement, p. 141; cf. *Eichrodt I, p. 50.

[28] Theology as History, p. 127; cf. Harvey, BTB 1 (1971), p. 22 on von Rad; facta and dicta must be held together (Sekine, ZAW 75 [1963]).

[29] Cf. Cupitt's criticism of the idealist notion of history, espoused by Collingwood (Christ and the Hiddenness of God, pp. 127–129).

larly in excluding the kerygmatic aspect to events and the deeper dimensions to texts – indeed, in excluding God from history altogether. This explains a major element in the difference between history as related by the OT and by the modern historian.[30]

Yet this bias of critical history cannot be blamed for some of the more troublesome gaps between the OT picture and the historian's reconstruction of Israelite history, such as the problematical links between patriarchal and settlement traditions, or between exodus and Sinai traditions, on which depends the theology of promise and fulfilment, or of grace and law. A case can be made on critical grounds for linking these traditions and the events they relate; but the evidence is such that no one approach to these issues can at present commend itself along a wide front of scholarship.

So while faith is impossible if it has no historical grounds, the historian cannot offer us proof or disproof of the historicity of these early acts of God in Israel's history.[31] If I carry on believing that these events took place and that the message based on them is true, even though I cannot prove it, the basis of my belief must lie elsewhere than in historical evidence itself. It may lie in the later realities of the prophetic experience of God: their relationship to history is more certain but they overtly build on the hexateuchal tradition, suggesting that the latter must reflect real acts of God. It may lie in Christ's acceptance of the OT as God's word, which reassures me of the reliability of its historical material – for if it were not reliable he would not make the mistake of acknowledging it. It may lie in my own knowledge of God's acts in Christ and in the Christian community, which leads me into fuller insight on God's earlier acts. It may lie in the fact that the truth of the hexateuchal traditons keeps proving itself in my own experience and life, enabling me to understand the whole of reality more convincingly and thus

---

[30] See *von Rad II, p. 418; *EvT* 24 (1964), pp. 391–393. It would thus be odd to seek to base a *heilsgeschichtliche* theology on history as reconstructed by modern scholars rather than as the OT portrays it, as Hesse once urged (*KD* 4 [1958]; *ZTK* 57 [1960], pp. 24–26; also in *Westermann, pp. 24–26), since God is on principle excluded from the former. See further *Hasel, pp. 31–34, 83–89/²pp. 59–62, 131–137. Part of *Barth's aversion to 'history' derives from this problem (*e.g.* III, 2, pp. 440–455; *cf.* Ogletree's discussion, *Christian Faith and History*, pp. 192–201).

[31] Pannenberg, *Theology as History*, pp. 272–275.

testifying to its own truth.[32]

On such bases I may maintain the conviction that salvation history happened, even when I cannot demonstrate this by historical methods. Two final comments then need to be made. One is that such faith-convictions cannot make historical investigation redundant. A historian may begin from an intuition about an event and its meaning, but such intuitions have to be tested by being confronted by concrete data. Indeed, the biblical sources themselves point us to real events and invite us to investigate their historicity so that we can believe on the basis of them. We cannot have history's benefits without its risks.[33]

The other comment is that OT interpretation is nevertheless concerned not only with investigating the historical events to which its narratives testify, but also with understanding the OT narratives themselves. If their writers were seeking to write pure 'history' and failed, it is difficult to take their work seriously. But if they were telling a story with a message, it is their story that we have to interpret. The text points us to an event, but it is the text that tells us the event's revelatory significance.[34] This leads to our next question.

c. How do God's acts relate to his words?

Those who emphasize that the OT is the story of God's acts often do so overtly as an alternative to seeing it as God's word. Revelation lies in history, rather than in word.[35]

But to emphasize history *rather than* word is to overreact from theologies that emphasize word at the expense of event, replacing *sola scriptura* by *sola historia*.[36] In the OT itself words have great

[32] See respectively Porteous, *ASTI* 8 (1970–1) (*cf.* Davidson, *ExpT* 77 [1965–6], pp. 101–102); Goldingay, *TynB* 23 (1972), pp. 91–93; Richardson, in *Anderson, pp. 46–47; Pannenberg, *Theology as History*, p. 133.

[33] See *Pannenberg I, pp. 50–51, 70–72, 78, following Collingwood; Jepsen in *Westermann, pp. 267–271; Voegelin, in *Anderson, pp. 64–89; Cupitt, p. 121; contrast Barth.

[34] *Amsler, p. 162.

[35] Wright, *God Who Acts*, p. 12; *Pannenberg I, pp. 15–80; II, pp. 19–26; the whole symposium *Revelation as History* (*e.g.* Rendtorff, p. 47).

[36] *Gunneweg, p. 192, also p. 199, *Amsler, p. 172, sees the historical method's preoccupation with the event behind the text, rather than the text itself, as parallel to allegory.

prominence as God's means of communicating with his people. After all, a person's words are his most characteristic form of communication.[37] His acts reveal his character,[38] but generally this is incidental to their actual aim; like anyone else, God acts in order to achieve something and speaks in order to communicate something, even though his actions can confirm his words and his speaking can be his way of seeing that his aims are put into effect. Actions are not self-explanatory, and neither are events such as Israel's escape from Egypt, her exile to Babylon, or her return to Palestine; you can know about the event but not know Yahweh.[39] The process of understanding Yahweh's purpose moves from theological convictions to the interpretation of event at least as much as vice versa. Further, revelation in word can be relatively independent of historical events. This is clearly the case with wisdom and law, and also with much prophetic material.[40] Indeed, even biblical narrative is not always seeking to be historical, but can use material of varying relationship to what we call history to embody a vision in a story.[41]

In actual fact, von Rad and Pannenberg allow for the word. Von Rad sees Israel's history as brought about by God's word and as mediated to us through Israel's verbal tradition, but he is less clear on the relative significance of word and event.[42] According to Pannenberg, 'the word relates itself to revelation [in history] as foretelling, forthtelling, and report', but it is not integral to revelation. The prophetic announcement of future events, for instance, is not essential to their having revelatory value; it is a concession to Israel's unbelief.[43] History, not word, thus receives the emphasis.

[37] Grobel, *Theology as History*, pp. 157–166; *Albrektson, pp. 118–122; *Barr, pp. 77–82.

[38] Pannenberg, *Theology as History*, p. 235.

[39] *Albrektson, pp. 113–114; de Vaux, *Bible and Ancient Near East*, pp. 52–53; Stoebe, Hertzberg volume, p. 208.

[40] *Cf.* Fohrer's comments on prophecy's emphasis on word, *BZAW* 99, pp. 287–288.

[41] *Cf.* *Barr, pp. 68–70; *JR* 56 (1976), pp. 5–8; Coggins, *JSOT* 11 (1979); Frei, *Eclipse of Biblical Narrative*. In encouraging us to look on the OT as story, however, Barr is inclined to have in mind the OT as a whole, an abstracted overarching story rather than the story told by particular narratives; while Coggins compares the OT with Shakespeare, whereas a better comparison might be with Thucydides or Herodotus. *Cf.* Smend in *D. A. Knight, pp. 49–50.

[42] See von Rad in *Westermann, pp. 25–26, with *Westermann's comments, pp. 46–49; also *Gunneweg, pp. 90–91.

[43] *Revelation as History*, pp. 152–155; *Theology as History*, p. 129.

Perhaps this stress on history is culture-relative, reflecting as it does our own historical awareness. 'History is God nowadays.'[44] Pannenberg himself hints at this. He accepts that the Bible speaks in terms of word as well as of event; yet he refuses to give word prominence in his own theology, on the grounds that it involves an authoritarian claim to revelation which is unacceptable to post-Enlightenment men.[45] The word can bring out only the inherent meaning of an event, which is visible to all men. It cannot have an authority of its own, independent of that history to which it points.

But is revelation as word inherently more authoritarian than revelation as event? Pannenberg himself notes that this may not necessarily be the case.[46] Indeed Scripture itself commonly says not 'Believe this because I say so' but 'Believe this because it makes sense in the following way, because it is proved true by the following. . .'. The authority of the word then lies in that to which it refers and that which it interprets. It is not inherently authoritarian.

Admittedly the truth of the word may only be self-evident in the context of the whole of history, and individual words presuppose that total context. It is this that partly explains the way 'the promises do not enter so literally into a fulfillment as one would assume that they would if they were the word of God effecting history'.[47] The problem is not actually that history 'overtakes' the promises, but that it falls behind them. Pannenberg himself recognizes that the prophetic word points to the ultimate fulfilment – that ultimate fulfilment anticipated in Jesus, who is thus the confirmation of them (2 Cor. 1:20). But when we say that the individual word has its context in the whole of reality and derives its authority from its relationship with the whole of reality, we are simply applying to the word the principle Pannenberg himself applies to the individual event as a means of revelation.

The function of the word, then, is to set an event in that universal context which is not yet complete. It is not merely a concession to unbelief (only the unique rebukes of Isaiah 48 make this point). It is a concession to the incompleteness of any historical perspective,

[44] See Reumann, *NTS* 13 (1966–7), p. 147; *cf.* *Gunneweg, p. 209; Thompson, *BZAW* 133, p. 328; *Kraus, p. 314; Geyer, *EvT* 25 (1965), p. 214.
[45] *Theology as History*, pp. 226–230.
[46] *Theology as History*, pp. 227–228, n. 4.
[47] Pannenberg, *Theology as History*, p. 259.

and brings out an event's inherent meaning in the light of the whole of history. It is revealed by the Spirit now, though this does not in itself mean that its authority finally rests on this (predicated) origin. Its authority rests on whether it corresponds to reality. This correspondence may not be complete, until history is complete. But it must be adequate, and more satisfying overall than alternatives.

Behind the question whether revelation is to be found in events or in words lies the question whether language or history is more fundamental to reality. Is hermeneutic to embrace history by interpreting language as event, or is history to embrace word by interpreting event in the context of tradition?[48] We shall more likely do justice to reality by letting these two interact and refusing to let one subsume the other. The danger of the new hermeneutic or of Brevard Childs' canonical criticism (see sections 5abc) is that it underestimates history. The danger of Wright or Pannenberg is that they devalue the word. History is a necessary condition of the truth of OT faith (as we saw in section 3b), but not a sufficient condition of it.

There needs to be a match of theological concept and historical fact. Fact and word (facta and dicta) have to be held together; 'facts without words are blind; and words without facts are empty'.[49] Similarly in relation to the NT, the importance of the OT is not soteriological (in revealing the Torah as the means of salvation), nor is it merely historical (in constituting Act I to the NT's Act II); it is hermeneutical (in embodying the forms of speech in which the Christ event could be articulated as the definitive act of the God of Israel).[50]

d. Is salvation history distinctive to the Old Testament?

One of the attractions of the salvation history approach was that the belief that God revealed himself in once-for-all events seemed to constitute a concept which was of central importance in the OT and at the same time distinguished Israel's faith from those of other nations with their mythical thinking.[51] *Bertil Albrektson's *History and the Gods: An Essay on the Idea of Historical Events as Divine*

---

[48] *Cf.* J. M. Robinson, *Theology as History*, p. 2.

[49] Braaten, *History and Hermeneutics*, p. 23, paraphrasing Kant; *cf.* Morgan, *Nature of NT Theology*, pp. 29, 157; Sekine, *ZAW* 75 (1963); Cupitt, *op. cit.*, pp. 113–116, 123–126.

[50] Geyer, *EvT* 25 (1965), p. 237.

[51] *E.g.* Noth, *Laws in the Pentateuch*, p. 195.

Manifestations in the Ancient Near East and in Israel attempts a quiet but comprehensive demolition of the beliefs behind such an assumption.[52] He demonstrates that the gods of the ancient near east were involved in history as well as in nature (though these two realms were probably not distinguished as they are by us). These gods used human kings as their instruments, as Yahweh did. They executed their control over the events of history by means of their word, with its mighty and terrifying power, again like Yahweh. They, too, worked purposefully in history and could be pictured as overseeing the unfolding of events from creation to a writer's own day. Likewise they thus revealed themselves (their power, their anger, their love) in these historical events.

Admittedly, Israel's views should not be assimilated to those of other nations; her emphasis on divine activity in history remains striking.[53] But her distinctiveness should not be overstated. Yet why does distinctiveness matter? The claim that Israelite faith is unique is an important part of the apologetic of scholars such as G. E. Wright. Is it important that Yahweh alone made this claim about his sphere of activity?[54] It is possible to make a unique claim, and to be wrong; it is possible to make a unique claim, and be right, but for the claim to be not worth making; it is possible for two people to express the same significant insight, and for both of them to be right; it is possible for two people to make the same significant claim, and for only one of them to be right. The question of uniqueness actually arises in the OT in claims such as 'Yahweh alone has ultimate power', 'Yahweh alone rules in history'. The fact that other nations make this claim for their gods is more likely presupposed than denied by such statements. There is no need for Yahweh's claim to be unique. What matters is whether he is right.

Perhaps the traditional stress on uniqueness confuses meaning and reference. It claims that the concept of a God acting in history was

[52] *Cf.* also Gese, *Journal for Theology and Church* 1 (1965); Dentan, *Idea of History*; Saggs, *Encounter with the Divine*, pp. 69–92; Clapham, G. E. Wright volume.

[53] Although *Albrektson recognizes this (p. 115), Lambert suggests that he underestimates Israel's distinctiveness (*Orientalia* 39 [1970]; *OTS* 17 [1972]); but Saggs (pp. 70–76) in turn questions Lambert's approach to this issue.

[54] Buss remarks, 'Uniqueness may enhance individuality, but it is not inherently related to theological truth or to moral validity'; and anyway true individuality 'lies positively in wholeness rather than negatively in idiosyncrasy' (*Encounter with the Biblical Text*, pp. 21, 22).

known only in Israel, when the more important claim is that this concept (which might have been widely known) had only one true referent, namely the God of Israel. Perhaps the former claim came to seem important because of a confusing correlating of the notion of uniqueness with the notion of revelation. To put the point in traditional categories, the Bible is God's revelation; what it reveals is the only way of redemption. G. E. Wright, like many others since the nineteenth century, wished to locate the revelation in the redemptive events rather than in the Bible, and the uniqueness belonging to the redemption has thus come to be attached to the revelation. The excessive importance attached to the theological concept of revelation in recent centuries compounded this problem.[55]

Albrektson's work, then, points towards a greater precision over the distinctiveness of the Israelite idea of God acting in history. But even if that distinctiveness were to be quite eliminated, this would not threaten the viability of the concept of salvation history as a category for OT theology. The question is not, 'How many religions believe that their gods control history?'. It is, 'Which religion (if any) truly claims that its God controls history?'

e. Is 'salvation history' still meaningful?

Talk of God acting in history commended itself in an age that emphasized history. But what does such talk actually mean? L. B. Gilkey[56] has pointed out that while scholars such as G. E. Wright and B. W. Anderson still use the biblical *language* of God himself acting and speaking, they do not themselves believe that God acted or spoke as this language describes him doing. The 'acts of God' either did not occur or were quite natural events; the 'words of God' were not really miraculous audible voices but human testimonies to what faith believed that it perceived. OT faith emphasized the recital of God's acts, but it is doubtful if our faith can.

In response to Gilkey's argument, S. M. Ogden and G. Kaufman[57] have pointed out that we do not see God's activity only in isolated

---

[55] Cf. Braaten, pp. 11–16. Buss (pp. 21–22) notes that the emphasis on peculiarity is a feature of historical criticism.

[56] JR 41 (1961); cf. Naming the Whirlwind, especially pp. 80–101.

[57] Ogden, JR 43 (1963); Kaufman, HTR 61 (1968); see also JR 36 (1956) and his Systematic Theology.

events separated from regular history. All history reflects God's activity, as a man's whole life is that man's activity. A disadvantage of this response, however, is that it turns attention from the special events that salvation history has usually denoted to the regular events that constitute providence rather than *Heilsgeschichte*; instead of wisdom with its concern for the regular and for cause and effect being neglected, it seems to have taken over.[58] But Ogden and Kaufman do not merely see events in general as God's acts. Rather there will be certain events which particularly manifest his characteristic concerns as creator and redeemer, and which are thus 'the acts of God' in a special sense – as certain activities may be especially characteristic of a man and may be seen as *his* acts in a way that other aspects of his activity are not. There will also be certain events which play a key role in the achievement of God's purpose, which especially further his aim in all his activity (*i.e.* history as a whole). Such events need not emerge immediately from the divine will independently of the context of other finite events within the cause-effect nexus; but they are crucial steps towards God's ultimate objectives, and in this sense are special 'acts of God'.

The approaches of Ogden and Kaufman help to clarify a confusion between 'mighty acts' in the Bible's sense and 'miracles' in ours, a confusion which contributes significantly to the problem of the 'acts of God'. In the Bible God's mighty acts are distinguished from his more everyday ones. They are extra-ordinary; but ordinary events are just as much his acts. 'Miracles' are difficult to define satisfactorily, though discussion of them usually assumes an understanding such as Hume's.[59] This speaks of events which are contrary to natural law as acts of God, whereas ordinary events may be explained by natural law without appeal to God.

Now Gilkey seems to reckon that the exodus, as the paradigmatic mighty act of God, needs to have been a miracle, and that Wright is, or ought to be, embarrassed that we cannot believe it was. This seems to be mistaken. The marvel was not essentially something

---

[58] *Cf.* *Hesse, p. 56; Buss's remarks on Pannenberg, *Theology as History*, p. 149; Pannenberg's on von Rad in *Gerhard von Rad*; *cf.* Janzen, G. E. Wright volume, p. 501: 'we have traded the problem of a *deus ex machina* for that of a *deus absconditus intra machinam*'. Note also Gilkey's essay on providence, *JR* 43 (1963). *Fohrer (p. 44) notes that the OT does not see God as always at work in history, but rather as alternating between inactivity and activity.

[59] *An Enquiry Concerning Human Understanding*, section X.

quite inexplicable, but something quite unexpected. It intervened to break the bounds of what could have been envisaged in the situation, and Israel responded with wonder. It was not all in their minds. Something happened to which faith responded; but it need not have been a 'miracle'.[60]

But suppose that the exodus event consisted in a happy co-inci-dence of strong east winds which favoured the Israelites and sank the Egyptians. Why should it be described as a mighty act of Yah-weh? The Exodus narrative itself suggests that this was a natural reaction because the Israelites already knew something of Yahweh and had already been promised that he would enable them to escape from the Egyptians. Part of the problem with Wright's understand-ing of the acts of God is that he excludes this element in the picture; the event itself is the revelation.[61] We have already seen reason to question this (section 3c). Rather, the exodus event, or complex of events, is identified as a special act of God because it is an extraor-dinary event which fulfils a plan of God already announced through his messengers and which gives expression to this saving purpose.[62]

The exodus event may, then, have been capable of 'natural ex-planation', without thereby losing its status as a mighty act of God. But we should question the assumption agreed on by Wright, Gilkey, Ogden, and Kaufman, that this must have been the case, the 'miraculous' being methodologically excluded. With regard to the climactic salvation event in Christ, and specifically to his resurrec-tion, *Pannenberg has questioned the principle associated with Troeltsch, that we can never allow for an event in the past which is without parallel in our own experience.[63] No OT 'miracle' is as well-evidenced as Jesus' resurrection. But once we allow this 'mir-acle' at the climax of the story of the acts of the God of Israel, it may be appropriate to be more open to 'miracle' at earlier stages in that story. It is not obvious that a mechanistic model of the universe should be taken for granted if one believes in God; a personal model

---

[60] Cf. Rogerson, *The Supernatural in the OT*, pp. 3–9, 44–46; Ellul, *Politics of God*, p. 186; Buber, *Moses*, pp. 75–76.

[61] Cf. Gilkey, *JR* 41 (1961), pp. 201–202.

[62] Wyatt (*ST* 33 [1979], pp. 56–59; cf. *ZAW* 91 [1979]), however, presses the question whether such announcement of God's purpose really took place. This takes us back to the issues discussed in section 3b. The OT's own understanding of the acts of God depends on its having taken place.

[63] I, pp. 45–49; cf. Fuller, *JBR* 34 (1966); Peters, *CBQ* 35 (1973).

such as the OT's own is then at least as appropriate, and this leaves open the question of 'miracle'.[64]

Pannenberg is concerned to exclude the negative use of the principle of analogy ('this event cannot have happened because it is unparalleled in our experience') and promote its positive use ('where do we find parallel reports to the ones we are examining?' – in myths, or accounts of visions, for instance?).[65] With regard to the OT, a narrative such as Exodus 1 – 15 is commonly described as 'saga' or 'legend'; such terms have implications for the degree of historical truth that is therefore reckoned to lie behind it.[66] On the other hand, such judgments can be made too hastily. They may, indeed, follow from the conviction that the exodus never happened the way it is described, rather than lead to it. More conservative writers have suggested that to designate OT narratives as saga, legend, or folk-tale is to impose on them alien categories.[67] In other words, the positive analogy is not there. Whether or not, however, miracles took place, 'mighty acts' did. These do have an important place in salvation history.

But there is a further aspect to the question whether it is still meaningful to speak of God acting in history. Suppose we can affirm that God acted in OT times; can this belief be applied to the contemporary world? Does God act today, or does such talk strike the average congregation as meaningless?[68] If God's activity is not to be confined to 'miracles', there is less problem here. Thus D. N. Freedman[69] suggests that events such as the American Civil War or World War II can be analysed in the light of the OT approach to history.

But are principles at work in Israel's history universalizable? Do they apply to other nations or only to the chosen people?[70] This question became a living issue in the 1970s in connection with liberation theology: was the exodus uniquely part of God's work for his chosen people, or can it be a paradigm for God's acts (and men's

---

[64] I think I owe this point to a remark by Dr Henry McKeating.
[65] Cf. Peters, pp. 480–481.
[66] Cf. Koch, *Growth of the Biblical Tradition*, pp. 111–158; Rogerson, *op. cit.*
[67] So Kitchen, *The Bible in its World*, pp. 59–65.
[68] So *Childs, pp. 82–87.
[69] *Int* 21 (1967).
[70] So Stott, *Christian Mission*, pp. 95–97; contrast Miranda, *Marx and the Bible*, pp. 90–97.

acts) in Latin America today? Amos 1 – 2 implies that there is an analogy between God's judgment of the nations and that of Israel, while Isaiah and Habakkuk imply that Yahweh the God of justice operates in the same way in relation to the nations as he does in relation to Israel. Genesis 12:1–3 suggests that Yahweh's blessing of Israel is something that other nations may naturally covet for themselves.

Such passages support the suggestion that God's ways with Israel offer insights into his ways with other nations, and also provide the (otherwise unstated) theological foundation for applying understandings of the nature of man from Genesis 12 – 50 to men generally, and for applying Israel's theology of the land to other peoples in their need of land.[71] Although God's acts in relation to Israel fulfil a special function in terms of salvation history, they nevertheless (and perhaps precisely because of that) embody his way of dealing with all his creatures.

f. Can history really bring salvation?

In the view of *F. Hesse, the OT is not concerned with salvation in the true sense of the word. By salvation it means as much the deliverance of the nation from defeat and of the individual from illness as the granting of a relationship with God; salvation in the Christian, NT, sense is essentially a spiritual matter.[72] Indeed, even if the two Testaments had the same understanding of salvation, then the concept of salvation history gives the OT an inferior position, because it presupposes that Israel lived in a 'not yet' situation. If salvation history comes to a climax in Christ, OT believers who lived before this climax cannot really have enjoyed salvation. History is the embodiment of human action and experience, an aspect of 'this world', an expression of sinful man's hunger for life. By definition it cannot produce salvation. The OT is actually the story of unsaved man, open to the saving act of God. Christ then rescues us from history; he is the end of history, as he is the end of the law.[73] Indeed,

[71] Cf. Westermann, *1000 Years and a Day*, pp. 20–53; Brueggemann, *Land*.
[72] *Hesse, pp. 8–15; cf. Saggs, pp. 66–67.
[73] *Gunneweg, pp. 180–181, 207–209; Fuchs, *EvT* 8 (1948–9); Buss, *Theology as History*, pp. 144–148 (he compares *von Rad II, pp. 117–118). Cf. also Sontag, *RelS* 15 (1979), who suggests that we today should treat the question whether history reflects God's activity or human sin as a more open one.

on the OT's own testimony, salvation even in its worldly sense is not consistently enjoyed in OT times. Salvation is either hoped for in the future (*Heilseschatologie!*) or looked back to as characterizing Israel's beginnings.[74]

Hesse's views were in part a development of those of F. Baumgärtel and R. Bultmann. Bultmann, too, felt distaste for the OT's 'worldliness'. He takes the idea that the OT is the story of *Unheilsgeschichte* rather than *Heilsgeschichte* as the key to understanding the OT's significance. The OT relates man's discovery that the people of God, the covenant, and the rule of God canot be realized in history. OT history in itself leads to a dead end; it thus comes to a climax in Christ in the paradoxical sense that here God makes a new beginning after this miscarriage.[75] Baumgärtel sees salvation and salvation history as defined by the NT; sometimes the OT may help us to grasp this salvation, but all too often its self-understanding is alien to it.[76]

The OT sometimes speaks of its own story as one of sin and judgment. For instance, the book of Judges' final assessment of the period it covers is a negative one (*cf.* Jdg. 21:25). Indeed, the larger whole to which Judges belongs, the story from Joshua to Kings, itself suggests that Israel's history came to a dead end in the exile. The prophets, too, in general 'deny the efficacy of the old divine actions for their contemporaries, and . . . perceive God's rising up to completely new acts in history'.[77] Amos, Hosea, and Isaiah picture history as the story of Israel's disobedience and resistance to God's gracious acts, which leads to the judgments she has already experienced and towards final judgment in the future.[78]

Further, it is striking that when OT interpreters who emphasize salvation history actually practise their craft, it is often the contrast between the Testaments that they take up. The wrongdoing of OT heroes is reckoned to hint at the need of a work of salvation; Israel

[74] *Hesse, pp. 19–30.

[75] 'Prophecy and fulfilment', in *Westermann; *cf.* *G. A. F. Knight, p. 8, on God's failure in his purpose to reach the world through Israel which led to his acting in Christ. Delitzsch ridicules the OT's so-called God who could not execute his will more effectively or choose himself a better means of revelation than sinful Israel (see *Kraeling, pp. 152, 160–161)!

[76] See Baumgärtel in *Westermann, pp. 144–156, also his *Verheissung*; see further section 1c above.

[77] *Von Rad I, p. vii.

[78] Vollmer, *BZAW* 119; *cf.* Fohrer, *ThL* 89 (1964), columns 273–282.

is guilty and liable to death, except for the fact of the cross.[79] Here, of course, such interpreters are reflecting a strand of the NT's attitudes, where it sees the Christ event as something radically new which is thus set sharply against the history of the Jews. For Stephen (Acts 7), the story which begins with 'our father Abraham' is nevertheless a history of the rebellions of the people of God, an *Unheilsgeschichte* (cf. Lk. 11:49);[80] for Paul the OT law, even though originally God-given, has a predominantly negative significance.

This, however, cannot be treated as *the* NT attitude to the OT. At other points the OT is seen as leading to Christ in a more positive sense. Indeed, this is where the the NT begins, with a genealogy of Jesus which demonstrates his historical link with the history of Israel and works back through the exile and King David to Abraham, with whom the story of redemption started.[81] Luke brings out the link in a different way, with his OT-like narrative portrayal of a priest functioning in the temple, which takes up where Chronicles (the last book in the Hebrew Bible) leaves off. Again, the NT people of God is seen as historically linked with OT Israel. The people of God is like a tree planted by him. The Jews' rejection of the messiah means they are (for a time) rejected by God; they are branches pruned out of the tree. Other, Gentile, branches are then grafted into their place. Yet there is only one tree, only one people of God, planted by him in Israel's history and continuing to grow in the life of the messianic people (Rom. 11:13–24).[82]

Bultmann's view takes one strand of OT and NT and uses it to characterize the whole. This results in a picture which is over-simplified in one direction, as a hard-line salvation history approach is in another. The reality is more complex, as is reflected in the ambivalence of the OT's own attitude to its history, and in the ambivalence of the NT's attitude to it.[83]

Theologically viewed, history as the OT describes it results from

---

[79] Westermann, *1000 Years and a Day*, p. 34; Wolff, *Hosea*, pp. 23, 69, 229, on Ho. 1:2–9; 4:1–3; 13; and *Joel and Amos*, pp. 304, 333, on Am. 7:1–9; 8:4–14.

[80] See Stauffer, *NT Theology*, pp. 98–100; also Fuchs' comments (*Studies of the Historical Jesus*, pp. 174–177) on the break implied by passages such as Gal. 3 – 4 and Mt. 3:9.

[81] *Cf.* Smith, Stinespring volume, p. 47.

[82] On Rom. 9 – 11, see Voegelin in *Anderson, pp. 95–96.

[83] *Cf.* Zimmerli in *Westermann, pp. 118–119; in *VTSupp* 29 he develops the theme of history as the sphere in which God meets his people in judgment or grace.

the interaction of at least the following elements. On the one hand, there are divine initiatives such as the creation, the exodus, and the return from exile. These meet with imperfect human responses (see Genesis 3 – 11 or Judges) and fail in the short term. This failure is sealed by the more negative initiative of divine acts of judgment such as the exile, which threaten to bring the whole story to an end – though in fact it keeps picking itself off the floor again and restarting. Then, on the other hand, there are human initiatives such as Abraham begetting Ishmael or Moses killing the Egyptian, or human ideas such as appointing a king or building a temple. Sometimes, these human acts threaten merely to frustrate God's own purpose; but often they are accepted by him, becoming part of the salvation story, and they thus express God's willingness to condescend to man. They, too, tend to fail (as the monarchy does) and/or to find that their role is disputed (as was the case with the temple).

The complexity of the history that results from these factors is such that it cannot be dismissed as *Unheilsgeschichte* any more than it can be accepted without qualification as *Heilsgeschichte*. It is both. And thus we need to see it as a history that leads both to Christ and to the rejection of Christ, and to affirm both the positive character of what God accomplished in Israel before Christ came and that in Christ a new and in many ways surprising act of God took place.[84]

It is noteworthy that the OT's own nearest phrase to salvation history is the term *ṣidqôt-ᵃdōnay*, 'the saving deeds of the LORD' (1 Sa. 12:7 RSV; *cf.* Jdg. 5:11). But the word translated 'saving deeds' in this expression is not the one usually seen as equivalent to 'salvation', *yᵉšûʿāh*. It is a word that suggests an involvement with what is right. Used here, and frequently in Isaiah 40 – 55 and elsewhere, it suggests Yahweh's active concern for his people's rights. He has that concern because he himself is *ṣaddîq*, 'righteous' or 'just' (*cf.* Is. 45:21). This same righteousness of God issues in trouble for his people when they do wrong (*cf.* Dn. 9:14). 'Yahweh's acts of justice', then, constitute *Heilsgeschichte* when Israel is needy and pleading for help, but *Unheilsgeschichte* when she is arrogant and disobedient. 'Yahweh shows himself holy in justice' (Is. 5:16): both for Israel and for the nations that can be either good news or bad news according to their attitudes and deserts at a particular time.

---

[84] *Bright, p. 196; Porteous, von Rad volume, pp. 424–425.

The phrase *šᵉpāṭîm gᵉdôlîm*, 'great acts of judgment' (*e.g.* Ex. 6:6; Ezk. 11:9) is used in similar ways.

Nor is it strange to OT thinking to suggest that such events incorporate the acts of sinful human beings. The historical survey in which Samuel implements his intention to recount these 'acts of justice' includes such events as Israel's rebellion in the period of the judges and the recent granting of her request for a king, as well as the exodus and the deliverances of Jerubbaal, Barak, Jephthah, and Samuel; it is, however, difficult to know precisely how Samuel himself viewed the former events in this respect. Certainly unrighteous Assyria and Babylon were later the means by which Yahweh fulfilled his righteous purpose on unrighteous Jerusalem (Is. 10; Hab. 1 – 2).

The OT sees Yahweh's purpose of justice and salvation worked out by human agency in all its moral ambiguity. Perfectly consistent with this is the Christ-event, the paradigm righteous act of God at the climax of the *ṣidqôt-ᵃdōnay*, holding together God's act with man's, and righteousness-as-salvation with righteousness-as-judgment. In OT times God wills Israel's salvation and blessing (national, personal, and spiritual well-being) and seeks to grant it by his initiatives and by the way his providence takes account of the acts of Israel and of other nations. But that will to save and bless is never fully satisfied, and the Christ event is his final means of achieving it.

g. Is salvation history really 'history'?

But in what sense can we describe all this as history, as *Geschichte*? When we talk about history we normally mean a continuous chronological sequence of human acts, linked as cause and effect; when we speak of the history of this or that we have in mind the process whereby the object of our concern gradually came to be what it was and continued to develop. Salvation history, however, does not mean a continuous sequence but a series of punctiliar events, and it emphasizes God's acts more than man's. As we noted in section 3e, it may be reasonable to maintain that God acts in history; it might still not be true that the concept of history can involve explaining things in terms of God's agency. So is salvation history really history?[85]

[85] *Cf.* *Hesse, pp. 17–20, 49–59. *Spriggs (pp. 34–38, 56–59) maintains that von Rad's use of the term salvation history is thoroughly confused.

Oscar Cullmann recognizes that salvation history is not history in the modern sense: 'an unbroken, causally connected chain of historical facts that is controllable and provable in such a connection'; 'the law of continuity, important for all history' is ignored here.[86] History is seen as 'gathering at nodal points, and crystallizing upon outstanding figures' who mark 'great turning-points in the history of the race', and the meaning and interrelation of these moments is not calculable but revealed by God.[87] We have thus come a long way from the baptism of evolutionary views which, according to *Kraus, was involved in the work of the early 'salvation history school' of Oehler, Beck, and von Hofmann.[88]

Why hold on to the word history, then? Cullmann suggests three important features of history that salvation history manifests. First, we are talking about a connected series of events, in a chronological sequence. Secondly, this series of events involves historical contingency, and embraces the results of human sin – *Unheilsgeschichte* as a subordinate theme, as it were. Thirdly, these individual events belong to history; they are real events which actually happened.[89]

The second of these features may need further consideration. On one side, Cullmann alludes to human acts only in connection with their functioning as obstacles to God's purpose, whereas we have seen that they can also have a positive role to play in the execution of Yahweh's acts of justice. Salvation history does find it difficult to give due place to human actions. It interprets history primarily from God's standpoint and is inclined in practice to ignore man's role as creative participant in the making of history as well as the negative element of brokenness in history which results from man's sin.[90]

On the other side, Cullmann stresses the notion of a plan or

---

[86] Cullmann, *Salvation in History*, pp. 55, 77.

[87] Barrett, *From First Adam to Last*, pp. 5, 46. J. M. Robinson (in *Anderson, pp. 152–153) speaks of *Lichtungsgeschichte*, a series of patches of clearing in the jungle. *Cf.* also Goppelt, *Int* 21 (1976), pp. 321–322.

[88] *Kraus, pp. 102–103.

[89] Cullmann, p. 78; *cf.* pp. 152–165.

[90] *Cf.* Tupper's comments on Pannenberg, *Theology of Wolfhart Pannenberg*, p. 301. For an emphasis on the positive theological significance of human initiative see Seeligmann, *TZ* 19 (1963) on the role of human heroism; Coats, *e.g.* *VTSupp* 28; *CBQ* 39 (1977), on Moses as a hero; *Fohrer, p. 163 (also *BZAW* 99, pp. 289–291) on the OT as *Entscheidungsgeschichte* (decision history) rather than *Heilsgeschichte*. On the interplay of the free determination of man and the free decision of God, see Ellul, *Politics of God*, pp. 15–21.

purpose of God which was being worked out in OT times. He speaks of an unfolding development or a progressive advance, or states that 'the entire redemptive purpose of the OT tends towards the goal of the incarnation'.[91] He sometimes speaks of this as an understanding of the significance of OT history which is gained from the NT, but elsewhere describes the prophets themselves as revealing the divine plan concerning a particular event against the background of a total view of history.[92]

But does the OT see events working out according to an overall plan? In discussing this question, several versions of the concept of a divine plan need to be distinguished. It is otherwise easy to accept or reject evidence for or against a belief in such a plan through confusion over the meaning of the term. One version of the concept envisages God pre-determining history as a whole, so that each event takes place because it fits into his detailed master plan. *Albrektson makes it clear that the OT does not talk in these terms,[93] and the concept may be difficult to reconcile with the contribution made to the story, as the OT actually indicates, by human initiatives and responses. If the OT does not think in such terms, Pannenberg's key concept of universal history may lose its purported biblical mooring, though it would not thereby be rendered actually incompatible with the Bible's understanding of history.

A second understanding of God's plan connects it particularly with key events such as the exodus which are especially important to the fulfilment of his saving purpose. Yet we must be wary of attributing even to these a significance which takes away from their contingency. The act of exodus, for instance, is a response to the particular wilfulness of a specific generation of Egyptians. The divine commitment to David and to the temple comes about because in particular contexts Israelites ask for a king and propose the building of a temple. None of these events sprang *immediately* from God's decree.[94]

---

[91] *Christ and Time*, pp. 117, 135.

[92] *Christ and Time*, p. 135; *Salvation in History*, pp. 89–90.

[93] *Albrektson, ch. 5. Van der Woude (*VT* 19 [1969], p. 259) makes the rather nice claim that the idea of an immutable plan of God actually originates in the assurances of the false prophets, whence it is turned upsidedown by Micah (4:11–13) into an immutable plan of judgment.

[94] *Van Ruler (p. 69) sees even the Christ event as God's 'emergency measure' in response to the fact of human sin.

A third understanding is the view that God acts purposefully in individual events and in particular series of events, such as the creation – patriarchs – exodus – conquest sequence, without these being explicitly understood in terms of a detailed overall plan. The OT does not develop an explicit perspective of universal history, and even when an OT narrator opens up a long perspective (*e.g.* creation to the post-exilic period in Chronicles or the exile to the End in Daniel), his real concern is still with his own present.[95] In itself this does not make *Heilsgeschichte* an inappropriate category: earlier history is seen as a purposeful story which shows how God's saving acts in the past (and his other acts!) have led to the (partial) experience of his saving presence in the writer's day. Aetiology and *Heilsgeschichte* are not mutually exclusive; they can be explanations of the same reality at different levels.

A fourth understanding of God's purpose is the belief that God has an overall goal (or goals). His purposefulness in particular events or event-series is not random, but issues from his overall concern for justice, for the blessing of his people, and so on. OT narratives are implicitly set against this context, and at least sometimes imply that if the reader understands the purposive way in which Yahweh has been pursuing certain goals in the past, he will also be able to infer how Yahweh's purposiveness is likely to work out in the future. The prophets make this approach explicit. God's commitment to certain goals, then, does not compromise the contingent element in the way he seeks to achieve these goals.[96]

Finally there is the view that God foreknows all events. This belief may cause philosophical problems today, partly because it may seem difficult to reconcile with genuine human freedom and historical contingency.[97] But it was perhaps taken for granted by many OT writers (who nevertheless also took for granted human freedom and historical contingency), becoming most explicit in Daniel's visions.

We noted above that the nearest Hebrew phrase to *Heilsgeschichte*

[95] *Albrektson, pp. 77–88; cf. *Gunneweg, pp. 205–206; Thompson, *BZAW* 133, p. 328; *Fohrer, p. 44; Barr, *Judaism*, p. 13. Goppelt (*Int* 21 [1967], pp. 324–326) notes that Paul, too, speaks of the redemptive significance of particular epochs (Adam's, Abraham's, Moses') without treating these as part of an overall scheme.

[96] Process theology develops this point; cf. Ford, *Int* 26 (1972), pp. 206–209; Janzen, in G. E. Wright volume.

[97] *Cf.* Ford, p. 208; Hebblethwaite, *RelS* 15 (1979); Wyatt, *ST* 33 (1979), pp. 56–60, seeing it as a Deuteronomistic idea.

is *ṣidqôṯ-ᵃḏōnay*. It may be significant that Cullmann takes the nearest Greek word to be *oikonomia* (Eph. 1:10; 3:9),[98] an expression which is much more open to suggesting an overall detailed master plan which God is implementing in history. So, perhaps, is the word *prothesis* (Rom. 9:11; Eph. 3:11). On the other hand, *mystērion* (Rom. 11:25; 16:25; Col. 1:26–27; Eph. 1:9; 3:4, 9) is more common than either of these, and it suggests that even if God had a detailed master plan, this was not one that was immanent in or could be read off from history. It is a plan that can be known only through its being revealed. Paul believes that it was revealed to him. That implies that it was unknown before, and this in turn fits with the fact that the OT itself speaks of no such master plan.

Theologically, then, one might claim that in God's purpose the OT story 'leads' to Christ or 'looks towards' Christ, both positively when it describes God's acts of grace and negatively when it describes his acts of judgment. The OT itself, however, is not over-concerned with looking forward, and it may be more appropriate to speak of it as simply the time in which Christ is 'not yet'.[99] Yet God is involved in that history throughout, and he always knew that he would finally send Christ to bring it to its climax in the achievement of the purpose he had always cherished.

h. Does it help us appropriate the Old Testament today?

It has always been the hope and claim of historical study that opening up the historical significance of the biblical documents would help the modern reader to grasp their meaning for himself. *A. H. J. Gunneweg, however, develops the view that the entire attempt to look at the OT historically is at best irrelevant, at worst inimical to hearing its message for oneself. Von Rad's work, for instance, is still in the end history (the tracing of the messages of successive prophets or tradition circles), not theology; nor can this kind of historical study prove that Jesus is the climax of OT history. Stressing the historical nature of the OT actually imperils appreciation of its present, personal relevance. It turns real historical experiences into mere points in a sequence; it alienates the OT, relativizes its various witnesses, and relativizes man, who is swallowed up by history, that

[98] *Cullmann, pp. 75–76; for what follows, see Reumann, *NTS* 13 (1966–7).
[99] *Barr, pp. 152–153.

modern embodiment of the ancient god, Moloch.[100]

It is mainly to NT scholars that Gunneweg alludes at these points in his book, and we are actually hearing echoes of the great German debate over salvation history in the NT. Is salvation history *the* central category of NT thinking?[101] Is it, on the contrary, not really a NT way of thinking, even in Paul – perhaps not even in Luke?[102] On this view, the NT attaches no theological importance to the historical link between the history of Israel and the Christ event. What matters is the fulfilment of Scripture and the analogy of faith, not the completion of history. Or is salvation history admittedly a Pauline theme, but a minor one subsequently overemphasized by Luke (and Cullmann)?[103]

Robert Morgan has observed that behind the conviction expressed by Bultmann and Käsemann that salvation history is marginal to Paul's real theology lies the fact that it is not central to their own thinking. They do not regard salvation history as a viable category for contemporary theology. Gunneweg seems to share this conviction. Present appropriation of the message and real personal response to God are what matters. A concern with history represents an evasion of that commitment.[104]

It seems that here we are again being urged to make a choice between two alternatives, when truth is more likely to lie in combining them and seeking to be historical in both Pannenberg's sense

---

[100] *Gunneweg, pp. 91, 94–95, 216–217, 298, cf. *ZTK* 65 (1968), pp. 397–407; Coggins *JSOT* 11 (1979), p. 44. For similar observations on von Rad, see Keller, *TZ* 14 (1958), p. 308; Porteous, *ExpT* 75 (1963–4), p. 73.

[101] So Cullmann; cf. Goppelt, *Int* 21 (1967); Stendahl, *HTR* 56 (1963); also Bruce, *Man and his Salvation*, for a discussion of the debate from this perspective.

[102] So Klein, *e.g.* *ZNW* 62 (1971); Geyer, *EvT* 25 (1965); *Gunneweg, pp. 196–197, 204, 213–215; *Hesse, pp. 31–35; cf. Dahl, *Studies in Paul*, p. 175, on Gal. 3.

[103] So Conzelmann, *Theology of St. Luke*; cf. Bultmann, *NTS* 1 (1954–5); *History and Eschatology*, pp. 31–55; *Existence and Faith*, pp. 226–240; Käsemann, *Perspectives on Paul*, pp. 60–101 (a more mediating position); also Keck and Martyn, *Studies in Luke–Acts*, for contributions from varying perspectives.

[104] Cf. Morgan, *Nature of NT Theology*, p. 56. There is an atmosphere of *tour de force* about Klein's NT exegesis, as about *Gunneweg's statement (p. 214) that for Paul the Jews' link with Abraham is irrelevant (cf. Beauchamp, *Recherches de science religieuse* 67 [1979], p. 55), which may be explained by their need to make the NT fit their theological convictions. To *stress* salvation history no doubt also reflects theological preferences, of course.

and Bultmann's.[105] For on the one hand, biblical faith is based (among other things) on history. Now that is a notoriously ambiguous claim;[106] everything is based on history in some sense. The point to be made here is not merely that in the biblical period there emerged certain key insights into the nature of reality – insights accessible through these events, but possibly accessible also elsewhere, and in any case true whether or not these events took place.[107] It is rather that in the biblical period certain things happened upon which present salvation depends, so that their actual occurrence remains of key importance.

But it will not do if we stop there. Past factuality has to have its effect on the present. To say 'Yahweh brought our fathers out of Egypt' or 'God raised Jesus from the dead' must be to imply an attitude and a way of life in the present.[108] Thus worship and ethics bring home the present implications of God's past and future acts of salvation, the one as ground for praise and prayer, the other as ground for commands. There can thus be such a thing as a 'salvation-historical existentialism'.[109] Actual events of the past and appropriation and application in the present thus have to be held together.

There is a further tension we have to accept. As well as that between past and present, there is that between the self-existent witness of particular past events considered alone, and the need to see these events in the context of others before and after them. In the first perspective, there is an absolute authenticity about their

[105] Cf. Schmidt, EvT 35 (1975), pp. 133–134; Reventlow, JSOT 11 (1979), p. 12. Rylaarsdam (Journal of Ecumenical Studies 9 [1972]) suggests that in the OT history is the major theme, eschatology the minor one, while in the NT the reverse is the case; hence Bultmann's emphasis on eschatology and (e.g.) Zimmerli's response stressing history (in *Westermann, pp. 118–120). The canon as a whole incorporates both, so the theological challenge is to relate them.

[106] See Wiles, Theology 81 (1978); cf. *Herberg, pp. 132–137.

[107] So Wiles; also Harvey, The Historian and the Believer; Thompson, BZAW 133, pp. 328–330. Contrast *Gunneweg's awareness on this point (p. 43).

[108] Cf. Weippert's examination of how Israel's own historical narratives challenged to commitment and repentance as well as offering explanations of Israel's place in and subsequent loss of the land (VT 23 [1973]). Contrast Noth's view (in *Westermann, pp. 87–88) that all that is required in proclaiming the OT message is a recounting of the acts of God. It is doubtful whether this ensures that past factuality has its effect on the present.

[109] Cullmann, Salvation in History, p. 329; see further pp. 313–319, 328–338; also *Herberg, pp. 66–71 on Passover and Easter and pp. 40–42 on the need of response if historical events are to become redemptive for me (cf. *Porteous, pp. 43–44).

testimony to what went on between man and God at a particular moment, and we can relate to them as moments of meeting between the God we know and men like us. But in the second perspective they can be reduced to stages in a process and relativized. 'It is as though the scintillating music of a Mozart symphony were made a phase in the history of music between Haydn and Beethoven – interesting for the musicologist, but silent and unmelodious for the concert-goer'.[110]

On the other hand, there is clear value in seeing any event both in terms of the options, perspectives, horizons, and possibilities of its time, and in terms of wider perspectives or horizons and further options or possibilities known before and afterwards. Only in the light of both ways of looking at an event or a passage can I see how it may responsibly be related to my specific historical existence today. *John Bright offered the suggestive image of the story of salvation as a two-act play; in such a play, he noted, the significance of Act I is clearer in the light of Act II, just as Act II itself cannot be understood without Act I.[111] The danger of this image is that it may rob the earlier 'scenes' of significance in their own right; its value lies in reminding us of the need to see them in their wider context.

Thus when we seek to understand the exodus story we must concern ourselves with it as the account of a moment when God and Israel had real dealings with each other. It is not merely, for instance, the source of a piece of background imagery for understanding the Christ event. And yet, the exodus was followed by other events which cast light on its significance (as well as having significance of their own). These include not only Sinai and the occupation of Palestine (to which the exodus narrative itself refers) but also Israel's failure to live as Yahweh's subjects, which takes her back into that bondage to the nations from which the exodus had rescued her. At a literary level, the fact that Genesis to Kings is one coherent narrative invites us to see the exodus in this whole context, and the

---

[110.] *Gunneweg, p. 217. Thus a danger of Cullmann's approach is that the OT's significance may be simply to illustrate the Christ event (*Christ and Time*, pp. 134–137). Von Rad, however, despite his *heilsgeschichtliche* perspective, concentrates on interpreting authors in their context, and the depth of his work lies in his creativeness here.

[111] *Bright, pp. 202–203; *cf.* Wolff in *Westermann, pp. 186–187; Watson, *ExpT* 73 (1961–2), p. 198; Wright, May volume, pp. 302–303.

taking up of the exodus theme in chapters such as Isaiah 40 – 55 implies that these chapters are part of the context for understanding the exodus as well as vice versa.[112]

A willingness to look at the exodus-conquest narratives in a salvation historical way offers the most promising way of escape from an otherwise insoluble dilemma over these chapters. Merely to apply them figuratively (to spiritual redemption in Christ and to spiritual warfare against the devil) ignores their literal meaning. Merely to treat them literally either leads to liberation theology's God of violence or makes them impossible to relate to at all. But by taking them as records of God's real acts, in the context of a broader understanding of his acts from Scripture as a whole, we can avoid either absolutizing or ignoring them.

Does salvation history manifest development, then? Does salvation become fuller or nearer? *Gunneweg protests at the notion that people who lived later in OT times, or who lived after Christ, experienced salvation more fully than people who lived earlier. In both Testaments, he suggests, the purpose of linking past to present is to identify them – we experience the same salvation as they did (cf. Dt. 5:3) – not to picture the past as mere stages on the way to the present.[113]

In practice, no doubt, interpreters more often draw attention to the analogy between the contemporary situation and the biblical one than to the historical relationship between them. Thus we relate to the OT (and the NT) not merely by recalling a history which is part of the once-for-all past, but by recapitulating that history in our own lives.[114]

*Bright suggests that in recapitulating that history we also repeat in our own lives the salvation story as a whole. BC and AD themselves are not merely once-for-all historical epochs; our world still lives in a BC way, and even as believers in Christ we still stand with one foot in BC. We thus 'find ourselves' in the OT in its essential BC

---

[112] See further Goldingay, *TynB* 27 (1976); my paper in *Essays on the Patriarchal Narratives* applies a similar approach to Genesis 12 – 50. Thus while a Christological exegesis of the Genesis 1 creation story is artificial (*Barr, p. 154), to consider creation as the beginning of a story which continues via OT events to Christ and on to the End suggests insights both on creation and on those subsequent events.

[113] *Gunneweg, pp. 202–209.

[114] *Cf.* *Herberg, p. 69; *von Rad II, p. 383, developed by *Achtemeier, pp. 116–123.

quality; but then we are propelled beyond all BC to Christ.[115]

The problem with this view is that it once again implies that in OT times people did not actually enjoy salvation. If the situation should not, then, be described quite thus, what difference does it make that Christ has come? If it is possible to synthesize what the NT implies on this subject, one might do so by suggesting that whereas there was always only one way from man to God (by faith in the grace of God), that way is easier to find now that Christ has come; and similarly that the life of a believer can be lived more fully now that the Spirit is given.[116] Yet that Spirit himself is only the foretaste of something we still live in hope of. 'Martin Buber and H. J. Schoeps can rightly declare that the world is not yet redeemed,' *van Ruler observes; though he goes on, 'but they are wrong, it seems to me, when they add that they cannot therefore believe that the Redeemer has already come'.[117]

So a salvation historical approach grasps something important about the relationship between the Testaments. Christ's coming did make a difference. That difference, however, must not be expressed in such a way that we destroy the real analogy between how God related to Abraham, Moses, Jeremiah, or Ezra and how he relates to me, and that we thereby evade the challenge of their stories.

---

[115] *Bright, pp. 205–209, following Baumgärtel.
[116] See further Barrett, *CHB* 1, p. 410.
[117] *Van Ruler, p. 43. On the need to safeguard the newness of what Christ brought as well as the reality of what OT believers experienced, see *Eichrodt I, pp. 519–520 and *Cullmann, p. 54, over against *von Rad; Thielicke, *Ethics* I, pp. 100–106 and *Vischer, p. 23, over against *Barth.

Chapter Four

The Old Testament
as witness to Christ

Behold, I am doing a new   *All the promises of God find*
thing.   *(Is. 43:19)*   *their Yes in Christ.*
                             (2 Cor. 1:20)

In Chapter 3 we have considered the OT as the story of God's saving purpose at work in history before Christ. In the mind of God that history looked forward to Christ. So what reflections of that fact are present in the OT itself? In this chapter we consider the way in which the redemptive events and other realities of OT times may implicitly foreshadow the Christ event, and the way in which explicit promises of redemption appear in the OT. These two related forms of witness to Christ are often spoken of as typology and promise-and-fulfilment.

a. The nature of typology

'Type' comes from the Greek word *typos*. This word and related ones are used in several NT passages concerned with the connection between OT faith and Christianity. Thus 'Adam . . . was a type of the one who was to come', Christ (Rom. 5:14 RSV): Paul explains what he means by describing the comparison between the one man Adam's sinful act which brought condemnation and death to many, and the one man Christ's righteous act which brought acquittal and life to many. It is significant, however, that this seems to be the only passage in which the English translations render *typos* by 'type'. The Greek word is, in fact, a rather general one for pattern, image, mark, model, example; it is not a technical term in the NT.[1] Conversely,

---

[1] See *Baker, pp. 251–253; *Hanson, pp. 172–176; contrast Goppelt, *TDNT* 8, pp. 251–253.

many NT passages which refer to the OT have been described as typological even though they do not themselves use this term. Hebrews, in particular, uses words such as *hypodeigma* (copy), *skia* (shadow), and *parabolē* (symbol) as synonyms for *typos* (8:5; 9:9, 23–24; 10:1).

Paul himself uses the verb *allēgoreō* in Galatians 4:24 in connection with an interpretation which many modern interpreters regard as typological.[2] Further, while David, for instance, is not called a type of Christ, a number of NT allusions to him and his successors may be understood in this way. Thus Psalm 2 and Isaiah 7:14 were probably not originally understood by writer or readers as prophecies of the messiah; the former is a statement of faith and hope about the Davidic king, while the latter is perhaps a promise about the king who will follow Ahaz (though the passage is difficult to interpret). But both passages are applied to Christ typologically in the NT.[3] There is, in fact, a wide range of such typological material in the NT.[4]

When the NT interprets the Christ event in OT terms, it is following the way the OT itself interprets new events in the light of earlier ones. The OT utilizes the exodus from Egypt, for instance, to describe the promised later deliverance from Babylon; Abraham, David, the flood, the judgment on Sodom, the temple and many other features of OT times also function in this way.[5] We have here, then, an important aspect of biblical interpretation within Scripture. But what exactly typology involves is a subject of confusion, as the word is used in several different ways in modern literature.[6] In my view, the idea of a type is best seen as holding together three features.

1. *Typology and analogy.* In its outward forms, there are marked differences between OT and NT faith. Typology presupposes that nevertheless there underlies these outward differences a fundamental correspondence, and it seeks to bring to the surface the implicit

---

[2] So *Goppelt, pp. 5–6; Foulkes, *Acts of God*, p. 37; *Ellis, p. 53.

[3] *Cf.* Runia, *TSFB* 49 (1967), p. 13.

[4] The classic survey is Fairbairn's *Typology of Scripture*; *cf.* more recently *Grelot, pp. 209–247, 286–326; Daniélou, *From Shadows to Reality*; *Goppelt; *Amsler; *France, pp. 38–80; Woollcombe, *Essays on Typology*, pp. 35–69.

[5] See Hummel, *BibRes* 9 (1964); Anderson, Muilenburg volume; Foulkes, *Acts of God*; Zimmerli, Vischer volume; Daube, *Exodus Pattern*; Blenkinsopp, *Concilium* 10.2 (1966); Fohrer, *ThL* 85 (1960), columns 415–418.

[6] *Cf.* surveys in *Baker, pp. 239–270; Haag, Kornfeld volume.

parallels between OT and NT faith in the conviction that 'the same God who revealed himself in Christ has also left his footprints in the history of the Old Testament covenant people' (cf. Heb. 1:1).[7] Thus what can be said about Israel's relationship to God under the old covenant can be said about the church under the new covenant, and typology helps us to identify the correspondences. Indeed, this is true of Israel's failures as well as her faith: there is a typology of unbelief as well as one of belief.[8] Further, this fundamental correspondence finds expression in some analogies of a formal kind. Both the story of Israel and the story of the NT begin with a birth. The story of creation, the story of Abraham, and the story of Jesus (in Jn. 1) all begin with the word of God: creating, promising, and finally becoming flesh.[9]

This conviction that there is a fundamental analogy between different divine acts is expressed within the OT itself. As we noted above, the rescue from Babylon will be analogous to the rescue from Egypt. It will thus be a new exodus. But the analogy is not only one between past events and eschatological ones. The historical David is in effect pictured as a new Abraham (i.e. he enjoys a covenant like Abraham's and Abraham's blessing) before he is himself the type of a coming king.

The element of analogy is the aspect of typology especially stressed by some scholars: the unity of human experience is such that OT experiences can be seen as typical of human experience.[10] But this feature of typology is not its only essential one.[11]

---

[7] Von Rad in *Westermann, p. 36; cf. Fairbairn, p. 50; Lampe, *Essays on Typology*, p. 29 and elsewhere; Richardson in *Anderson, p. 45; Eichrodt in *Westermann, pp. 239–240, disputing the objections to typology on the grounds of the differences between OT and NT faith made by Baumgärtel in *Westermann, pp. 146–148 (cf. *Verheissung*). Examples in von Rad, *Genesis* (e.g. pp. 191, 245/[3] pp. 196, 250 on Gn. 16; 24) and his *Biblical Interpretations in Preaching* (e.g. p. 26 on Gn. 12; pp. 83–84 on Is. 40:3).

[8] Lampe, *LQHR* 190 (1965), p. 23.

[9] Westermann, *1000 Years and a Day*, pp. 20–22; further examples in *The OT and Jesus Christ*, pp. 37–41.

[10] So *Baker, pp. 268–270, arguing on theological grounds; *Gunneweg, pp. 214–215 (he quotes H. D. Preuss, 'Das Alte Testament in der Verkündigung der Kirche', *Deutsches Pfarrerblatt* 68 [1968], pp. 73–79; cf. Haag, p. 253), giving typology a more philosophical base.

[11] Cf. Eichrodt in *Westermann, p. 228, urging that typology be distinguished from paraenesis (i.e. using the OT for 'warning and advising models'); cf. Bultmann, *ThL* 75 (1950), column 212.

2. *Typology and salvation history.* Although types express the analogy between OT and NT faith, this is a matter of correspondence rather than of actual identity. The realities that are being compared are not contemporary with each other but follow each other; this alone makes differences between them inevitable, for history does not repeat itself. The OT's story is continued in the NT and parallel events occur; but the second event is not merely a repetition of the first. It is analogous, but heightened. Indeed, this second event takes place within the ongoing story of salvation history, in which more is realized at the End than had been experienced at earlier stages of the story. This was already so in the OT, where the new exodus is to be better than the original even though analogous to it (Is. 52:12). It is clearly so in Christ, who surpasses all that came before. So his act of redemption may parallel ones that came before, but is nevertheless greater.[12]

Typology's essential nature, then, involves this combination of analogy or anticipation with contrast. OT realities, while of real significance in themselves, also correspond and thus witness to something that comes about in Christ which is of a parallel religious and theological significance, yet is greater than what existed in OT times.[13]

If typology essentially combines both correspondence and intensification, then Hebrews' use of the Levitical priesthood and sacrifices to interpret the work of Christ provides a useful illustration of it: Christ recapitulates and renews in a far more profound sense the restoration of fellowship between God and man which was the

---

[12] *Cf.* von Rad in *Westermann, pp. 17–20, emphasizing that typology is concerned with historical analogies (between beginning and end), not with cosmological ones (between what is this-worldly and what is other-worldly). Usually these analogies are seen in OT persons and institutions as well as events (so Eichrodt, p. 225; Bultmann, column 205). Because of his stress on history von Rad (*II, p. 371) restricts them to events, but this seems unnecessary. Richardson (*History Sacred and Profane*, pp. 222–223) views typology merely as a way of writing history which sees the long-term outworking of the results of events.

[13] *Cf.* von Rad in *Westermann, pp. 20, 37; *Goppelt, pp. 18–19, 240, 244, 286; also *Int* 21 (1967), p. 317; Wolff, in *Westermann, pp. 180–181; *Lohfink, ch. 7; Eichrodt in *Westermann, pp. 226, 233–235. Contrast Bultmann, columns 205–206, who suggested that typology was concerned with repetition rather than fulfilment, and thus thought in terms of cyclic rather than linear time. Indeed *Pannenberg (I, pp. 28–30) thinks that von Rad allows too much space for the discovery of analogies between the Testaments, risking the loss of the historical connection to a purely structural similarity; though *Hasel (p. 73/²p. 113) thinks that von Rad is in the opposite danger!

concern of the Levitical system. In Romans 5 intensification becomes so marked that the typological correspondence between Adam and Christ is dominated by the note of contrast rather than that of analogy.[14] More commonly, however, the heightening is a matter of the NT making clearer or more explicit what was allusive or implicit in the OT, or providing one with a more satisfying coherence than that which one finds in the OT, or even enabling one to see as a whole what was quite fragmentary in the OT.[15]

If typology is essentially linked with salvation history, then objections to the notion of salvation history will also constitute objections to typology, though if one views the objections to salvation history as overstated (see ch. 3 above), then this obstacle to the typological approach will be removed.[16]

3. *Typology and symbolism.* If typology were only about analogy and salvation history, however, it would be a redundant concept, because its significance would be covered by these two notions, which we have considered already (see chs. 1 and 3). But typology also involves symbolism or metaphor. Now the NT uses the expression *to antitypon* to refer to two forms of typology, the 'horizontal' or historical (1 Pet. 3:21) and also the 'vertical' or cosmological (Heb. 9:24). The latter involves the assumption that heavenly realities are 'symbolized' by their earthly counterparts. It does not think in historical terms.[17]

In studying typology as an aspect of Christian interpretation of the OT, however, we are especially concerned with the more common

[14] Thus Müller (*ZNW* 58 [1967]) suggests that in effect Paul rejects Adam-Christ typology; *cf.* Bultmann, column 208.

[15] See respectively Wolff, *Hosea*, pp. 17, 22, 45, 63, 159, *etc.*, suggesting how passages such as 1:2–9; 2:2–15; 3:1–5; 9:1–9 foreshadow or point towards NT events and passages; Foulkes, *Acts of God*, pp. 34–40; Barton, *Theology* 79 (1976), p. 263. Wolff's typology works at the level of theological themes and, presupposing a unity of Scripture, sees individual treatments of particular themes in the light of a broad biblical context. Its approach is thus similar to that of the 'fuller sense' (see section 4b). Barton speaks of the adding of a quite new coherence in discussing the theme of promise and fulfilment.

[16] *E.g.* Baumgärtel questions whether unhistorical events and persons (*e.g.* he cites Adam) can have been 'typical' (*ThL* 86 [1961], column 906; *cf.* *Hanson, pp. 229–232) and accuses typology, like salvation history, of distancing the OT and turning it into intellectual information rather than moral challenge (*pp. 138–142; *EvT* 14 [1954], p. 305; *cf.* *Barr, p. 155, warning against devaluing the reality of the 'typical' situations as moments of real contact with God). But see Eichrodt's response to Baumgärtel in *Westermann, pp. 236–241.

[17] See Fritsch, Vriezen volume; Goppelt, *TDNT* 8, pp. 256–259.

phenomenon of 'horizontal' typology. But this, too, essentially involves symbolism.[18] One reason for this is that while there may be an inner structural affinity between events that are typologically linked, there is usually considerable outward difference. The original Israelite salvation event was a literal exodus, so exodus becomes a symbol for salvation and the Christ event is the effecting of a metaphorical exodus. The original messiah was a literal David, so David becomes a symbol for Israel's ideal leader and her hope for a new leader is a hope for a new David.

It is to be noted, however, that even before David became a future-oriented symbol (a type), his present kingship was already seen as the embodiment of something much more significant than it was historically. David is Yahweh's vicegerent, ruling the earth on behalf of the Lord of heaven and earth: the picture is larger than life, painted by faith in God who is Lord and who will surely one day manifest his Lordship thus. It is by means of the explicit hope of prophecy and the implicit hope of type that the NT then interprets the Christ event. The types are anticipatory symbols of it.[19] The event itself, of course, then transforms the meaning of the symbols, partly by bringing different symbols (David, Son of man, sacrifice, servant) in association with each other.[20]

Christian typology, then, studies OT realities that became symbols of something analogous to them (though greater than them) in the NT.

b. Typology, allegory and the 'fuller sense'

Typology is concerned with levels of meaning beyond the bare literal historical. That concern is shared by allegory, though advocates of typology usually insist on the difference between the two, and agree

[18] *Von Rad (II, p. 366; also in *Westermann, pp. 22–23) warns against turning typology into a general study of symbols and pictures enshrining timeless religious truths; it has to keep its link with concrete historical events of OT and NT times.
[19] Cf. *Lohfink, pp. 81–82, on the symbolic significance of the exodus, already in Ex. 15; von Rad in *Westermann, pp. 34–37 on the 'overdrawn' picture of events such as Israel's conquest of Canaan and on the typical significance of realities such as land, rest, and long life; Eichrodt, TZ 13 (1957), pp. 509–518 on the high priest Joshua as a promise/symbol of the messianic king to come. *Lohfink (pp. 131, 134) notes that this is a form of 'mythologizing' of Israel's history: key historical events take over the function of the primal age of creation (cf. *Pannenberg III, pp. 1–79).
[20] Barton, Theology 79 (1976), p. 264, following Farrer, The Glass of Vision.

with Bultmann on this (if on nothing else) that 'every form of allegory is idle play or nonsense'.[21]

Literal interpretation normally involves seeking to understand a text of univocal meaning; that meaning is the one natural to the text in its historical context.[22] Occasionally an author intends his work to be read at two levels (C. S. Lewis's novels offer an example), and literal interpretation may then concern itself with both of these. Such a work invites interpretation as an allegory, but the allegory belongs to the work itself. It is part of its intrinsic meaning in the context of its author and his readers.[23]

Allegorical interpretation (as applied to the Bible or any other document) involves attributing to a text a meaning which is extrinsic to the text itself, in that it is not the apparent meaning it would have had for writer and readers. It is brought to the text from elsewhere – from the interpreter's own mind, for instance, or by independent revelation from God (as he may believe), or from his theological tradition. The interpreter may understand himself as giving a new meaning to the text (allegorizing something of originally univocal meaning, we might say). Or he may see himself as unveiling a second meaning which is intrinsic to the text itself, whether as the words of its human author or as the words of the one who inspired the human author (who perhaps himself did not then understand the allegorical meaning of his words). He may see this second meaning as of parallel importance to the surface meaning, as of greater importance, or as of sole importance.

So how are typology and allegory to be defined in relation to each other?

1. Are we to understand that, where allegory emphasizes a meaning brought to the text from elsewhere, typology interprets texts literally, and then sees an analogy between their literal reference and what comes about in Christ? In fact, this distinction is more apparent

[21] Bultmann in *Anderson, p. 33.
[22] Cf. Brown, The Sensus Plenior, pp. 1–9; but for a discussion of the problems involved, see Childs, Zimmerli volume.
[23] One instinctively speaks in terms of what an author intended his work to mean; but the idea that meaning is determined by what an author intended has been under severe attack since Wimsatt and Beardsley's essay on 'The intentional fallacy'; D. Newton-De Molina (ed.), On Literary Intention, documents this debate. Although criticism of 'intentionalism' has generated insights on the meaning of meaning, it tends to imperil the objectivity of meaning; see the works of E. D. Hirsch (e.g. Validity in Interpretation; Aims of Interpretation).

than real, since the typological interpretation given to a text is still one which arises from convictions based elsewhere than in the text itself. Hebrews' interpretation of Psalm 8 (Heb. 2:5–9) and Matthew's interpretation of Hosea 11:1 (Mt. 2:15) are both brought to the text rather than suggested by it. Fundamentally they derive from the conviction that Jesus is the messiah; but they also commonly presuppose or imply certain further convictions, such as that Jesus is the representative or embodiment of Israel and indeed of true humanity (so that the passages in Hosea and Psalms referring to Israel or to man can be applied to him).[24] Certainly some of the NT's interpretation (1 Cor. 9:9 is a notable example) and some subsequent Christian interpretation, such as the understanding of the Song of Songs as a celebration of the love relationship between Christ and the church, may well seem both to ignore the text's natural meaning (as allegory does) and to have no real point of contact with typology.[25]

2. Is the difference, then, that typology concentrates on central, key features of a passage, while allegory can find great significance in smaller details of a text?[26] Again, one cannot make this distinction at all sharply. Many NT and modern typological interpretations appeal to details of the OT text which were not originally symbolic (e.g. Gal. 3:16; Heb. 7:1–6).[27]

3. Is the difference that typology works with the important biblical perspective of salvation history, while allegory sees salvation as timeless and universal?[28] But when Paul uses the verb allēgoreō (Gal. 4:21–31) he is not referring to a non-historical understanding of salvation, while Thomas Aquinas[29] and other medieval scholars refer to what we call the typological as allegorical. Conversely, allegory can appear within non-Christian typology. A Jewish targum

---

[24] See Runia, TSFB 49 (1967), p. 14; *Ellis, pp. 135–139; *Barr, pp. 108–112.

[25] Though see *Hanson's treatment of 1 Cor. 9:9 (pp. 161–166).

[26] See von Rad and Eichrodt in *Westermann, pp. 21 and 225–226; cf. *Barr, p. 107; R. P. C. Hanson's definition (Allegory and Event, p. 7) is comparable.

[27] *Barr, p. 113; Lampe, LQHR 190 (1965), pp. 20–21, Essays on Typology, p. 34. Strikingly, Melkisedeq's bringing out bread and wine is not taken up by Hebrews, though it is by *Vischer (p. 132) (cf. Bruce, This is That, p. 13)! For other modern examples, see Ellul on Elisha (Politics of God, pp. 9–12) and Jonah (Judgment of Jonah); *G. A. F. Knight (pp. 9, 202–217) on the parallels between the 'moments' of Israel's life and of Jesus's life.

[28] See von Rad in *Westermann, p. 21; *Goppelt, pp. 18–20.

[29] Summa Theologiae 1a Question 1, Article 10.

interprets the Song of Songs as an account of salvation history from the exodus (ch. 1), conquest (ch. 2), and building of the temple (ch. 3 – 4), through the exile (ch. 5) and return (6:1 – 7:11) to the Roman exile (7:12 – 8:14).[30] If typology is essentially concerned with history, this interpretation looks more like typology than the common Christian one which takes the Song as a celebration of Christ's relationship with the church. Yet the original reference of the Song of Songs is not to an OT event, person, or institution; if any interpretation merits the adjective 'allegorical', it is surely this targum!

While it may be of the essence of typology to be 'historical', it is not of the essence of allegory to be 'unhistorical'. Perhaps the impression that the latter is the case arises from a comparison of NT interpretation (which emphasizes history, because of the distinctive beliefs of Christianity) and Philonic interpretation (which does not emphasize history, because of Philo's distinctive beliefs).

Christian interpreters believe that the historical orientation of OT faith made a typological approach appropriate. Conversely, an allegorical approach to the OT is likely to be unhistorical. This is not because allegory itself is necessarily unhistorical; rather, allegory by definition reads a text in a non-obvious way, while the obvious meaning of the OT places an emphasis on history. Viewing typology as the characteristic NT approach to OT interpretation and seeing Philonic interpretation as the characteristic embodiment of allegory helped set typology and (Alexandrian) allegory over against each other. This may not in the end have been illuminating.[31]

Paradoxically, we might suggest that typology itself can become allegory (as in the targumic approach to the Song of Songs) if it overemphasizes history and starts operating as if salvation history were all that there is to Scripture. The appropriateness of typology derives from the fact that salvation history is *one* important strand in the OT. But it is not the most appropriate category for every text. Paul's allegorical interpretation of Deuteronomy 25:4 (1 Cor. 9:9) is essentially similar in argument to Philo's (*On the Virtues* 145 – 146; *cf. Special Laws* I. 260), though Paul's is applied to ministers, Philo's to men in general. A typological approach to the passage would not necessarily be more appropriate.

4. Is the difference between typology and allegory that typology

---

[30] Cf. Loewe, *Biblical Motifs*, pp. 159–173.
[31] Cf. *Barr's critique, especially pp. 104–107.

interprets a passage in the light of the Bible as a whole, while allegory interprets a passage in the light of other concerns (such as Philo's Alexandrian philosophy) that are alien to the Bible? On the Christian view, the Christ event is of key importance to God's achieving the saving purpose in history which he began to implement in OT times. A typological interpretation of the OT, which looks at earlier events in the light of this climactic event, follows from this view. It admits that connecting the Christ event to OT events adds something they do not refer to; but it believes that this is not to add something alien, whereas to interpret the OT in the light of Alexandrian philosophy is to read it in the light of alien beliefs.[32]

Certainly there is an ideological difference between Christian typology and Alexandrian allegory. But we have noted already that not all typology is Christian, and not all allegory is Alexandrian. There is Christian and non-Christian typology, Christian and non-Christian allegory.

Christian typology and allegory work with the presupposition that the OT and the Christ event belong distinctively together; rabbinic typology or Philonic allegory make different assumptions. The justification which the Christian claims for seeing a special relationship between the Christ event and something in the OT is theological, not hermeneutical; it claims that the God who did things in Israel was the God who then acted in Christ.[33] Similarly an allegorizing of the OT (e.g. treating the Song of Songs as a picture of the relationship between God and his people) could be legitimated by noting that other biblical passages (e.g. Hos. 1 – 3; Eph. 5) draw the analogy between that relationship and that of a man and a woman. So the allegorical interpretation is not alien to the thought of the Bible as a whole. On the other hand, Philo's allegory, or 'Bonaventura's attempt to wed the Hebrew Psalter to medieval Mariolatry . . . is not exegesis, nor even eisegesis; it is "metagesis" '.[34] But it is not wrong merely because it is allegory.

5. I think that the best way to formulate the distinction between typology and allegory is to see the former as an approach to theology and the latter as an approach to interpretation. Typology, that is,

---

[32] Cf. Eichrodt in *Westermann, p. 227; Daniélou, op. cit., p. 84; *Barr, p. 116.
[33] Cf. Markus, Communication of the Gospel, pp. 80–81.
[34] Jewett, WTJ 17 (1954), p. 12.

studies events, while allegory is a method of interpreting words.[35] Thus types are events, persons, or institutions, which are or become symbols of something brought about later which is analogous to, yet more glorious than, the original. As such, typology is a way of studying the actual subjects that OT texts refer to (the exodus, David, the temple sacrifices, and so on), not out of a concern with their original historical meaning but out of an interest in their symbolic significance.[36] Allegory, on the other hand, is a way of studying the texts themselves, a method of interpreting the actual words. It parallels typology in that it goes beyond a literal approach to them. Typology goes beyond the literal approach to events, allegory goes beyond the literal approach to texts.

From a Christian perspective, valid typology will then be limited to study which sees the Christ event as the ultimate event symbolized by the anticipatory types. Valid allegory will be biblical interpretation which understands a particular statement as an expression of truths found elsewhere in the Christian Bible, though not in the overt meaning of this particular statement.

There is then in the Bible (and elsewhere) typological allegory (interpretation which is concerned with the links between subjects referred to in texts) and non-typological allegory (interpretation which concentrates on the words of texts). It may, however, be doubted whether the NT writers made this distinction or felt the need for a distinctive rationale for either approach; it is unlikely that Matthew or Hebrews rationalized their interpretation of Hosea 11 and Psalm 8 in the way the modern interpreter does. Paul's use of the verb *allēgoreō* in connection with a piece of interpretation that various modern writers prefer to describe as typological (see section 4a above) 'is a parable' showing that the NT feels no need to distinguish a category such as typology from other interpretative procedures.

If we define allegory as an approach to textual interpretation which goes beyond the words' overt meaning, we can relate it to the study of the 'fuller sense' of scripture as this has been pursued mainly by

[35] Cf. Foulkes, *Acts of God*, pp. 35–36; Sowers, *Hermeneutics of Philo and Hebrews*, p. 97; Williamson, *Philo and Hebrews*, pp. 531–533; Stek, *CTJ* 5 (1970), p. 160.

[36] It concerns itself with them as they are described in the texts, however – with Melkisedeq or Jonah as Genesis or the Book of Jonah describe them (Brown, *The Sensus Plenior*, pp. 16, 114–119).

Roman Catholic theologians. The term *sensus plenior* or fuller sense was coined by A. Fernández to designate 'the deeper meaning, intended by God but not clearly intended by the human author, that is seen to exist in the words of Scripture when they are studied in the light of further revelation or of development in the understanding of revelation.'[37] Matthew's interpretation of Isaiah 7:14 (Mt. 1:23) again provides a stock example; another is the common interpretation of the decalogue as containing in germ the fuller revelation regarding God's standards contained in the Sermon on the Mount.[38]

More generally, this approach presupposes that the God-given unity of Scripture makes it appropriate to see particular references to grace or sin or faith as implying the fuller whole of the total biblical treatment of that topic. Another instance of it, however, is the 'Marian' interpretation of Genesis 3:15. This last example illustrates the importance that attaches to where 'further revelation' is believed to lie. Does it, for instance, lie only in the Bible or also in subsequent Christian tradition? Can the ordinary Christian claim spiritual insight into a new fuller sense of a biblical passage; or is this confined to the biblical writers themselves?

As R. E. Brown notes, typology and the fuller sense are related, but the former applies to things, the latter to texts.[39] This distinction is the same as the one proposed above for typology and allegory; the fuller sense in fact seems to be another description for Christian allegory. Both find extra meaning in texts in the light of subsequent revelation.

With allegory, we noted, there is an ambivalence over whether the meaning the interpreter brings to the text is one he sees himself as unveiling in the depths of the text somewhere, or whether he actually understands himself as bringing an extra meaning to a text of univocal nature. There is a similar ambivalence over the fuller sense. We may be inclined to see interpretations such as Matthew's or Paul's (*e.g.* Mt. 2:15; 1 Cor. 9:9) as re-applications of the original texts (albeit, we may believe, inspired ones), approaching them as we approach

[37] Brown, *Jerome Bible Commentary*, sections 71:56, 57; *cf. The Sensus Plenior*, pp. xiii, 92–93; he refers to A. Fernández, 'Hermeneutica', *Institutiones Biblicae* (Rome: PBI, 1925, ²1927), pp. 306–307. *Harrington and *Grelot summarize much of the recent literature; see also Coppens, *Concilium* 10.3 (1967).

[38] So Benoit, *RB* 67 (1960), pp. 182–183; Brown, *Jerome Bible Commentary*, section 71:59; *cf.* note 15 above.

[39] *Jerome Bible Commentary*, section 71:72; *cf. The Sensus Plenior*, pp. 114–119.

parallel treatment of the OT elsewhere (*e.g.* at Qumran).[40] Matthew and Paul, however, seem to have seen themselves as utilizing the texts' own meaning (the meaning it had for its divine author, perceived from further knowledge of his purpose in later events and scriptures), not as re-applying it.[41] Admittedly the distinction between re-application and fuller sense can be dissolved by defining meaning in such a way that it includes what a work 'means' to later readers who have found it 'meaningful'.[42] But this approach imperils the notion of objective meaning even more than recognizing the possibility of a fuller sense does.[43]

c. The use of typology and allegory

We have noted that the application of typology or allegory to the OT can be Christian only if it works within the boundaries of the overall Christian revelation. But, even granted this limit, are these approaches legitimate in principle if they introduce meaning into texts or events, rather than discover meaning from them? In facing this question we need to clarify two distinct activities: their application to the OT as a means of understanding *the Christ event* and its consequences, and their use as a means of understanding *the OT itself*.

1. Typology can help us to understand the Christ event. NT typology begins from the antitype and moves back to identify the type, not vice versa;[44] allegory and the fuller sense, too, are ways of letting the Christ event be illuminated by the OT. They are not systematic principles for interpreting the OT itself; they are selective in the passages they utilize, and selective in their approach to those passages. In taking up Isaiah 7:14 to throw light on the birth of Christ, for instance, Matthew appeals to only one aspect of Isaiah 7; he leaves aside the central thrust of that chapter with its challenge to

[40] *Cf.* Brown, *CBQ* 25 (1963), p. 267; Fitzmyer, *NTS* 7 (1960–1), p. 332.

[41] *Cf.* Brown, *CBQ* 25 (1963), pp. 279–280; *Hanson, p. 234.

[42] Robinson, *CBQ* 27 (1965), pp. 19–20; Bruce, *Epworth Review* 4 (1977); Eichrodt in *Westermann, p. 242.

[43] See note 23 above. Bruce (pp. 97–98) seeks to safeguard historical meaning by insisting that the germ of the fuller sense/re-application be present in the text's historical meaning, though it is not clear that this is necessarily so in the NT. *Cf.* also the discussion of typology as a way of understanding the OT itself, in section 4c below.

[44] *Gunneweg, p. 24; *Goppelt, pp. 242–243; Wolff in *Westermann, p. 190.

a costly and practical trust in God under the pressures of life in the world.[45]

Christian typology, then, is selective in its use of the OT. This does not mean, however, that it simply reads into the OT what it already knows.[46] The NT writers may choose texts that are patent of the Christian meaning they are seeking, may read Christ into a text, and may modify the form of the text to make the reference to Christ clear; but they do not manufacture their texts. The text includes a 'given' and this interprets the Christ event as well as being interpreted by it. The fact that the OT is being invited to comment on a question derived from outside it (i.e., What is the significance of the Christ event?) does not mean it is making no real contribution with regard to that question. Although it does not decide the overall nature of the question, it does decide the nature of the answer. The answer is not determined by the question.

Indeed, the potential answers that the OT can provide influence the actual shape of the question. Thus G. W. H. Lampe is concerned about typology not because it fails to do justice to the OT, but because it places regrettable limits on the way the NT understands the death of Christ, by causing this understanding to be so influenced by the nature of OT sacrifices.[47] The theology of Hebrews, Galatians, or Romans is not determined by the writer and then grafted on to the OT. It is formed by the interaction of OT and Christ event (and Holy Spirit) in the writer's mind. Setting alongside the Christ event some earlier reality which parallels it in a particular way does clarify the meaning of the Christ event. In a similar way, Jesus understands himself from the picture of the servant in Isaiah 53 at least as much as vice versa.[48]

So it is with typology within the OT. Although the exodus is used

[45] Cf. Westermann's typological interpretation of Judah's willingness to take Benjamin's punishment (1000 Years and a Day, p. 53), which utilizes Gn. 44 to illustrate for us the significance of Christ's death, but does not thereby illuminate that chapter's own meaning in its context in the Joseph story; also the allegorical application of OT warfare passages to the believer's spiritual warfare (e.g. C. S. Lewis on Ps. 137, Reflections on the Psalms, pp. 113–114).

[46] So Bultmann in *Westermann, p. 54. Since Bultmann believes that some NT narratives were created to provide fulfilments of OT passages (e.g. History of the Synoptic Tradition, p. 281), it seems perverse of him to deny that OT prophecies contribute to the NT's interpretation of the Christ event!

[47] LQHR 190 (1965), p. 23. Contrast *van Ruler (see n. 60 below).

[48] Haag, Kornfeld volume, p. 257.

to provide a retrospective interpretation of Abraham's journey to Egypt, it is more widely used to offer a prospective interpretation of a coming act of redemption, a new exodus.[49] Typology does move from type to antitype. Another way to express this conviction is to speak of typology as not strictly an aid to exegesis (a way of moving towards an understanding of a text) but rather as an aid to exposition (a way of showing how the text applies in some new context).[50]

Von Rad notes that typological interpretation takes place in the Spirit, and he has been criticized for this remark.[51] But all our application of Scripture is intuitive, and the nature of the application is bound to reflect the person, assumptions, conventions, and tastes of interpreter and his audience, to whom the Holy Spirit graciously condescends. Perhaps Paul implies this in Galatians 4. Does he mean 'these things can be taken allegorically (if the audience finds that form of interpretation convincing)'? Today, too, whether forms of application of Scripture appeal to a listener or reader is in part a matter of taste; so it is with typology, allegory or the fuller sense.[52]

But if our concern is with interpreting the OT itself, there are limits to what these approaches can achieve, if they allow the OT to illuminate the Christ event in certain ways only, without necessarily allowing the OT to speak for itself. Their situation-centred approach to the text ('How does it relate to Christ?') has to be complemented by a text-centred approach ('What is the text itself saying in its own right, what is its own agenda?'). We need to understand Isaiah 7 or Genesis 44[53] for themselves; a typological approach does not necessarily help us to do this. Similarly, concern with the 'fuller sense' or 'spiritual meaning' becomes lack of interest in the literal meaning.

Yet it was in the words of a human writer communicating with his readers in a particular situation that the Holy Spirit actually spoke; so, it is normally through understanding these words in that context that we understand what the Holy Spirit meant through

---

[49] Haag, p. 252.

[50] France, *TSFB* 56 (1970), p. 15; *France, pp. 41–42.

[51] Von Rad in *Westermann, p. 38; see Baumgärtel, *ThL* 86 (1961), column 902; *van Ruler, p. 67; Stek, *CTJ* 5 (1970), p. 154, contrasting von Rad (for whom typology is our way of appropriating or proclaiming God's revelation in history) with Fairbairn (for whom it is God's way of teaching us). (Brown [*The Sensus Plenior*, p. 12] also notes that it is God's will that determines the presence of a type).

[52] See *e.g.* those referred to in notes 7, 27, and 45.

[53] See again the passages referred to in notes 7, 27, and 45.

them. The spiritual interpretation of the text is the literal one, the meaning the Spirit himself inspired.[54] The need to give the text itself priority is also clear when we consider allegory, for allegory may enable us to maintain a formal commitment to the Bible's words when we actually believe different things from what it says; we may assimilate the text to our understanding rather than our understanding to the text, and fail to keep testing our so-called biblical theology by reference to the Bible itself.[55]

So typology, allegory, and the fuller sense can help us utilize the OT in order to interpret the Christ event. But fully to interpret Christ in the light of the OT involves interpreting him in the light of the OT's literal meaning.

This is true even insofar as the Christian's interest in studying the OT is to see what light it throws on Christ. If the OT offers an anticipatory witness to the Christ event, then the whole of it, in its natural meaning, should be considered for its relevance to that subject. This concern takes us back to the study of OT theology. As our grasp of the OT's intrinsic meaning grows, so should our understanding of Christ against this context.[56] Again here we see reason not to allow excessive scope to these interpretative approaches which begin from the Christ event, for they make the interpretative process a circular one. Typology, for instance, is less concerned with the type's intrinsic meaning than with what the antitype says more clearly. While seeming to interpret the OT and to attribute authority to it, it actually derives its interpretation from the NT and finds authority only there. Allegory, typology, and the fuller sense thus become Marcion in another form.[57] They imply that the whole of Christianity is to be focused on Christ, so that the OT must be full

---

[54] Vawter, *CBQ* 26 (1964); *van Ruler, p. 62; *Amsler, p. 167; against *e.g.* Coppens, *Concilium* 10.3 (1967), p. 64. *Cf.* the questioning of typology by Drane (*EQ* 50 [1978] and Rössler (von Rad volume, pp. 156–158), who wonders why one needs to preach on an OT text at all if one interprets it typologically; though von Rad himself stresses the need to pay attention to the OT text itself and not merely to the text as used in the NT (see *Biblical Interpretations in Preaching*, pp. 98–99, on Is. 61).

[55] *Amsler, pp. 164–167; Barrett in *CHB* 1, pp. 377–379; *Barr, p. 116. This discomfort with the text is overtly the basis of C. S. Lewis's allegory (*loc. cit.*).

[56] *Cf.* *von Rad II, p. 386; *Barr, p. 145; Fohrer, *EvT* 30 (1970), pp. 294–298; *van Ruler, pp. 67–72.

[57] *Cf.* *Gunneweg, pp. 144, 211–212; Michalson in *Anderson, p. 62; *Fohrer, p. 15; Davies, *ExpT* 67 (1955–6), p. 6.

of him if it is a Christian book.[58]

But if the OT is itself Scripture, the whole of it contributes to an understanding of the faith. In the light of the NT's use of these methods, we may hesitate to repudiate them. But the NT is concerned with how Christ is to be preached, and a Christian concern with OT interpretation is broader than this. We are not Jews trying to understand one who has just come as the (alleged) messiah; we must ask what the OT means for us, not merely for such a person.[59]

2. But typology is also a way of understanding the OT. We have noted that the primary function of methods such as typology is to utilize certain aspects of the OT in order to interpret the Christ event, and we have emphasized that this is a different task from interpreting the OT itself. Despite this, typology can help us with the latter task. Perhaps it is inevitable that if we interpret one thing in the light of another, the process of interpretation is two-way. If the OT is set alongside the Christ event as a means of interpreting the latter, the OT itself is inevitably thereby also interpreted by the Christ event. The belief that Christ is the climax to which the types pointed functions as a pre-understanding for approaching the OT itself, and (in the way that a pre-understanding does) may thus open our eyes to aspects of texts or of events that we might otherwise miss.[60]

Exponents of the fuller sense make a similar claim for this approach. A prophet characteristically believes that his message has been 'given' him; he may well himself then grant that its meaning goes beyond what he can indicate. Nevertheless, a passage's fuller sense will be one of which the historical sense is a less complete version, not an unrelated one. OT history's portrayal of events 'larger than life' and its use of symbols, indicating that it is written by faith

---

[58] Cf. *van Ruler, p. 68.

[59] Haag, p. 256; Fohrer, *EvT* 30 (1970), p. 293.

[60] Cf. Eichrodt in *Westermann, p. 243. Examples in *van Ruler, p. 40 (the NT's use of OT cultic material to interpret Christ's death drives us to take this element more seriously than scholarship with its stress on the prophets and ethics often does); *Vischer, pp. 207–208 (the NT enables one to perceive incompleteness in the OT's testimony which the text itself is at least half aware of – *e.g.* Ex. 32 – 34); Wolff in *Westermann, pp. 182–185 (the NT understanding of promise and law helps us to perceive the OT's approach to this, and a typological perspective encourages us to be less dismissive of OT stories such as Ehud – God still works through such moral ambiguity).

and by hope, illustrates a parallel phenomenon.[61] Thus a typological perspective brought to passages such as Isaiah 9:6–7 and 11:1–9 may help the interpreter to hear the passage itself better.

It may also help us to understand the actual subjects referred to in texts, which are typology's particular concern. Who did Jacob actually wrestle with (Gn. 32:22–32), and was that a unique event or one with analogies elsewhere? Were the affliction of Joseph and the self-offering of Judah of any paradigmatic significance? Genesis is equivocal over whether Jacob fought with man, angel, spirit, or God, and typology cannot force Genesis itself to be less equivocal. But typology can seek to interpret the event itself in the light of the whole of Scripture and on that basis identify Jacob's opponent and draw lessons from the event.[62] It thus makes a contribution towards the interpretation of the OT events themselves by providing a further context which suggests aspects of what was going on and reveals that it was not an event outside any meaningful pattern of human experience. Of course such interpretations cannot be proved right;[63] the reader is invited to consider whether a particular patterning provides a satisfying interpretation of a collection of open data.

Typology often leaps straight from an OT event to Christ; but the pattern may have several OT elements, as in the accumulating portrayal of the 'humanity' of God which 'anticipates' the way the incarnation pictures an entire human life fully 'embodying' God to man, or in the OT instances of vicarious suffering (Moses, Hosea, Jeremiah, Ezekiel, the servant).[64] These could be missed if one were not looking back from the perspective of the cross; this enables one to see them in a context.

[61] For the distinction between prophecy and history, see Vawter, CBQ 26 (1964), pp. 91–93 on prophetic and scriptural inspiration; for the similarity, see Coppens, Concilium 10.3 (1967), pp. 66–67.

[62] Thus *Vischer (pp. 153–154) identifies the opponent as Jesus, and sees the Christian believer as, like Jacob, wrestling for Abraham's blessing with the one weapon of God's word of promise. But Westermann (1000 Years and a Day, p. 39) sees the link as between Christ and Jacob himself, wounded yet victorious and receiving a new name. The possibility of diverse interpretations is a problem with typology, though it is a problem with literal interpretation, too!

[63] Cf. Baumgärtel's criticism (ThL 86 [1961], column 906) of von Rad's seeing the theological conclusion of the Joseph story (Gn. 50:20) in the context of the Christ event (*von Rad II, p. 369; cf. Genesis, pp. 433–434/³pp. 438–439 – with significant revisions).

[64] See respectively Mauser, Int 24 (1970), also Gottesbild und Menschwerdung; Eichrodt, Int 20 (1966), p. 317.

Typology is currently unfashionable. But when von Rad tells us that the angel who seeks out Hagar is a type or shadow of Christ, or when Vischer asks, 'Is there not hidden in the depths of these ancient accounts [*i.e.* Gn. 21] the paternal joy of God, the joy of the father in heaven over the birth of His own Son as Son of man and Son of Abraham?',[65] such comments (understood as interpretations of OT events rather than of OT narratives) may indeed contribute to a fuller rather than a narrower interpretation of the OT's significance by enabling us to see these events as part of a pattern.

d. The Old Testament's explicit forward look

The conviction that the coming of Christ brings the fulfilment of OT prophecy is clear in many places in the NT: in Jesus' own use of OT prediction as described in the synoptic gospels, in the apostolic preaching described in Acts, in 1 Peter, in Hebrews, and elsewhere.[66]

Nevertheless, this way of looking at the relationship between the Testaments has been questioned as radically as any. From the perspective of exegesis, it has been noted that many of the prophecies allegedly fulfilled in the NT are not actually eschatological or messianic predictions at all. Matthew (1:22–23; 2:15, 17–18; 3:3) begins with several notable examples. Conversely, if one looks at prophecy within the OT itself, one finds that much of it, such as the promise of the extent of Israel's empire, of the destruction of Babylon, of the fall of Tyre, and of the mass return of the exiles to Palestine, simply failed to come true, at least in the precise way the prophets describe these events.[67]

From the perspective of the history of religion, understanding the prophets as foretellers of the future was succeeded by seeing them as forthtellers of the will of God in the present. Insofar as they speak

[65] Von Rad, *Genesis*, p. 189/³p. 194; *Vischer, p. 139.

[66] See respectively *France, *e.g.* pp. 97, 150, 159 (on Jesus); *Amsler, pp. 63–69 (on Acts) and pp. 28–31 (on 1 Peter); *Longenecker, p. 185 (on Hebrews). Wolff illustrates how a modern interpreter sees prophecy fulfilled in Jesus: the promise of God's personal coming and dwelling on Zion in Joel 3 was fulfilled in Jesus (*Joel and Amos*, p. 85); the prophecy of judgment on those who turn away from God's message (Hosea 9) was or will be fulfilled in Jesus (*Hosea*, p. 159).

[67] *Cf.* Bultmann in *Westermann, pp. 50–54 (the NT reads the OT as prophecy only by allegorizing it); *Barr, p. 153 (there is no prediction of Jesus in the OT); *Delitzsch I, pp. 34–41; II, pp. 22–31 (unfulfilled prophecy in the OT); *cf.* Carroll, *When Prophecy Failed*; *Fohrer, pp. 11–12, 27–28.

of what is to come, it is characteristically of judgment rather than of blessing, and it is of the imminent future which relates closely to their contemporaries. Eschatological prophecy is a late development in OT religion, a by-product of a crisis, and messianic prophecy itself is a subordinate aspect of this by-product. Historically, the NT relates more directly to inter-testamental Jewish hopes than to the OT.[68]

From the perspective of theology, Bultmann posited that the NT's 'allegorizing' of OT prophecy had the purpose 'of demonstrating that the events of the present are based – and so predetermined – on God's plan of salvation, thus taking from these events any offensiveness that might be theirs, and indeed turning the offense into its opposite, into a confirmation of the certainty of salvation'. But then he asked, 'is that theologically tenable? Can the offense of the cross of Jesus be overcome by recognizing it as long-prophesied and decided upon by God – or only by grasping its meaning and significance?'[69]

From the perspective of philosophy, the possibility of prediction – outside a deterministic universe – has been questioned. R. P. Carroll describes the idea of God knowing and revealing the future as an archaic metaphor and a notion lacking coherence, and quotes the alleged Chinese proverb, 'Prediction is a very difficult business, especially predicting the future'.[70]

Bultmann's own solution to the dilemma posed by the fact that many OT texts appealed to by the NT are not themselves explicitly forward-looking is to take up the thesis of J. C. K. von Hofmann in his *Weissagung und Erfüllung* (Prophecy and Fulfilment) (1841–4), 'that it is not the *words* of the Old Testament that are really prophecy, but the *history* of Israel, to which the Old Testament testifies'. This prophetic history is 'fulfilled' in the NT events – in its inner contradiction or miscarriage, in Bultmann's view.[71] But does

---

[68] *Cf.* *Clements, pp. 132–134; Fohrer, *EvT* 30 (1970), pp. 282–286.

[69] Bultmann in *Westermann, pp. 51, 55. Baumgärtel, too (in *Westermann, p. 143) questions whether the NT's proof from prophecy can bring us into encounter with Christ.

[70] *When Prophecy Failed*, p. 4; see further, pp. 29–35. Carroll expresses sympathy for a view of God expressed in the terms of process thought, according to which God can foresee the range of things that may happen, but not what actually is to happen, which will depend on the exercise of human freedom (p. 227) (see further section 3g above, with notes 96 and 97).

[71] Bultmann in *Westermann, pp. 55, 72. *Bright (p. 193), too, sees OT history as promise, NT history as fulfilment.

it really mean anything to say that an event or a writer is pointing towards something future, when this is not explicit in what is actually said? Does the actual proclaimed word lose its significance in any stress on salvation history which locates the promise in the events themselves and not in words offered at the time? Is it in principle right to appropriate a concept by means of a piece of redefinition that turns it into something so different?[72]

Part of the background to this questionable re-interpretation of the notion of prophecy and fulfilment, however, is that Bultmann exaggerates the problem raised by the NT's references to OT prophecy. Their motivation is surely not to offer rationalist proof or to satisfy curiosity, but to interpret the significance of the Christ event and to challenge and encourage a response to Christ which is not so different from the one Bultmann looks for. Further, the NT is actually rather restrained in quoting 'messianic' prophecies. It does not refer to many of the texts which were later appealed to by Christians, but whose messianic reference historical criticism questions (e.g. Gn. 3:15; 49:10; Nu. 24:17; Is. 9:6; 32:1–2), nor even to many of the texts that scholarship does regard as originally messianic (e.g. Is. 11:1–5; Je. 23:5–6). It is at least as interested in non-messianic eschatological texts.[73]

Conversely, even if there is little explicitly messianic prophecy in the OT, nevertheless an orientation towards what God is going to do in the future characterizes most expressions of OT faith and is bound up with the idea of covenant in its various biblical forms.[74] The theme of promise and fulfilment runs through the OT narrative from Genesis to Kings, as Yahweh keeps declaring his will and fulfilling it. Yet each such event makes Israel look the more to the future for this pattern of experience to continue, so that each fulfilment in the past becomes promise for the future. The OT is thus a book of ever increasing anticipation, a story moving towards a goal which lies

---

[72] For these questions cf. *Barr, pp. 152–154; *Gunneweg, p. 180; and the comments on the re-definition of salvation history by Rendtorff and Pannenberg in section 3b above.

[73] Cf. Hertzberg, *Beiträge*, pp. 149–152; *France, pp. 83–163. *Hanson, indeed, comments (p. 181) that 'Paul is not greatly interested in the predictive element in the Scriptures'.

[74] Cf. Preuss, *Jahweglaube und Zukunftserwartung*; Fensham, *TZ* 23 (1967).

beyond itself.[75] In a sense the prophets (in the strict sense) simply make this implicit hope explicit.[76] So promise can even be identified as the centre of OT thinking[77] and further as the key link between the two Testaments.[78]

Nevertheless 'the Old Testament never mentions Jesus Christ, nor does it visualize such a man as appears in the Gospels and Epistles', and NT 'fulfilments' often differ from what the prophets envisaged; so how can they be seen as genuine fulfilment?[79] Von Rad's answer is that even within the OT itself hopes often find realizations that are very different from what was expected. They are still seen as fulfilments of *those* hopes; yet the fulfilment nevertheless leads to a re-interpreting of the hope. So when the fulfilment in Christ is different from the promise articulated in the OT, this is comparable with the changes the promises undergo within the OT. Nothing in principle novel is involved then.[80] So one could not have 'deduced' Christ from the OT promise material; there is a sovereign freedom about the divine fulfilment, as the prophets themselves were aware. Yet faith in Christ finds the OT 'a book full of genuine allusions to Jesus Christ';[81] the Christian re-interpretative process is not alien to the thought of the OT promise.[82]

So Bultmann is right that you cannot 'prove' Christ by appeal to

[75] Cf. *Von Rad, II, pp. 319–335; 357–387; von Rad, *Genesis*; *Studies in Deuter-*. *onomy*; von Rad and Zimmerli in *Westermann, pp. 25–26, 89–113; *Amsler, pp. 127–128.

[76] This means there is something new about them, of course; the explicit promise element in Kings is much less prominent than the explicit portrayal of human sin (cf. *Gunneweg, pp. 203–204).

[77] See *Kaiser, also Kaiser, *Themelios* 10 (1974); Moltmann, *Theology of Hope*, p. 43; cf. *von Rad II, p. viii; also p. 428.

[78] Cf. Jasper, *ExpT* 78 (1967), p. 270; Verhoef, *New Perspectives on the OT*, pp. 280–303; Bruce, *Biblical Exegesis in the Qumran Texts*, p. 88; Stendahl, *IDB* 1, p. 423; cf. *Grelot's survey, pp. 327–403.

[79] *Von Rad II, p. 319; examples in Wolff's treatment of Ho. 1:10 – 2:1; 11 (*Hosea*, pp. 29, 204) and of Joel 2:32 (*Joel and Amos*, pp. 69–70; see also p. 15: 'The Christ event has . . . altered Joel's expectation'); cf. note 67 above.

[80] *Von Rad II, pp. 319–335. Cf. *Clements' treatment (ch. 6) of the development of OT hope towards the more overtly eschatological form strongly represented in the shape of the OT canon; see further section 5b below.

[81] Zimmerli in *Westermann, p. 120.

[82] Cf. Gese's various studies, *e.g.* his observation that the virgin birth motif in the gospels remains subordinate to a central concern with the birth of a new David; its significance is to help to underline the fact that this is God himself coming into the world, and it thus deepens the OT understanding of the son of God rather than turning this into something alien ('Natus ex virgine', von Rad volume).

the OT; nor can you 'disprove' Christ in such a way. 'The argument is at least as much about the claim of Jesus to be a definitive revelation from God and hence the key to the Scripture, as it is about the reference of the Scriptures, considered as infallible oracles, to Christ. The process is a two-way one; but on the whole Christ, rather than the Scriptures, is the given – even in arguments ostensibly relying on scriptural proof texts.'[83] The OT offers a many-coloured picture of the consummation of God's sovereignty. Some aspects of it link closely with claims made in connection with the Christ event, but others do not, and thus it is not self-evident that Christ is the fulfilment of OT hopes. Whether one recognizes him as such will be dependent on whether one is willing to acknowledge him for his own sake.[84]

What is one then to make of the actual OT promises, whose content is in many respects very different from what Christ was and achieved? At least three responses to this question are possible.

The view suggested by the approach just described, which follows hints in the NT itself, declares that the promises have been fulfilled, in a figurative sense. A vast increase is promised to Abraham, and it comes about through the preaching of the gospel through the whole world. A secure homeland is promised to Israel, and she finds this 'rest' in Christ. As is the case with typology, once it is claimed that Christ is the fulfilment of OT hopes, then the nature of OT hopes demands to contribute to our developing understanding of the significance of Christ.[85] In order that it may do so, the study of prophecy, recognizing that its application to Jesus often involves a transposition of its meaning, must respect the original word (just as typology must respect the original event) in its God-given meaning.[86] Only thus will OT hopes fully contribute to our understanding of Christ.

A second response is to infer simply that OT promises do not correspond to what happened in Christ because they were mistaken. Those who take this view sometimes emphasize that the important

---

[83] Barton, *Theology* 79 (1976), p. 261. Thus it is an over-simplication to say that the OT reveals what Christ is, the NT who he is (*Vischer, p. 7); he transcends OT hopes and categories even though he arises from them (*McKenzie, pp. 322–323; Porteous, *OT and Modern Study*, p. 337).

[84] Cf. *Eichrodt I, pp. 501–511.

[85] Zimmerli in *Westermann, pp. 115–116.

[86] *Amsler, p. 151.

feature of OT promises is not the concrete predictions, which, if they came true, functioned primarily to authenticate the one who made them. Nor, however, is it the specific undertakings which God is said to have made, usually about earthly blessings, even though the actual content of the prophecies, positive or negative, is more important when someone undertakes a commitment than it is when he merely makes a prediction. The important feature is the overall single promise of a personal relationship between God and his people. It is this last promise which is fulfilled in Christ.[87] But, while this distinction is useful, the Bible itself does not suggest that predictions (or concrete undertakings) are insignificant or dubious and can be ignored as long as the central promise is treasured.[88]

A third approach to unfulfilled OT prophecies is taken by A. A. van Ruler.[89] He agrees with F. Baumgärtel that OT promises cannot all be seen as aspects of one larger promise fulfilled in Christ. But van Ruler believes that a promise which is not in any direct sense fulfilled in Christ (e.g. that of the land) nevertheless does retain significance: the promises of OT times are still to be fulfilled.

But in what sense can we still look for a fulfilment of OT prophecies? One answer to this question appears in the scores of paperbacks lining the shelves of religious bookshops, which utilize biblical prophecy to interpret and to forecast present-day events in the Middle East. But there are several problems about this approach. First, it seems in principle unlikely that the God of the Bible would reveal future events in this way. He is not inclined to give signs or reveal dates (cf. Mk. 13:32–37; Acts 1:7). When he makes statements about the future, they are not so much an unveiling of a history that is predetermined to unfold; rather, they are promises, warnings, challenges designed to call those to whom they are addressed to a repentance, faith, and hope which can face an unknown future trusting in him. Bultmann's theological critique of certain approaches to OT prophecy[90] is relevant here.

Secondly, if prophecy is designed to challenge its hearers in the

---

[87] Cf. *Baumgärtel (pp. 15–36, 47–71) and Moule (NTS 14 [1967–8]); also Dahl, Studies in Paul, pp. 121–136; Carroll, When Prophecy Failed, on how prophets and their followers responded when event did not match prediction.

[88] Cf. *Westermann, pp. 128–133, on Baumgärtel; Miller, JSJ 2 (1970–1), pp. 80–81, on Moule.

[89] *Van Ruler, pp. 45–47.

[90] See note 69.

present, it is to be expected that biblical prophecies related to the people to whom they were addressed. This is clearly the case with chapters such as Ezekiel 34 – 48, much of which has been referred to contemporary events in the Middle East. These chapters take up God's ancient promises regarding people, land, kingship, temple, her relationship with the world, and so on, and reaffirm them in a context when they seem threatened or actually suspended. The purpose of the prophecies derives from that historical context; their inspired meaning derives from their function as a piece of communication between a sixth century Jew and his sixth century hearers, which could not as such have referred to 'the fatal collapse of the Red Army' or 'the use of tactical nuclear weapons'.[91]

Thirdly, a major apparent strength of this literalist interpretation is that it does believe in an eventual fulfilment of prophecies that were not completely fulfilled in their day. Yet this strength is only apparent, for it assumes that prophecies have to be fulfilled as if they were bare predictions. This is not the case. They are God's statements of intention, but God can change his mind, as the story of Jonah illustrates (Jon. 3:9–10) and as the ministry of Jeremiah states as a principle (Je. 18:7–10).[92] Whether or not they are fulfilled depends in part on the response they meet with. If they are not fulfilled at the time, there is no presumption that they ever will be, and no ground for an essentially allegorical appropriation of them in the context of events today.

Yet these prophecies stand as statements of the purpose of God, not merely random resolutions. They represent God's ultimate purpose, and the principles they embody can be re-applied in the future. This is the process which we have observed in the NT re-application of OT prophecy to Christ, and which we need to continue as we seek to live by OT prophecy. It is often referred to as a non-literal fulfilment of prophecy, but it is more appropriately seen as a re-application of prophetic principles and imagery, which must of course take place in the context of the broader insight into God's purpose that we now have through Christ.[93]

[91] So Lindsey, *Late Great Planet Earth*, pp. 160, 161.

[92] *Cf.* *Amsler, p. 125; Roberts, *Int* 33 (1979), pp. 243–244; Overholt, Rylaarsdam volume, noting the way in which prophetic revelation and proclamation is reshaped by the 'feedback' a prophet receives from his audience; see also the comments on process philosophy in section 3g above, with notes 96 and 97.

[93] See Roberts, pp. 245–253.

Our relation to apparently unfulfilled prophecy in fact resembles our relation to apparently fulfilled prophecy; the Christian believer is in a parallel position to the OT believer. The fulfilment of God's promises in Christ introduces him to a further stage of looking for yet another fulfilment as he 'comes to stand in a new way under an arc of tension between promise and fulfillment.'[94] The kingdom is come, yet we still pray 'thy kingdom come'. In this sense OT promises are fulfilled in the NT by being proved true and reaffirmed, so that they can be the basis of our hope. In the light of the coming of Christ, faith can now become expectant faith. In Christ all God's promises find their 'Yes' (2 Cor. 1:20): that is, not that in him they are all kept, but that in him they are all confirmed.[95]

Thus the NT itself can see an OT prophecy as both fulfilled in the work of Christ and as nevertheless still to receive a fulfilment (see the quotation of Je. 31:34 in Heb. 8:12 and Rom. 11:27).[96] On a broader scale, Revelation embodies a thoroughgoing future-orien-tated understanding of OT prophecy, in contrast to the present- or past-orientated emphasis of the rest of the NT.[97] Here very clearly, the coming of Christ enables faith to become expectant faith.

This hope, indeed, comes to be the focus of the Christian gospel for our age in works such as J. Ellul's *Hope in Time of Abandonment* and J. Moltmann's *Theology of Hope*, which emphasize (in the context of a widespread feeling of hopelessness in the world and the church) that the God of Christianity is the God of Israel, the God who promises and challenges his people to advance in faith towards a masked future.[98] OT prophecy bears witness to Christ, but not merely by pointing to a coming historical event. It ever calls people to look at the future in the light of the past, so as to see how to live in the present.

[94] Zimmerli in *Westermann, p. 114.

[95] *Vischer, p. 23, referring to Barth, 'Verheissung, Zeit – Erfüllung', *Münchner Neueste Nachrichten*, 23.12.1930; Dahl, *Studies in Paul*, p. 136; *Vriezen, pp. 100–101/²pp. 123–124.

[96] *Cf.* Wolff's application of prophecy not only to what God did in Christ but also to the position of believer and church now, living in hope but still open to standing under judgment (*e.g. Hosea*, p. 29; *Joel and Amos*, pp. 53, 70, 86).

[97] *Cf.* Smith, Stinespring volume, p. 63.

[98] Ellul, *Hope in Time of Abandonment*, p. 229.

Chapter Five

The Old Testament as Scripture

*Open my eyes, that I may
behold wondrous things out
of thy law.* (Ps. 119:18)

*Whatever was written in
former days was written
for our instruction, that by
steadfastness and by the
encouragement of the
scriptures we might have
hope.* (Rom. 15:4)

A term such as 'the scriptures' suggests a particular collection of writings which a religious community has accepted as a norm for its faith and life. This community will characteristically believe that God's providence and initiative lay behind the emergence of its scriptures, and that is certainly the present writer's conviction about the scriptures of OT and NT. Yet the development of the canon is at the same time a process which can be studied historically. As one can investigate the human origins of individual biblical books while at the same time recognizing that they also embody God's word, so one can study the historical development of the canon while at the same time believing that God's purpose was at work in this process.

The development happened over a long period, however, and discussion of this process can seem confusing, because the idea of 'canon' means various things at different stages. The process begins when Israel first recognizes that it possesses stories, laws, and instruction expressing God-given truths about faith and life, and that the community has to hold on to and live by these. As the community applies these insights to new situations and experiences, this tradition develops, and within the context of the tradition as it stands at a particular point, God speaks. The history of the canon thus begins with Israel passing on stories about what has gone on between her and God (and retelling them), passing on laws that God gives her (and applying them to new circumstances), passing on the wisdom of her elders (and amplifying it on the basis of new experiences), passing on the words God gave to her prophets (and seeing how they speak beyond the situations to which they were first addressed), and passing on the prayers, praises, and other expressions of her worship (and adapting them so that they express what the later community wants to say to God).

But the scriptures themselves are documents, not oral traditions. The development of the canon thus sees this material reaching a final written form, though documents do not necessarily become canonical as soon as they are completed (as we see in the case of some books that were eventually accepted into the NT). The story from Joshua to Kings probably reached its final form by 550 BC, but it may not necessarily have become canonical until some time later; the literary history of the biblical documents is not the same as the history of the canon. On the other hand, sometimes the final form of a text reflects a canonical process – that is, the text has been visibly shaped so as to speak not merely in one historical situation, but in others.

Thus, when traditions are put into writing, the canonical process may continue. This may happen by their being treated as canonical and as such becoming the object of interpretation in a new situation. Alternatively they may be revised in their written form so that they may better fulfil an ongoing role. Either way, once material has this written canonical form, questions about its interpretation take a different form, since people will have higher expectations of it and a higher degree of commitment to accepting what it says. Interpreting OT Scripture is thus not the same as (though it overlaps with) interpreting Jewish religious documents of the pre-Christian period.

As the canonical process continued, written scriptures came to be collected into groups of documents. This raises the question, how many of them are there and how do they relate to each other? It is this process that may be most commonly understood as the formation of the canon – the establishing of a clearly defined and circumscribed list of normative documents accepted by the community and given a distinctive status in relation to other material. Such canonization is the end of a process. The process begins when the community is gripped by the intrinsic qualities of the actual material, which has commended itself to the community and influenced it in informal ways; it ends when official authorization gives it formal canonical status.[1] A canon of Scripture in the narrow sense thus comes into existence. And as tradition functions differently once it becomes Scripture, so Scripture functions differently once it bears the burden and responsibility of being *the* canon. Further, demarcating canonical writings in this unequivocal way raises the question of the relationship of canon and inspiration. Are the two coterminous, or is one category broader than the other?

In this chapter we shall look at the various aspects of this process by which the OT canon came into existence, and note some of the implications that the canonical process has for OT interpretation.

a. The growth of the biblical tradition

In theory, the notion of canon suggests a legal norm, a yardstick for behaviour. The development of Israel's tradition[2] included the growth of covenantal/legal material, beginning in the exodus period and reaching important moments at the reforms of Josiah and Ezra. But when Israel began to preserve material of ongoing significance for her faith and life, the memories of her history were embodied in her tradition, at least as much as her knowledge of God's law.[3] She understood herself on the basis of her knowledge of events such as the promise to the patriarchs, exodus, Sinai covenant, wilderness wanderings, occupation of Palestine, promise to David, and building of the temple. This she did not merely once and for all, but afresh in different contexts. This process lies behind the narrative from Genesis to Kings (and later that from Chronicles to Nehemiah) as we know it. It also contributes to the prophetic books, because they, too, keep one eye on what *has* happened as they explicitly concern themselves with what must and will happen. Further, the new ways in which individual prophets express themselves in turn become the

[1] Sanders, Morton Smith volume, p. 79.

[2] The title 'the growth of the biblical tradition' is taken from that of a book by K. Koch, entitled in German *Was ist Formgeschichte?* This discipline (and *Überlieferungsgeschichte* or *Traditionsgeschichte* which developed from it) traces the process whereby experiences, images, insights, or ways of expressing something are taken up, developed, and re-applied over the centuries within a community. See also Rast, *Tradition History and the OT.*

[3] 'The canon is a memory before being a rule' (Jacob, *VTSupp* 28, p. 107).

125

old ways which subsequent prophets can take up and re-apply to themselves and their contexts.

The traditio-historical approach to the OT also assumes that legal, cultic, wisdom material, and so on, were transmitted and developed in such interpretative traditions. The theological implications of understanding the OT as the deposit of the growth of Israelite tradition are systematically explored in *Gerhard von Rad's *Old Testament Theology*. As we noted in section 1b, von Rad considers that the proper task of OT theology is to follow the ongoing chain of testimony to Yahweh's activity in history, crystallized in Israel's traditions.[4]

One set of criticisms of this approach centres on the relationship between tradition, revelation, and theology; for tracing the development of Israel's traditions may seem to raise as many theological questions as it answers. First, in what sense, or on what grounds, can we say we have made a theological statement, when we have made a statement about the development of Israel's tradition?[5] Perhaps von Rad's implicit response to this question is that he is willing to let the OT (as he interprets it) make its own claim upon the reader. If it has something compelling to say, it will carry conviction.

Secondly, what is the relationship between the concept of tradition and the concept of revelation? The latter long seemed an important key to understanding the OT's status, but has more recently been sharply questioned;[6] in effect, tradition constitutes an alternative model for understanding the OT's status. The revelation model emphasizes the conviction that biblical insights came through a divine initiative. The tradition model stresses that these insights were mediated, expressed, and developed through human channels.[7] The faithful response of the people of God contributed to the process of communication between God and man which is reflected in Scripture as a whole.

The revelation model fits well those moments when authors describe themselves as receiving words direct from God; applied to the more prosaic development and composition of narrative material

[4] See also Gese, *ZTK* 67 (1970) and Gese in *D. A. Knight. *D. A. Knight's symposium develops the theological issues involved in this approach.
[5] *Childs, p. 68; Kraus, *EvT* 36 (1976), p. 502; Baumgärtel, *EvT* 14 (1954), pp. 298–303. See also Zimmerli, von Rad volume.
[6] See especially *Barr, pp. 15–33.
[7] *D. A. Knight, p. 144.

such as Kings, it can be adapted to signify a divine providence that works through human initiatives and insights. The tradition model fits well this material whose development naturally invites understanding in human terms; where there is something 'revolutionary' about Israelite tradition or where the prophets say 'No' to Israel's traditions,[8] the notion of tradition can be adapted to cover the emergence of creative, new insights which inevitably have tradition as their background or locus.[9]

Both models, however, tend to imply a universal claim, and look as if they exclude the other. Once the notion of revelation swallowed up that of human development; now the notion of tradition threatens that of revelation, as if the growth of the OT material were an immanent evolution or the unfolding of something whose ultimate implications could be found in its beginnings.[10] The situation here is parallel to, and inter-related with, the understanding of history as the sphere of God's and of man's activity, examined in chapter three above.

Some aspects of the relationship between tradition and revelation within Scripture can be seen as matters of linear sequence. At any given moment the people of God live by what has been passed down to them. However 'supranaturally' one is to understand the origin of a particular prophetic word or the occurrence of a particular saving event, it is passed on to the next generation by a human process. This tradition is then the background and context for understanding new situations, new words, and new events. The exodus, for instance, finds its meaning against the background of the story of the patriarchs; the oracles of Jeremiah presuppose the background of Israelite history, law, and earlier prophecy. It is thus in dialogue with the resources of the tradition that a prophet's revelation can be most profoundly expressed, partly because the tradition is the repository of past revelation. It is no co-incidence that chapters of such depth as Isaiah 40–55 have such manifold links with Israel's traditions of narrative, prophecy, and psalmody. These constitute a store of creative insight and a 'springboard for revelation.'[11]

Nevertheless, while it is quite possible to say that from tradition

---

[8] Harrelson and Zimmerli in *D. A. Knight, pp. 25, 69–70.
[9] *D. A. Knight, pp. 164–178.
[10] See Kraus's critique, *EvT* 36 (1976), pp. 501–502, 506.
[11] *D. A. Knight, p. 167.

insight can emerge, to say that revelation emerges from tradition seems less appropriate.[12] It has reductionist implications: 'What people call revelation is really only human insight emerging from tradition'. Revelation suggests 'the concrete communication of positive substantive and expressible content' from God to man.[13] It builds on what the tradition has already given to the human speaker and hearer, but with its characteristic 'Thus Yahweh says' it can add something by way of both authority and content which insight emerging from tradition would lack. This is made clearer by the fact that often these words announce what Yahweh is about to do, explaining its significance and demanding the appropriate response.

When such an event has actually taken place, a third form of word may be heard, which looks back to this event and proclaims its meaning and demand. The OT, like the NT, is not only the end-product of the formation of a tradition; it is also the written record of the proclamation of God's acts.[14] Like revelation, proclamation is a 'word-event', by which God makes things happen. But like the development of tradition, proclamation is a human activity, a response to revelation.[15] As this proclamation ceases to be a direct word of address and becomes a record of proclamation, it is recorded in traditional forms and joins the existent body of tradition.[16] This expanded tradition sets the existent tradition and the events to which it refers in a new context, and can even open up their meaning more fully.[17] And as the deposit of tradition and revelation, it makes its ongoing demand on the community's life, constitutes the locus of future revelation, and (like the tiger's cage) is always capable of springing a surprise on the person who is willing to open it up.[18]

Fortunately or unfortunately, however, the housewife's larder may be as appropriate a metaphor for the community's accumulated tradition. It provides the raw materials for a large variety of recipes, but whether the menus are appropriate to the occasion depends on

---

[12] *D. A. Knight, pp. 164–180, comes so close to this without actually saying it that he may himself be aware of the point.

[13] Scholem, *The Messianic Idea in Judaism*, p. 284; *cf.* *McKenzie, pp. 65–66; Kuntz, *The Self-Revelation of God*, pp. 40–41.

[14] *Gunneweg, p. 207.

[15] Jeremias, *ExpT* 69 (1957–8), p. 339.

[16] *D. A. Knight, pp. 153–158.

[17] *Pannenberg I, pp. 133–134.

[18] Scholem, pp. 282–292.

the cook's insight. A revelatory word from God may be expected to have power and relevance beyond its original context; indeed, the prophets sometimes make that point explicit (Is. 8:16–20; 30:8; Jer. 36; Hab. 2:2).[19] Yet there is a certain tension between the notions of 'prophecy' and 'canon', for a prophetic word is given to a particular set of circumstances, and may not apply outside them.[20] Normative tradition (such as past words of prophecy) can be appealed to in a way that frustrates God's purpose in the present, as well as in a way that furthers this purpose.

This does not mean that sin has affected the content of the tradition itself;[21] the tradition embodies the way God *has* led and spoken to his people thus far. It does mean that the tradition can be the springboard for error as well as for revelation. The insight that served one generation's liberty can be the next generation's bondage.[22] By nature a community will tend to notice the aspects of the tradition that legitimate its present beliefs, attitudes, and practices. But God's word is as likely to come from aspects of the tradition that confront the community.

'Tradition is a mode of hermeneutics'[23] and thus studying the 'canonical hermeneutics' embodied in the biblical tradition itself can provide guidelines for our own interpretation of Scripture.[24] Canonical hermeneutics characteristically uses the tradition to encourage those who are down but confronts those who are secure. It offers prophetic critique to its own community and safeguards the freedom of God himself rather than assuming he is tied to us; it encourages us to see ourselves in those who oppose the truth rather than in those who stand for it; it offers mirrors for identity rather than

[19] See *von Rad II, pp. 39–49, on the putting of prophecies into writing.

[20] Jacob, *VTSupp* 28, pp. 112–113.

[21] So *Barr, pp. 32, 190–191; *D. A. Knight, pp. 174–175.

[22] *D. A. Knight, pp. 175–176. The controversies between prophets (*e.g.* Micah or Jeremiah and their opponents) concern at least in part which aspect of the tradition formed its cutting edge at that point (see van der Woude, *VT* 19 [1969]; Davidson, *VT* 14 [1964]; Zimmerli in *D. A. Knight); one piece of normative tradition can be open to appropriation at one moment but not at another (contrast the attitude to God's pomise to Abraham in Ezk. 33:23–29 and Is. 51:1–3; *cf.* Sanders in *Coats and Long, pp. 31–33, also *IDBS*, pp. 404–405). It is on the basis of the OT tradition that Jesus finds his calling and is recognized by some, but also on the basis of this tradition that he is resisted, condemned, and executed by others (*Barr, pp. 27–28).

[23] Fishbane in *D. A. Knight, p. 286.

[24] For what follows, see Sanders in *Coats and Long, pp. 35–40; *IDBS*, pp. 403–407; Morton Smith volume, pp. 94–104; Hyatt volume, pp. 247–253.

models for morality. In order to see how to apply the Bible's own hermeneutical method, we need to watch as closely as possible as it operates thus in specific contexts.

The answer, therefore, to the question 'Is it possible to understand the text without knowledge of its prehistory and the situations which produced it?'[25] is surely 'Some understanding is commonly possible, but understanding will usually be increased by looking at it in the light of these insights.' Thus a major concern of OT study has been the investigation of the 'kerygma' of various biblical traditions in their context in the history of Israel.[26] Studying the process of creative kerygmatic reinterpretation within the OT tradition helps us both to appropriate its witness within its own historical context and to follow it as a model for our exposition of Scripture.

Brevard Childs, however, questions whether this OT process of actualization is the key to contemporary OT interpretation. He does not believe that it works: so often the historical-critical approach 'sets up an iron curtain between the past and the present'.[27] The reason it fails to work is this: in going behind the actual text to supposed original historical situations only dimly reflected in it, scholarship ignores the believing community's witness in the text itself to the way the historical word is actualized; instead, it settles for an investigation into original historical contexts whose theories about the origins of biblical material are often very fragile.

Yet this argument carries less weight when the canonical form of the text itself, as is commonly the case with the prophetic books, directs us to particular historical contexts in which to listen to the text's kerygma.[28] Further, while the canonical form of the text may add something to its earlier form (if Childs' own fragile theories regarding the canonical process are correct), this is not necessarily a critical judgment on an earlier stage of the tradition. Rather, by preserving material the canon acknowledges its authority and invites the reader to submit himself to the message it brings – which commonly pre-supposes a specific context in which it is to be under-

[25] *D. A. Knight, p. 5.

[26] E.g. Brueggemann and Wolff, *The Vitality of OT Traditions*, and the articles on the 'kerygma' of various books and traditions in *Int* 20–25 (1966–1971).

[27] *Childs, pp. 141–142; for what follows, see Childs in Zimmerli volume, pp. 90–93; *Introduction to the OT as Scripture*, pp. 74–77.

[28] Tucker in *Coats and Long, pp. 56–70; cf. Jepsen in *Westermann, pp. 250–257, with his quotations from Luther's Preface to Isaiah.

stood. Indeed, in his concern to commend the text's final form, Childs seems to undervalue the considerable theological insights which emerge from the kind of hermeneutical approach he is criticizing. The historical approach has often set up a wall between past and present, but the work of writers such as von Rad and Wolff shows that it need not confine itself to the elucidation of philological and historical points; it can go on to help a reader face a text's theological dimensions and through it meet the God who met his people in the original historical situation.

For von Rad also understanding the OT as the growth of the biblical tradition provides the key to perceiving the relationship of the two Testaments; for what is the NT but another 'actualization' of the OT tradition in the light of a new event? This new event, of course, is so new that it demands contrasting with the old; yet it is at the same time in continuity with it, and can take over the OT tradition only because the latter is open to it. Von Rad's approach to biblical theology has been taken up by others. Scholars such as Hartmut Gese and Peter Stuhlmacher have applied it fruitfully to distinctively NT-looking topics like the virgin birth, the suffering of Christ, and the resurrection; they have sought to approach these topics biblically and view the whole biblical tradition as the unfolding of God's revelation until it reaches its goal in an understanding of the Christ event. The total biblical tradition then provides the context within which one particular embodiment of it is to be understood.[29] Comparable features about the approach to the development of biblical themes are to be found in the work of non-German scholars who do not necessarily presuppose a traditio-historical perspective.[30]

The traditio-historical approach to the relationship between the Testaments is suggestive, though it makes too exclusive a claim. The NT is a selective actualization of the OT, rather than an inevitable goal to which the whole OT is manifestly aimed. There is material in the OT which is not actualized in Jesus, and there is a real development of OT tradition in Judaism outside Jesus. The NT is *an* actualization of OT tradition, but the view that it is *the* climax of that tradition's

[29] *Von Rad II, pp. 322–335; Gese, *Vom Sinai zum Zion*; *Zur biblischen Theologie* (see also n. 4 above); Stuhlmacher, *ZTK* 70 (1973); Seebass, *EvT* 37 (1977); Pannenberg, *Theology and the Philosophy of Science*, pp. 381–391.

[30] *Porteous, p. 27, also pp. 93–111 (on the symbol Jerusalem-Zion); Bruce, *This is That*; Hooke, *Alpha and Omega*; Ellul, *The Meaning of the City*; *Smart, pp. 153–159 (on the re-application of the motifs of creation, Abraham, and the servant).

development is a statement of faith, made retrospectively in the light of Christ. The traditio-historical approach thus does presuppose a specifically theological position.[31]

b. The earliest Old Testament interpretation

Understanding the Bible as the unfolding of a tradition process has been subject to a further criticism: though appropriate enough for earlier stages of the development of some biblical material, it ignores the fact that, by a natural process of development, within OT times much of this material, which had proved it could speak in different situations, ceased to be malleable oral tradition; it was already becoming written Scripture. When tradition crystallizes as Scripture, it becomes a constant, a 'given' for faith, which henceforth exercises a more dominant critical and creative function in a community; it is appropriated and applied according to a different dynamic. Prophecy ends and textual preaching begins.[32] Interpreting the OT, then, means interpreting written scriptures, not the traditions behind the texts, any more than the theology which underlies them or the events they relate.

Like the canonical instinct, the instinct to put traditions into writing goes back many centuries in OT history.[33] This applies to narrative, law, prophecy, and no doubt other material such as psalmody. Narrative tells the story which identifies Israel and her God, and reminds the hearer of what may be expected of each party because of the relationship between them. Law acts as an explicit norm for Israel's behaviour; one can see the written law functioning canonically in the times of Josiah and Ezra. Prophecy, especially insofar as it survives the falsification test of exile, is preserved in the conviction that, as God's word, it has power to speak again.

OT tradition, therefore, had long existed in written form when later parts of the OT were being composed, and was studied in ways that parallel the approaches eventually taken to what was formally designated as Scripture. Thus 'the earliest Old Testament interpre-

[31] *Childs, pp. 68, 122; *Gunneweg, pp. 207–208; *Kraus, p. 507; Barr, *Judaism*, pp. 12–13.

[32] Barr, *Judaism*, pp. 14–15; Mays and Sanders in G. E. Wright volume, pp. 514–515 and 541–543; *cf.* Gese himself in *D. A. Knight, pp. 318–319.

[33] Anderson, *CHB* 1, pp. 117–118; Freedman, *IDBS*, pp. 130–131; Sanders, *IDBS*, pp. 403–404 and G. E. Wright volume, pp. 534–552; *Kraus, pp. 337–338.

tation'[34] took place within the OT itself, as later writers studied, pondered, applied, expounded, and quoted earlier ones.

One can see this process behind the production of OT narrative. Chronicles, for instance, can be described as an exposition of earlier OT texts, especially Samuel-Kings.[35] A parallel approach may be taken to the origin of the various pentateuchal law codes: Deuteronomy is an example within the OT of the sort of exposition, clarification, and expansion of law which appears later in the Mishnah.[36] The study and re-application of OT prophecy within the OT is explicitly instanced in Daniel 9:24–27 and less explicitly elsewhere in Daniel and other books: Apocalyptic has been described as an exercise in inspired biblical interpretation.[37]

Within individual prophetic books, 'secondary material' or 'glosses' can be seen not as alien and intrusive but as another form of inspired updating, explanation, and re-application of a word from God which enables it to continue to speak to the people of God during the 'post-history' of a document (the converse of its 'pre-history').[38] This same process can also be perceived in the Psalms, especially in their headings,[39] and continues in the work of the scribes who transmitted the scriptures and produced the Masoretic Text.[40] Narrative, law, prophecy, and other material is thus continually re-applied on the presupposition that its significance for Israel was not limited to the situation in which it first arose. It is of ongoing importance as God's word.

This attitude prepares the way for the view that it is canonical in a further sense: it has a distinctive status and is permanently binding

[34] Bruce, OTS 17 (1972); cf. Seeligmann, VTSupp 1 (1953); Weingreen, IDBS, pp. 436–438; Vermes, CHB 1, pp. 199, 228–229.

[35] Willi, Die Chronik als Auslegung; Ackroyd, JSOT 2 (1977); Goulder, Midrash and Lection in Matthew, pp. 3–4, 28–46; Goldingay, BTB 5 (1975). Cf. Sandmel's approach to the origin of the pentateuchal narrative (JBL 80 [1961]).

[36] So Weingreen, From Bible to Mishna. Fishbane (in *D. A. Knight, pp. 276–286) shows how the various elements in the Decalogue are taken up, explained, amplified, re-interpreted, and even transposed elsewhere in the OT.

[37] Willi-Plein, VT 27 (1977); Seeligmann, pp. 170–171; Bruce, p. 38, also his Biblical Exegesis in the Qumran Texts, pp. 16–17.

[38] Hertzberg, BZAW 66, with examples especially from Isaiah; Willi-Plein, BZAW 123, systematically examining this phenomenon in Amos, Hosea, and Micah; Grech, Augustinianum 9 (1969).

[39] Childs, G. E. Wright volume, also JSS 16 (1971); Bruce, OTS 17, pp. 44–52.

[40] Koenig, RHR 161–162 (1962); Barthélemy, VTSupp 9.

on Israel. Brevard Childs[41] suggests that such a canonical instinct has left its marks on the form of the scriptures themselves. As we noted in section 5a, he believes that the final form of the scriptural text is the right object for the interpretative efforts of synagogue and church. He commends it not on literary or historical grounds,[42] though he does believe that a historical-critical understanding of a biblical book should take this aspect of its actual form and intention seriously; rather, he commends it as the form that was given to the material in order that it might fulfil the ongoing canonical function which synagogue and church ascribe to it. 'The heart of the canonical process lay in transmitting and ordering the authoritative tradition in a form which was compatible to function as scripture for a generation which had not participated in the original events of revelation. The ordering of the tradition for this new function involved a profoundly hermeneutical activity, the effects of which are now built into the structure of the canonical text.' Thus 'an adequate interpretation of the biblical text, both in terms of history and theology, depends on taking the canonical shape with great seriousness'.[43]

The hermeneutical implications of the canonical process have also been studied by *J. A. Sanders, who added 'canonical criticism' to the glossary of OT study. Sanders' interest lies not so much in the 'canonical shaping' of individual books as in that of the canon overall, with its implications for our understanding of the OT as a whole. He considers that the opening books of the OT were reshaped in the post-exilic period, when the continuous story from creation to the exile was divided at Deuteronomy, and notes how significant this development was. Although this reduced both the Pentateuch and the 'Former Prophets' to dismembered torsos, the move made hermeneutical sense to those who wished to give special emphasis and authority to the Torah as the basis for the life of Judaism. Christianity in effect reverses this movement, re-emphasizing the *mythos* (gospel-story-identity-*haggadah*) element within Torah rather than

---

[41] *Introduction to the OT as Scripture*; also other works cited in the bibliography.

[42] *Cf.* the interest in the text's final form which is taken by redaction criticism, rhetorical criticism, and literary approaches to the Bible (*cf.* Barr, *BJRL* 56 [1973], pp. 10–33). The tradition process, too, can be studied from a literary perspective (see Steiner, *After Babel*, pp. 424–470).

[43] *Introduction to the OT as Scripture*, p. 60. The body of the volume outlines what this means for each of the books of the OT.

its *ethos* (law-ethics-lifestyle-*halakah*) element.[44]

Yet seeing the Pentateuch as Torah has justification in the material itself. Although Genesis to Kings has a narrative structure, Genesis to Deuteronomy is dominated by torah or instruction material (the conventional translation 'law' is misleading). It describes the way Israel is to live as the covenant people. Further, although there is a more radical side to prophecy, the 'Former Prophets' themselves present the prophets as preachers of repentance who called Israel back to the Mosaic torah; while Deuteronomy (and thus Torah), through being linked with the Former Prophets and thus with the Latter Prophets and their hopes, is set in the context of a promised final realization of the covenant, so that the perspective assumed by Paul (1 Cor. 10) is present in the canonical structure of the OT itself.[45]

The question of the relationship between Torah and Prophets in the canon as a whole is taken up by *Joseph Blenkinsopp. Torah stands for 'normative order', needed to undergird the life of the community; prophecy exists to ensure that the normative order is free to change rather than to freeze in a form that is appropriate only to circumstances now past, yet to change without merely assimilating to the patterns of a new set of circumstances. Torah becomes canon only after it has allowed itself to take account of prophecy and the prophetic perspective; prophecy, too, finds a place in the canon alongside Torah, though the price of this status is its independence. Overall the juxtaposition of law and prophecy within the canon suggests 'an unresolved tension, an unstable equilibrium between rational order and the unpredictable and disruptive, between the claims of the past and those of the present and future'.[46]

*R. E. Clements draws attention to another feature of the canonical form of the prophetic books. A threatening message of judg-

---

[44] So Sanders, *Int* 29 (1975); *cf.* Davies, *NTS* 24 (1978), pp. 38–39.

[45] See *Clements, pp. 104–30; also Clements, Torrance volume; Clements disputes Sanders' view that the reason for seeing the Pentateuch as torah is that this means 'teaching' in a sense which can include kerygmatic narrative. Kline sees the connection between covenant and canon which emerges especially clearly in Deuteronomy as the key to interpreting the OT (and NT) canon as a whole: it comprises covenantal law, history, prophecy, praise, and wisdom (*Structure of Biblical Authority*, pp. 45–75 = *WTJ* 32 [1969–70], pp. 179–200). But there is little overt indication of this perspective in the material itself. For other emphases on Deuteronomy's key place in the OT, see Herrmann, von Rad volume; *Deissler, p. 7.

[46] *Blenkinsopp, p. 151.

ment dominated the preaching of the pre-exilic prophets themselves; yet in the canonical form of all the books appears a message of hope which speaks of rebirth as well as of death, stemming from the conviction that this is God's word through prophecy as a whole – as the NT also understands it to be. Conversely, this understanding of the future as God's promise means, for instance, that royal psalms that are interpreted messianically in the NT may have been included in the Psalter precisely in the belief that 'Israel would again need them'.[47]

Studies such as these have opened up interesting questions concerning the relationship between narrative, law, and prophecy within the first two divisions of the Hebrew scriptures. It is much more difficult to see an internal coherence in the third division, the Writings (which are also often regarded as of rather inferior importance), and thus to postulate a shape to the canon as a whole. Two recurrent ways of doing this are to see the three divisions as referring to 'the past', 'the future', and 'the present' or as relating 'God's deeds', 'God's words', and 'man's response';[48] but neither of these exactly corresponds to the actual divisions of the canon. The basis for those divisions perhaps lies in historical and/or liturgical considerations (the Writings are the books which entered the canon last and/or are those which are not used in the weekly lectionary), rather than in matters of content or even of relative authority.

It is easier to see a structure based on form or content in the canonical arrangement of English Bibles: narrative (or Law – history) – poetry – prophecy, or past – present – future. This order, which has come down to us via the Septuagint, has often been assumed to be secondary, but it may actually be as old as the Hebrew order.[49]

---

[47] *Clements, p. 151; *cf.* pp. 131–154 generally, also Clements in *Coats and Long, pp. 42–55; Sawyer, *From Moses to Patmos*, pp. 108–118. Sawyer also notes (pp. 32–34) the appropriateness of calling Joshua to Kings 'prophecy', given its links with prophecy in subject matter, style, and date, its emphasis on 'Davidic soteriology', and its interest in prophecy and its fulfilment.

[48] *E.g.* Wolff, *The OT*; Westermann, *What Does the OT Say about God?*

[49] So Katz (*ZNW* 47 [1956]), noting that the Hebrew canon artificially separates Joshua-Kings from Genesis-Deuteronomy and Daniel from the prophets, as well as placing Chronicles after Ezra-Nehemiah. Lebram (*VT* 18 [1968]) believes that the oldest approach to the canon emphasizes its prophetic aspect, as testimony to the work of God's spirit in Israel. Law is linked to prophecy from the beginning of the canon's history, and the nomistic understanding of the canon is introduced only by Ben Sira.

The extant canons may reflect several historical shapings, and the differences in approach to the overall structure of the canon which we have been surveying do not, therefore, necessarily indicate that attempts to understand this structure are inherently subjective.

The various views on the shape of the OT canon also suggest different ways of seeing its relationship with the NT. The traditional understanding that the Hebrew canon emphasizes the Torah encourages a law-gospel contrast; though if the stress on law can indicate a concern with the way the covenant people are to live before God, then this understanding need not be read legalistically: the function of Torah may not be so different from the function of the epistles. If, however, the opening books are instead seen as God's deeds, these are continued in the gospels and Acts, while God's words are continued in the rest of the NT. Alternatively, one may view the OT narrative as beginning a story taken up in that of Christ and the church, to which prophecy explicitly looks forward;[50] placed at the end of the canon, prophecy thus leads into the NT particularly well.[51]

These questions about the shape of the canon, however, raise a further one. An emphasis on the final form of scriptural documents is a different matter from using a particular collection of these as the normative context for understanding each document within it;[52] since the invention of the printing press made it possible and natural to disseminate the scriptures in one volume, the question what are *the* scriptures may seem more pressing than it was when documents were copied separately (or in small collections of shorter books). So is there a defined canonical collection, and if so, what does it comprise?

---

[50] Might OT narrative be seen as tragedy, its prophecy as comedy? On the categories of tragedy and comedy, see Via, *The Parables*; *Kerygma and Comedy in the NT*.

[51] According to Sawyer (p. 32), the past-present-future arrangement should be the starting-point for any Christian study of the Bible. Protestant scholars have often seen the prophets as the theological, religious, and ethical highpoint of the OT (cf. recently *Fohrer, ch. 3). Westermann emphasizes Isaiah 40 – 55, holding together as it does the approaches of history, prophecy, and psalms in such a way that here 'the relation of the message about Christ to the OT is clearest and most unequivocal' (*The OT and Jesus Christ*, p. 19).

[52] Cf. Barr, *JTS* 25 (1974), p. 274.

c. The defining of the Old Testament canon

The usual historical picture[53] of the canonization of the OT has suggested a three-stage process reflected in the three-fold division of the Hebrew canon. The status of Torah and Prophets is taken to be clearly established well before the Christian era;[54] the more complex issue is the contents of the canon beyond that.

In the contemporary church, there are several opinions about this. Protestantism has traditionally accepted the books we have referred to as the Hebrew canon, though differently ordered. Roman Catholicism accepts in addition Tobit, Judith, Wisdom, Ben Sira (Ecclesiasticus), 1 and 2 Maccabees, and certain additions to the versions of Jeremiah, Esther and Daniel in the Hebrew canon. The Greek Orthodox Church uses the Septuagint, which includes this longer canon, plus also 1 and 2 Esdras, the Prayer of Manasseh, Psalm 151, 3 Maccabees, and (in some versions) the Odes of Solomon, the Psalms of Solomon, and 4 Maccabees. The Ethopian Orthodox Church also includes 1 Enoch and Jubilees.[55] Generally these different groups also give some status to further books, often called apocrypha, which are regarded as useful and edifying, but not necessarily as fully binding; usually one group's longer canon is someone else's apocrypha! It is not clear that the differences in belief or practice between these groups relate markedly to the differences between their canons.[56]

Behind this canonical diversity in the modern church lie two facts.

[53] Cf. Pfeiffer, IDB 1. Anderson's useful summary in CHB 1 reflects some subsequent insights; Childs, Introduction to the OT as Scripture (pp. 72–76) reviews various theories.

[54] Freedman (VTSupp 9; IDBS) interrelates the canonization of Torah and Prophets and locates this event soon after the exile. Koole (OTS 14 [1965]) associates the second stage of canonizing with the third-century Jewish revolt. Vermes (CHB 1, p. 199) believes that all the books except Daniel were canonical by 200. Leiman (Canonization of Hebrew Scripture, p. 131) thinks the canon reached its final form by about 150. But Lightstone (Studies in Religion 8 [1979]) questions whether the status of even Torah and Prophets was finalized before the Christian era.

[55] Formally, the Greek Church gives a lower status to books in the longer canon (see Istavridis, Orthodoxy and Anglicanism, pp. 73–74; also the Orthodox Church Interorthodox Commission report Towards the Great Council, pp. 3–4, and their references). On the complications of the Ethiopian canon, see Cowley, Ostkirchliche Studien 23 (1974); Kealy, BTB 9 (1979). These complications reflect the looser attitude to the concept of canon which lives on in the Orthodox Church.

[56] Though 2 Maccabees 12:45 used to function as a proof text for prayers for the dead. It was rejected as apocryphal by Luther (Luther's Works 32, p. 96).

The first is that the Hebrew canon is the one which was accepted in the synagogue. The other is that the church in Greek-speaking countries (specifically in Egypt) used a broader range of Jewish writings which was not precisely delimited until well into the Christian era; the longer canons just listed are only some versions instanced from this period.

It has been maintained that the 'Alexandrian canon' was itself a Jewish one, more extensive than the Hebrew canon. But more likely this collection became a canon as such only within the church. *A. C. Sundberg argues that neither the Hebrew nor the Alexandrian canon existed in the first century AD; all Jews recognized the Torah and the Prophets, but the bounds of the rest of the scriptures were not yet determined. Rabbinic Judaism eventually settled on what we call the Hebrew canon, while Christianity settled on what we call the Alexandrian canon, one version of the wider range of Jewish books which were treasured in Palestine (e.g. at Qumran) as well as in Egypt.

Sundberg has securely established that the wider canon was a Christian creation. The question whether the Hebrew canon was unknown in the first century is more open. The textbook answer to the question 'When did the Hebrew canon come to be accepted in the synagogue?' is 'at the synod of Jamnia at the end of the first century AD'.[57] The statement is misleading.[58] According to the rabbinic sources, after the fall of Jerusalem Rabban Johanan ben Zakkai re-established a theological community (*yeshiva* or *beth-hammidrash*) at Yavneh, south of present Tel Aviv. The community was also allowed to function as a religious court (*beth-din*), and thus to fulfil some of the functions of the former Sanhedrin, during the period between the two Jewish wars. To refer to it as a 'synod' or 'council', however, gives the wrong impression.

Our knowledge of deliberations at Yavneh comes from scattered references in the Talmud. The Talmud alludes to various discussions of whether certain books (Ezekiel, Ecclesiastes, Proverbs, Song of Songs, Ben Sira) should be 'withdrawn'. The meaning of this term is uncertain, though it does not seem to refer to either the bestowing or the revoking of canonical status. But in any case, the Talmud

---

[57] So *Sundberg, pp. 113–128; Pfeiffer, *IDB* 1, p. 150.

[58] For what follows, see Leiman, *op.cit.*, which includes relevant texts; Lewis, *JBR* 32 (1964); Saldarini, *CBQ* 37 (1975), pp. 348–353; Newman, *WTJ* 38 (1975–6).

does not connect these discussions with Yavneh. Elsewhere the Talmud alludes to decisions as to whether certain books are amongst those which 'defile the hands' (that is, in some way their sanctity means they require special treatment), like the rest of the scriptures. These books include Ruth, Ecclesiastes, the Song of Songs, Esther, Ben Sira and other books written after it, the Gilyonim and the books of the heretics (the gospels and other Christian documents?) and Homer. It is again questionable whether the issue here is canonical status.[59]

In any case, only one of these discussions, concerning the Song of Songs and Ecclesiastes, is said to have taken place at Yavneh, on the day that Rabban Eleazar ben Azariah temporarily replaced Gamaliel II (Johanan's successor) as head of the community, some time between AD 80 and 117 (Mishnah Yadaim 3:5).[60] The sum total of direct evidence for the fixing of the OT canon at Yavneh about AD 90 is this sole reference to some occasion of unknown date during those thirty-eight years, when the Sages there discussed a particular aspect of the status of these two books. Even over this matter they apparently made no binding decision, because other talmudic passages show that such questions continued to be discussed in the next century. Their deliberations no more prove that a canon did not yet exist and was then delimited, than does Luther's later discussion of the status of books such as James. Nor, of course, do they presuppose that the Hebrew canon already existed. They are simply irrelevant to the question.

In consequence, nor is there concrete evidence for seeing the rabbis at Yavneh delimiting a canon of scriptures which deliberately omitted writings that the church especially valued.[61] Indeed, not only have we no evidence that the Hebrew canon was formed or ratified at Yavneh, we have 'no evidence whatever of any official or public activity at any time in history that could be called the "canonization"

---

[59] Leiman suggests that what makes a book defile the hands is not whether it is canonical but whether it was given by divine inspiration. The Talmud itself was canonical (normative or binding) but not directly inspired, and Leiman believes that the question under discussion within the Talmud is whether this is true of these other books.

[60] Danby, *The Mishnah*, pp. 781–782.

[61] Cf. Stemberger, *Kairos* 19 (1977); Schäfaer, *Judaica* 31 (1975); Davies, *ExpT* 59 (1947–8), pp. 235–237.

of Scripture or the "closing of the canon" '.[62] It is easy to suggest religious, political, social, intellectual, and emotional factors that may have led to canonizing activity after AD 70, or in the Roman period or in the Maccabaean period, or earlier; but these suggestions remain hypotheses.

Whatever event led to canonizing activity, however, there are some indications that about the time of Yavneh the Hebrew canon had come into existence. The primary pieces of hard evidence lie in references in Josephus (*Against Apion* 1:8) and in 1 Esdras (14:45) to a 22- or 24-book canon. The difference in computation reflects different ways of dividing the books, not variation in the actual components of the list.[63] The diversity of first-century Judaism is such that one should not assume that all Jews recognized this canon,[64] but at least we can say that many did; Josephus claims to speak as a Pharisee.

Many witnesses testify to this canon both in Palestine and in Alexandria from then on.[65] These are the first unequivocal references to a canon we can identify with that of the Hebrew scriptures.[66] They imply that it had existed for some years – it was not being promulgated at this moment – but we do not know at what point any Jewish groups passed from commitment to the Torah and the Prophets and less formal recognition of various other scriptures, to explicit acknowledgement of this (or any other) longer canon. References to the Torah, Prophets, and 'other writings' in the prologue to Ben Sira and in Philo (*On the Contemplative Life* 3:25, *cf.* Luke 24:44) may or may not indicate a defined threefold canon whose third section lacks a shorthand title.

The evidence of the NT is for the most part compatible with recognition of the Hebrew canon, though it does not require it. The NT quotes nearly all the Hebrew scriptures, though it also quotes from other works, and it does not always make clear whether a work cited is seen as 'Scripture' or not. But it does not quote from works

---

[62] Gowan, *Bridge between the Testaments*, p. 315.
[63] Anderson, *CHB* 1, pp. 135–139; Leiman, *op.cit.*, p. 152.
[64] Lightstone (*op. cit.*) emphasizes this point.
[65] See Katz, *ZNW* 47 (1956), pp. 199–200; Leiman, pp. 41–50.
[66] According to Charles (*Apocrypha and Pseudepigrapha* II, p. 15) Jubilees 2:23 (dating from the second century BC) refers to a 22-book canon; but the point depends on Charles' reconstruction of the text.

that were included in any of the longer canons (except 1 Enoch),[67] and Jesus' reference to the martyrs from Abel to Zechariah (Mt. 23:35; Lk. 11:51) may suggest allusion to the first and last martyrs of the Hebrew canon (Gn. 4:1–10; 2 Ch. 24:20–21). Indeed, when Jesus spoke of 'the Law and the Prophets', the phrase may have covered the 'Writings' too, as was the case in later times (*e.g.* Irenaeus, *Against Heresies* I. 1:6). Philo presents a similar picture to the NT, though his quotations concentrate in the Torah.

Within NT times, some early Christian documents themselves come to be regarded as among the 'scriptures', along with the documents which appear in the Hebrew canon (*cf.* 2 Pet. 3:16). When we move back to a consideration of the Qumran scrolls, we find a similar situation reflected there. At Qumran, too, most of the books which appear in the Hebrew canon were well-known, and there are references to the Torah and the Prophets as collections (Damascus Document 7:14–18; Manual of Discipline 8:15–16). But the covenanters apparently attach similar importance to Jubilees and Enoch, and to their own Manual of Discipline and Damascus Document, as they do to some of the writings that appear in the Hebrew canon.

Here, too, the evidence does not exclude the possibility that the Hebrew canon as such was known at Qumran, but neither does it point towards it. The community may just not have been thinking in these terms.[68] On the other hand, if it is difficult to instance recognition of the Hebrew canon before the late first century AD, the thesis that at this time a wide religious literature without definite bounds circulated throughout Judaism as Holy Scripture is imperilled by the fact that works from the wider canon are never cited as Scripture in Philo, Josephus, the NT, Ben Sira, Maccabees, Hillel, Shammai, or any of the first century Tannaim.[69]

Historically, then, between 200 BC and AD 500 'the OT canon' meant different things to various different Jewish and Christian groups. We can sometimes guess at the reasons for giving canonical

[67] There are verbal parallels in the NT with books outside the Hebrew canon (see *e.g.* *Sundberg, pp. 52–55), but verbal parallels do not imply scriptural status. Of course some of the Prophets and Writings are not actually quoted in the NT, either.

[68] *Cf.* Eybers in *Leiman.

[69] Leiman, *op. cit.*, p. 39; Leiman does not refer to Jude's quotation from Enoch. On Ben Sira's status, see his discussion on pp. 92–102; Leiman's view is supported by R. T. Beckwith's arguments in an unpublished paper on 'The Old Testament canon in the teaching and background of the New Testament'.

status to one book or one collection rather than another, but we rarely have grounds for great confidence in our guesses. Nor is it always possible on grounds of content to account for the inclusion of one and the exclusion of another. It is interesting to note that all the canons seem to be 'fuzzy at the edges'.[70] The marginal books, however, are not always those that strike us as more doubtful in content (Ruth is under discussion in the Talmud and is not quoted in the NT); conversely, books of unquestioned canonicity are among those that raise problems for some people today (Judges, Obadiah, Nahum).

But what is the significance of surveying the history of the canonization process? It implies that deciding which books belong in the OT canon and which do not is a question of history. The decision is not really a task for the contemporary church; the latter has to follow decisions handed down from the past. The broad basis for the church acknowledging a canon of Jewish and early Christian books is their connection with the story that comes to its decisive point in Jesus Christ. In this sense, even if closing the canon ran counter to the dynamic nature of tradition growth, it was consonant with the nature of Christianity as essentially a story, a message about certain past events. There *was* something unique about the biblical period.[71] Perhaps taking decisions about the extent of this canon also belongs essentially to the past story of the people of God.

On a basis such as this the Alexandrian canon can be commended as the form of the canon once determined by the Christian Church itself; whereas the Hebrew canon was a Jewish creation whose contents may have been decided at least in part by anti-Christian polemic. The Church's decision is buttressed by the fact that the additional books in the Greek canon provide an important link between Judaism and Christianity, in developing such doctrines as the resurrection, angelology, judgment, and the personalization of wisdom, in the apocalyptic and wisdom books. On the basis of this canon, Christ would appear as the end and goal of a single tradition process, whose embodiment in written scripture would be inter-

---

[70] Cf. Gowan, p. 333.
[71] See Cullmann, *Salvation in History*, pp. 293–304; Kraus, *EvT* 36 (1976), p. 500; Pannenberg, *Theology and the Philosophy of Science*, pp. 375–376; contrast Laurin in *D. A. Knight.

rupted if we confined the Jewish scriptures to the Hebrew canon.[72]

The Hebrew canon, however, can claim relative antiquity; it alone has a plausible (though unproved) claim to have been recognized in NT times, and thus to be the form of the OT scriptures that Jesus passed on to us. The church's eventual canonizing of a longer canon may have been an accidental consequence of using the Septuagint; the evidence that the Hebrew canon was shaped by anti-Christian polemic is circumstantial. Further, the suggestion that the canon ought to comprise a continuous tradition from Jewish to Christian writings ignores the fact that the early Christians were themselves reading the scriptures as a set of writings, not continuing an ongoing tradition process; there is no need for a canon to include all the other documents that may have constituted its antecedents, influences, and background. Theologically, there is an appropriateness about Christianity accepting the same canon as Judaism; for by accepting a collection of Hebrew scriptures Christianity confesses its identification with Israel, its historical origins in Judaism and its invitation to Judaism to look at its own scriptures in the light of the coming of Jesus.[73]

A third position, however, is to advocate an 'open canon'. That means abandoning the quest to delimit a precise selection of books as having a unique status, and taking serious note of the wide range of Jewish religious literature of the period we are considering. One can then recognize all the documents that bridge OT and NT and thus acknowledge the importance of the Judaism that produced them. Thereby one is not limited to those that appear in either the Hebrew or the Alexandrian canon, and can take a position that is not vulnerable to the historical uncertainties of the situation in the first

---

[72] So Gese, ZTK 67 (1970), pp. 419–424, also in *D. A. Knight, pp. 321–324; cf. Mowinckel, The OT as Word of God, p. 113. The intertestamental writings' importance is also reflected in Stuhlmacher's work (e.g. ZTK 70 [1973]), and in Barr's (see JTS 25 [1974], pp. 275–277; RTP III. 18 [1968]); cf. also *Ebeling, p. 92. Elsewhere *Barr (p. 156) comments that the growth of the Jewish tradition 'provides the matrix for the coming divine acts and the impulse for their very occurrence': it helps to bring salvation about. Ross (Theology 82 [1979], pp. 190–191) argues that accepting the longer canon rescues us from the narrowness of the Hebrew outlook and from treating the whole OT as having any higher position than the secondary one which protestantism gives to the apocrypha!

[73] Childs, Introduction to the OT as Scripture, pp. 661–669; cf. the notion of the scriptures as Israel's statement of her identity (Jacob, VTSupp 28, pp. 104–105; *Barr, p. 165, also Barr, JR 56 [1976], pp. 16–17).

century AD.[74]

The disadvantage of this view is that it is in effect an abandonment of the idea of canon – that is, of commitment to a particular group of writings as *the* paramount source and final norm of a community's faith and life. It thus corresponds to our own theological climate, but not to that of OT or NT times. The acknowledging of specific traditions or scriptures as a norm for the belief and behaviour of the community is of long standing in the biblical tradition. This canon of material that is not only inspired and authoritative, but circumscribed and set over against other traditions or documents, is not necessarily ultimately exclusive, as is shown by the addition of the Writings to the Torah and the Prophets, and later by the giving of canonical status to the Talmud and the NT in Judaism and Christianity respectively.[75]

Nor does the acknowledgment of such a canon exclude the possibility that God has also spoken elsewhere. One may indeed find God's word in other Jewish and Christian writings, traditions, or statements, as Jude does explicitly in a passage from Enoch (Jude 14–15) and as other NT writers may in other writings that we cannot now identify (see *e.g.* 1 Cor. 2:9; Eph. 5:14; Jas. 4:5). Rabbi Joseph's rule can be generalized to other writings: 'even though the rabbis withdrew the book of Ben Sira, we expound all the good passages in it'.[76]

The canonical writings, then, are those concerning which the people of God have had sufficient confidence that here God has spoken to declare that they comprise *the* scriptures; they are then a norm for evaluating what one finds in other words that have some claim to be the words of God. One cannot prove that Judaism or Christianity made right or wrong decisions in recognizing particular documents as canonical. Like all such acts of discernment, acknowledging a canon of Scripture is a declaration made by faith, not by sight.

---

[74] See Ackroyd, *Colloquium* 3 (1969–70); Barr, 'Biblical theology', *IDBS*, pp. 109–111; *JTS* 25 (1974), pp. 275–277; *RTP* III.18 (1968), pp. 214–217.

[75] Contrast Dungan, *Int* 29 (1975), p. 350, who assumes that a canon must be closed and exclusive.

[76] Sanhedrin 100b; *cf.* Leiman, *op. cit.*, p. 95. See further Sundberg, *Int* 29 (1975), pp. 370–371.

d. The interpretation of the Old Testament as Scripture in New Testament times

Whatever precise books counted as Scripture for the various Jewish groups of NT times, these Jews certainly had scriptures, regarded them as the written word of God, and sought to frame their thinking and their lives by them. One particular block of writings which reflect this commitment and concern is the early Christian documents which themselves came to be canonical for the Christian Church as the NT.

But the NT's interpretation of Scripture needs to be seen in the context of approaches among other Jews of the period. This survives in six main blocks of material. Three of these blocks, targumim (Aramaic interpretative translations), midrashim (biblical commentaries), and the Talmud (teaching collected in subject-centred or problem-centred form in the Mishnah and interpreted further in the Gemara), have come down to us via rabbinic Judaism, but they are in part the deposit of oral teaching from the period before AD 70. The other three blocks were for the most part actually written during this earlier period. They are the Greek Bible and the pseudepigrapha, the Qumran scrolls, most of which are biblical manuscripts or works based on Scripture, and the writings of Philo and Josephus.[77]

In this literature, the word 'midrash'[78] is sometimes used to denote biblical study in general (*e.g.* Ecclus. 51:23; Manual of Discipline 8:12); but subsequently the connotations of 'midrash' were determined by the nature of the later midrashim, which were nominally scriptural commentary but were full of legend and fable. Under the influence of Renée Bloch's work, however, midrash has been rehabilitated as a general term for all Jewish endeavours, within the canon as well as outside it, to make Scripture intelligible, coherent, acceptable, and relevant to a later audience, in the conviction that it is God's inspired word and can be expected to be meaningful to

---

[77] For introduction, sources, and bibliography, see *IDBS* on 'Dead Sea Scrolls' (G. Vermes), 'Interpretation, History of', at Qumran and in the targums (G. Vermes) and early rabbinic (K. P. Bland), 'Judaism' (M. J. Cook), 'Midrash' (M. P. Miller), 'Pseudepigrapha' (M. E. Stone), 'Septuagint' (E. Tov), and 'Targums' (M. McNamara); *IDB* on 'Josephus' (J. Goldin), 'Philo' (E. R. Goodenough), and Talmud (I. Epstein); also *CHB* 1; Gowan, *Bridge between the Testaments*; Bavier and Townsend in *The Study of Judaism*.

[78] On terms used in scriptural interpretation see Gertner, *BSOAS* 25 (1962).

every generation.[79] Defining midrash in this broad way encourages one to look comparatively at Jewish interpretation in general. But its disadvantage is that midrash becomes as vague a word as its modern equivalent, hermeneutics, and this vagueness leads to disputes over whether this or that document (*e.g.* within the NT) is midrashic, which are partly or entirely mere matters of definition. If midrash is to be given a very broad meaning, then we need to make various distinctions within midrash.[80]

1. There are many *midrashic genres.* These include the biblical text itself as it is modified in the course of transmission, biblical translations such as the targumim and Septuagint, close textual commentary such as the Qumran pesharim, discursive commentary such as Philo on Genesis, legal commentary such as the legal midrashim, anthologizing of Scripture, homily, retelling of biblical narrative such as the Genesis Apocryphon, expansion of biblical books, 'testaments' and visions attributed to biblical figures, instances of genres which are themselves biblical and reflect biblical language such as 1 Maccabees or the Qumran Hodayot, and community rules such as the Talmud or Manual of Discipline. All these contain explicit or implicit biblical interpretation, though different genres work in different ways. Broadly, those nearer the beginning of this list give more priority to the biblical text, while those nearer the end are to a greater extent using the text as the vehicle for new material which may have little connection with the text.[81] In practice, however, commentaries (whether closely textual or discursive) may be doing the same thing, while a community rule, for instance, may stay close to the spirit of Scripture without actually basing itself on it in an explicit way.

2. One may distinguish two *aims of midrash*, within its overall purpose of creating a bridge between the biblical text and the life,

[79] See Bloch, in *Approaches to Ancient Judaism*; *cf.* Le Déaut, *Int* 25 (1971). Much of the study of midrash since Bloch has concentrated on the targumim and has assumed as a working hypothesis that the basic targum tradition is pre-Christian. But dating criteria for targumic material have not yet been worked out, and this working assumption may be incorrect (*cf. e.g.* York, *JSJ* 5 [1974]; acknowledged by Le Déaut, *BTB* 4 [1974], p. 23).

[80] *Cf.* *Patte, pp. 315–324.

[81] Within a composition, scriptural material may appear as quotation, allusion, choice of theological terms, or mere language colouring (*cf.* *Ellis, pp. 10–11). On these various genres in general, see Gowan, pp. 339–378.

attitudes, questions, and needs of a later reader.[82] Expository midrash aims to clarify questions that arise from the text itself: obscurities, lacunae, uncertainties of application, tensions between different passages, and so on. Although, like all midrash, it is concerned with understanding and applying Scripture as God's living word to the interpreter's own day,[83] expository midrash has its explicit focus in the text itself.[84] It thus contrasts with situational midrash, which focuses on particular questions of behaviour or belief which have arisen in some later context and for which illumination or justification is sought from Scripture. This may simply amount to a writer's instinctive use of biblical language (and thus at least his adoption of broadly biblical parameters) as a means to expressing his own concerns, beliefs, or piety.[85]

3. The *interests of midrash* are classically distinguished as ḥalakah ('walking') and haggadah ('telling'). The first is concerned 'to show how the original revelation of Torah was to be applied in the constantly changing situations of life', the other 'to inspire and to encourage people to accept and follow those decisions'.[86] These definitions reflect the focus of rabbinic midrash in behaviour; even narrative is ultimately concerned with how the reader lives before God, not with revelation divorced from life. A third interest, much more common in the pseudepigrapha and at Qumran than in the rabbinic or Philonic material,[87] is a concern to appropriate biblical prophecy as the key to understanding contemporary events and persons. But perhaps this prophetic midrash is to be seen simply as a kind of haggadah.[88]

4. Contemporary application of Scripture was facilitated by the

---

[82] Cf. Vermes, *CHB* 1, pp. 203–228.

[83] Cf. Loewe, *Papers of the Institute of Jewish Studies London* 1 (1964), emphasizing that this is true of even more exegetical-looking study.

[84] A. G. Wright (*CBQ* 28 [1966]) confines the term midrash to this expository study.

[85] 'Anthological style' (*Patte, pp. 172, 184–185, and elsewhere, following Robert, *DBS* 5).

[86] Bowker, *The Targums and Rabbinic Literature*, p. 43; cf. Loewe, *JTS* 21 (1970), p. 462.

[87] Though not absent from these: see *Hanson, pp. 254–255; Holtz, *ThL* 99 (1974), columns 25–26; Vermes, *Scripture and Tradition in Judaism*, pp. 34–35.

[88] Contrast Stendahl, *The School of St. Matthew*, p. 184 ('midrash pesher') with Ellis, *Prophecy and Hermeneutic*, pp. 189–190.

use of various *midrashic techniques*.[89] Frequently all that was needed
was literal application of laws or theological statements. But where
necessary, expositors utilized scholastic methods, applying obvious
rules of logic to the text, looking at it in its own context and in that
of other texts, and so on. These, formalized in sets of rules attributed
to Hillel and later rabbis, are similar to the principles of hellenistic
legal interpretation.[90]

In principle they sound quite modern; in practice, however, they
are the means of finding significance in aspects of a text which had
no such meaning when treated contextually, and thus facilitate the
'atomistic exegesis'[91] for which Jewish interpretation is often criticized. What we might call re-application of biblical texts is well
instanced from Qumran: passages that originally referred to a prophet's own day, or to God's future acts of judgment and salvation
(*e.g.* Is. 40:3; Am. 9:11; Mal. 1:10; Habakkuk) are applied to the
covenanter's own era, in accordance with what they took to be the
passages' original (in a sense literal) meaning, which the author and
his first hearers could not see. Figurative interpretation takes originally non-symbolic passages in a symbolic way (in Damascus Rule
6:3–11 the well dug at Beer, Numbers 21:18, becomes the Torah
studied by the covenanters), understands passages which may have
been symbolic in a different symbolic sense (in Josephus' *Antiquities*
2.7 the tabernacle portrays the structure of the universe, in the *Letter
of Aristeas* the Levitical uncleanness laws refer to moral behaviour),
or adds a second-level figurative meaning to a text which is also
applied literally (classically in Philo's allegorical interpretation).[92]
Finally, midrashic technique extends to how the interpreter actually
reads the text: his own understanding of the God who inspired
Scripture and of the message entrusted to the writer enables him to
choose the 'right' reading if various possibilities are available to him

---

[89] See *Longenecker, pp. 19–50; Fitzmyer, *NTS* 7 (1960–1); Slomovic, *RQ* 7 (1969–
71); *Doeve, pp. 52–90; *Ellis pp. 41–42.
[90] See Daube, *HUCA* 22 (1949), also in Lewald volume; Lieberman, *Hellenism in
Jewish Palestine*, pp. 47–82.
[91] Moore, *Judaism* I, p. 248. Sanders sees this process as built into the freezing of
an inspired/canonical text, if it is to continue to speak to new situations (G. E. Wright
volume, pp. 531–543; *JBL* 98 [1979], pp. 22–26).
[92] According to Loewe (*Biblical Motifs*, p. 159), Philo introduced the actual term
allegory to Jewish exegesis (*cf.* Williamson, *Philo and the Epistle to the Hebrews*,
pp. 519–520).

or to adapt the text to make the meaning he sees in it clearer.[93]

5. It is, however, *the resources of midrash* that generate the hunch as to a text's overall interpretation, which is then worked out in detail by means of exegetical techniques.[94] These include the creative imagination which is important to any form of interpretation, and which contributes especially to the development of haggadah and to the interpretation of prophecy, though less to halakah because of its direct practical significance.[95] What we might see as a theology of the creative use of imagination is provided by the belief which the Qumran covenanters shared with Philo that God reveals the meaning of Scripture to the inspired interpreter by a process that is not very different from the original author's inspiration.[96] Imagination or inspiration is stimulated (and checked) by Scripture itself, in that an interpreter will often turn to other passages of Scripture for the answer to questions raised by a text, may base an allegorical interpretation on the direct meaning of some other passage, or may interpret Scripture by Scripture by means of typology.[97] But the interpretation of Scripture by Scripture is complicated by the fact that the Bible is read through spectacles provided by the way it has traditionally been interpreted; the conviction that the living tradition breathes in the present the life of the inspired word means that interpreting Scripture by Scripture may be difficult in practice to distinguish from interpreting Scripture by tradition.[98]

6. Ultimately, however, it is the different *ideologies of midrash* that determine the kind of overall interpretations generated. Interpreters may share broadly the same genres, aims, interests, tech-

---

[93] Examples in *Longenecker, pp. 36–40; *Patte, pp. 55–58; Finkel, *RQ* 4 (1963–4), pp. 367–369; Brownlee, *BA* 14 (1951); Talmon, *ASTI* 1 (1962); Wernberg-Møller, *ST* 9 (1955); *cf.* Sanders (see n. 91).

[94] *Cf.* Silberman, *RQ* 3 (1961–2).

[95] Lowy, *ALUOS* 6 (1969), pp. 121–122; *Doeve, pp. 64–65; examples in Vermes, *Scripture and Tradition in Judaism* and *Post-Biblical Jewish Studies*; also Levine, *Concordia Theological Monthly* 40 (1969); Jacobs, *Jewish Biblical Exegesis*.

[96] Barrett, *CHB* 1, pp. 377–378; *Longenecker, p. 44; Silberman, pp. 327–331; Finkel; Bruce, *Biblical Exegesis in the Qumran Texts*, pp. 7–19; Betz, *Offenbarung und Schriftforschung in der Qumransekte.*

[97] *Patte, pp. 159–164, 237–241, 264–266, 291–293; Le Déaut, *La Nuit Pascale*; Sanders, *JR* 39 (1959), pp. 232–233; Hanson, *Allegory and Event*, pp. 13–19. Typology is thus not unique to Christianity (so Lampe and Woollcombe, *Essays on Typology*, p. 42).

[98] Le Déaut, *RHPR* 51 (1971), pp. 33–34; Lowy, pp. 124–128; Vermes, *Scripture and Tradition*, p. 177; *Patte, pp. 90–115.

niques, and resources, but they understand Scripture very differently because of the differences between the beliefs, concerns, and commitments they bring to the text. Their interpretation has as much of their concerns in it as it has of Scripture itself. Within the writings we have been considering, three particular ideologies are easy to distinguish: those of Pharisaic Judaism (of which rabbinic Judaism saw itself as the successor), of Qumran, and of Philo. If the differences between these groups are at one level conflicts over the right interpretation of Scripture,[99] behind these conflicts are differences of current faith.

Pharisaic Judaism saw itself as the lineal successor of OT Israel and saw its teaching as the contemporary application of God's revealed law. Its calling was to live in the light of this teaching. The Qumran community in turn believed itself to be the true Israel and that its own particular understanding of halakah had God's authority; its belief that the End was near and that God was active in contemporary history was of key importance to the way it interpreted Scripture.[100] To use categories we have used earlier in this book, as well as seeing itself as committed to the same faith and way of life as those Scripture speaks of, it also read Scripture from a perspective of salvation history, typology and prophecy. Philo of Alexandria believed that the wisdom of God was reflected both in the law of nature (studied by hellenistic philosophy) and in the written law (transmitted by Moses), and wanted to hold both together. An allegorical approach to interpretation enabled him to find Scripture in general instructive with regard to his philosophy (e.g. On the Preliminary Studies, where he deals with Genesis 16, the passage Paul allegorizes in Gal. 4:24), and to make silk purses out of sows' ears by finding such illumination even in passages that otherwise seemed irrelevant or embarrassing.[101]

The ideologies, resources, techniques, and interests that are brought to the text mean that Jewish biblical interpretation is not merely a matter of letting the text speak. Like the interrogator on

---

[99] Brownlee, pp. 58–59; Betz, pp. 59–60.

[100] Elliger, Studien zum Habakuk-Kommentar, pp. 150–164; Silberman, p. 329; *Patte, pp. 311–313. Pharisaism had an eschatological perspective, but it was not a central feature of its ideology: see Davies, ExpT 59 (1947–8); Osswald, ZAW 68 (1956); Saldarini, CBQ 37 (1975); 39 (1977).

[101] Cf. Williamson, pp. 523–528; Nikiprowetsky, Le commentaire de l'écriture chez Philon d'Alexandrie.

the late night film, the interpreters 'have ways of making you talk'. On the other hand, one should not imagine that as a result nothing is found in the text but what the interpreter brought to it. The text itself is a given which imposes exegetical constraint and makes its own contribution. Its detailed understanding is generated by the words themselves.[102]

How does NT interpretation of Scripture appear in this context? The NT's major *genres* are new. The gospel, however, is related to scriptural narrative models, and both gospels and epistles include many scriptural quotations and sections of explicit midrash (*e.g.* Mt. 4:1–11; 2 Cor. 3:7–18; Heb. 7:1–10) or 'covert midrash'[103] (*e.g.* Jn. 1:1–18 in relation to Gn. 1:1–5 and Lk. 9:51 – 18:43 in relation to Dt. 1 – 26). But the NT lacks consecutive commentary work, and its characteristic *aim* is situational rather than expository: it is concerned to interpret themes arising out of its own questions rather than directly out of Scripture (see *e.g.* Rom. 9 – 11, or Hebrews and Revelation generally). In a sense, therefore, the NT is a midrash on Christ, rather than on the scriptures.[104]

The *interest* of NT interpretation lies much less in halakah than is the case with the other bodies of writings, and much more in haggadah. Christianity brought a 'Copernican revolution' to Jewish biblical interpretation by concentrating on the Bible as history (notably Genesis-Exodus) and as testimony to God's promise (notably in the prophets); the NT does discuss questions of behaviour, but not usually in halakic fashion.[105] Most of the midrashic *techniques* utilized elsewhere appear in the NT.[106] Many scholars find the NT more contextual in its approach, though there is a number of standard examples of less literal interpretation (*e.g.* Mt. 22:32; 1 Cor. 9:9; Gal. 3:16; 4:21–31; Eph. 4:8; Heb. 7:1–3). As regards the *resources*

---

[102] *Cf.* Nikiprowetsky, pp. 184, 238 (Philo); Silberman, p. 332 (Qumran).

[103] Gertner, *JSS* 7 (1962); surveys in Smith, Stinespring volume; Miller, *JSJ* 2 (1971).

[104] Le Déaut, *Int* 25 (1971), pp. 275–276. Perhaps partly as a consequence, it does not merely use the scriptures to reinforce the status quo (as midrash easily does); it takes up the confrontational aspect of canonical hermeneutics (see section 5a and note 24). It may thus in the end do more justice to Scripture itself than more (theoretically) Scripture-centred midrash does.

[105] *Amsler, pp. 97–98; *Ellis, pp. 28–32; *von Campenhausen, pp. 24–50; Meier, *CBQ* 40 (1978). Paul's use of Genesis and Exodus thus differs markedly from Philo's in its interest (though see Barrett, *CHB* 1, pp. 396–399, on halakah in the NT).

[106] Examples in *Ellis; *Longenecker; *Doeve; Fitzmyer, *NTS* 7 (1960–1); Barrett, *CHB* 1.

for interpretation, the NT too, interprets Scripture by Scripture; yet it, too, inherited an interpreted Bible and often presupposes the way Scripture is understood in Jewish tradition.[107] Presumably it was creative imagination or spiritual insight that led to the way passages were brought to bear on issues and incidents, and the scriptures had to be read in the Spirit – which may refer to charismatic interpretation,[108] or may only mean reading the scriptures with eyes opened by the Spirit to the fact that Jesus is the key to understanding them.[109]

This leads us to consider the *ideology* that the Christians brought to Scripture. Although the profile of genres, aims, and so on that characterizes Christian interpretation is distinctive, so is that of Qumran or of Philo or of Pharisaic Judaism. But these profiles reflect the interpreters' varying ideologies; it is the beliefs that the Christians brought to the scriptures that contributed most to their distinctive interpretation of them.

Like the Pharisees and the Qumran community, they identified with the faith and way of life of the scriptures, and believed that they were *the* true Israel. Like the Qumran community, they believed that they could see God at work in the events of their day and that the End was near – indeed, was actually present – and thus that OT history and prophecy led and pointed towards their day.[110] Like the Qumran community, their own leader was of great importance to their biblical interpretation; but Jesus, and his death and resurrection, are much more central to the NT than the Teacher of Righteousness is to Qumran.[111] It was in the conviction that God had done something decisive in Christ that the Christians wrote gospels rather than midrashim on Genesis, that their interpretation

---

[107] Le Déaut, *Int* 25 (1971), p. 277; examples in *Hanson and in McNamara's works.

[108] So Ellis, *Prophecy and Hermeneutic*; *Longenecker, pp. 151, 206–209.

[109] So *Hanson, p. 189.

[110] *Cf.* Metzger, *JBL* 70 (1951), pp. 306–307; Barrett, *CHB* 1, pp. 399–401; Holtz, columns 25–29. This point is made in different books in different ways: Matthew and Paul emphasize fulfilment of prophecy, Luke and Paul the continuation and climax of history, John and Hebrews a typological link (see further Smith, Stinespring volume; *von Campenhausen; *Longenecker).

[111] Gärtner, *ST* 8 (1954), pp. 6–12; Sanders, *JR* 39 (1959), p. 240; Bruce, *Biblical Exegesis in the Qumran Texts*, pp. 36–37; *cf.* the Christian belief that Christ was actually present in OT times (*e.g.* Jn. 12:37–41; 1 Cor. 10:4; Heb. 12:22–27) (see Hanson, *Jesus Christ in the OT*).

was situational rather than expository, that they stressed haggadah (narrative and prophecy) rather than halakah.

Does this mean that the differences between NT biblical interpretation and other contemporary approaches simply reflect an arbitrariness about the whole procedure of interpretation? Is everyone reading a message into the text rather than reading one out of it? To interpret a document in the light of something outside it may seem a dangerous proceeding, but it need not necessarily mean misinterpreting it. The question is whether there is, as a matter of fact, a 'match' between the text and what is brought to it, and whether the text is allowed to 'speak back'.

The NT's claim is that the Christ event is the actual key to the OT's significance, and that it enables one to do justice to the OT's own concerns. It is the 'pre-understanding' (Bultmann's term) which opens up the OT, not an alien ideology like Philo's hellenism. Jesus *is* the messiah; the Teacher of Righteousness is not. While faith in Jesus is in one sense brought to the OT, in another sense it derives from it, because the OT provides many of the means for working out who Christ is and the implications of his coming. A real 'merging of horizons' (Gadamer) takes place as the OT is interpreted in the NT. Thus the NT's approach can in fact be instructive for our own task of interpretation.[112]

If the NT's own explicit interpretative work is entirely situational, it nevertheless presupposes the expository study of Scripture which has shaped the overall cast of mind of Jesus and the NT writers. Further, because the latter direct our attention to the OT and claim to stand in continuity with it as a whole, the fact that they do not explicitly expound the significance of Ruth, Nehemiah, or Job is the reason we must do so, rather than the reason we need not.[113]

The techniques of NT interpretation often strike the modern reader as odd.[114] We have seen that these are simply the interpretative methods of the day. They may thus be significant for us only in the same way as the NT use of Greek as a language, of the Septuagint as a Bible translation, and of Jewish or Greek community leadership

---

[112] Grech, *NTS* 19 (1972–3); *BTB* 5 (1975); M. Barth, Piper volume; *cf.* Bultmann's essays in *Existence and Faith* and *Essays Theological and Philosophical*; Gadamer, *Truth and Method.*

[113] *Amsler, pp. 103–104; Sanders, *JR* 39 (1959), pp. 233–236.

[114] *E.g.* Bultmann in *Anderson; Braun, *ZTK* 59 (1962).

structures for the ordering of its own community life.[115]

Perhaps a better analogy is the NT's acceptance of the institution of slavery. As we noted in sections 2e and 2f, there is a tension between this attitude and the radical rejection of slavery implied by some OT and NT texts. The NT did not work out the full implications of the belief that all men are one in creation and in Christ; there were other things to do. Similarly, the Bible contains within itself the basis for a more consistently historical and contextual approach to biblical interpretation than the one it practises. It portrays God speaking through human beings in particular historical contexts, and thus implies that the appropriate way to hear the word of God is by listening to the human word understood as a piece of human communication in those contexts.[116] If this is so, then the concern of modern techniques with historical and contextual interpretation relates to biblical hermeneutics as the abolition of slavery relates to bibilical ethics.

Not that this is merely the happy discovery that modern hermeneutics was biblical all the time. The more overt side to midrash is the conviction that the subject of its study is the word of God. Whatever apparent problems, uncertainties, or irrelevancies may seem to be present in the text, it is actually a divine word which can and must speak to God's people in whatever context they find themselves. Thus all forms of midrash aim at a persistent dialectic between ancient text and contemporary situation, based on the conviction that this word of God can and must speak to any such context; any situation, therefore, has the potential to provide an entry into grasping the word of God and being addressed by it.[117] The challenge to contemporary OT interpretation thus arises from the twofold nature of these scriptures. It is so to use the techniques appropriate to the study of the human words, that the divine word which they constitute may speak to us who live this side of the coming of Christ.

---

[115] McKenzie in *Anderson, pp. 102–103; *Longenecker, pp. 218–220 (cf. TynB 21 [1970], p. 39).

[116] Likewise, the theological significance of 'literary approaches' to the Bible has its basis in this consideration. In order to hear a biblical book as God's word we need to read it as a literary work. See e.g. Alter, Commentary 60:6 (December, 1975).

[117] Childs, Enslin volume, p. 52.

Bibliography

*E. Achtemeier, *The Old Testament and the Proclamation of the Gospel* (Philadelphia: Westminster, 1973).
— 'The relevance of the Old Testament for Christian preaching', *A Light unto My Path* (J. M. Myers volume, ed. H. N. Bream and others; Philadelphia: Temple UP, 1974), pp. 3–24.
P. R. Ackroyd, 'The place of the Old Testament in the church's teaching and worship', *ExpT* 74 (1962–3), pp. 164–167.
— 'The open canon', *Colloquium: The Australian and New Zealand Theological Review* 3 (1969–70), pp. 279–291.
— 'The Chronicler as exegete', *JSOT* 2 (1977), pp. 2–32.
*B. Albrektson, *History and the Gods* (Lund: Gleerup, 1967).
R. Alter, 'A literary approach to the Bible', *Commentary* 60.6 (December 1975), pp. 70–77.
*S. Amsler, *L'Ancien Testament dans l'église* (Neuchâtel: Delachaux, 1960).
— 'La motivation de l'éthique dans la parénèse du Deutéronome', *Beiträge zur alttestamentlichen Theologie* (W. Zimmerli volume, ed. H. Donner and others; Göttingen: Vandenhoeck, 1977), pp. 11–22.
B. W. Anderson, *The Living World of the Old Testament* (London: Longmans, 1958, ³1978) = *Understanding the Old Testament* (Englewood Cliffs, NJ: Prentice-Hall, 1957, ³1975).
— 'Exodus typology in Second Isaiah', *Israel's Prophetic Heritage* (J. Muilenburg volume, ed. B. W. Anderson and W. Harrelson; London/New York: SCM/Harper, 1962), pp. 177–195.
*— (ed.) *The Old Testament and Christian Faith* (New York: Harper, 1963/London: SCM, 1964; reprinted New York: Herder and Herder, 1969).
G. W. Anderson, 'Canonical and non-canonical', *CHB* 1, pp. 113–159.
H. Anderson, 'The Old Testament in Mark's Gospel', *The Use of the Old Testament in the New and Other Essays* (W. F. Stinespring volume, ed. J. M. Efird; Durham, NC: Duke UP, 1972), pp. 280–306.
*D. L. Baker, *Two Testaments, One Bible* (Leicester: IVP, 1976).
— 'Typology and the Christian use of the Old Testament', *SJT* 29 (1976), pp. 137–157 = *Baker, pp. 239–270.

156

K. Baltzer, *The Covenant Formulary* (ET Philadelphia/Oxford: Fortress/ Blackwell, 1971).

R. Banks, 'Jesus and custom', *ExpT* 84 (1972–3), pp. 265–269 = *Jesus and the Law*, pp. 1, 91–99, 237.

— 'Matthew's understanding of the Law', *JBL* 93 (1974), pp. 226–242 = *Jesus and the Law*, pp. 203–226.

— *Jesus and the Law in the Synoptic Tradition* (Cambridge/New York: CUP, 1975).

O. R. Barclay, 'The nature of Christian morality', in *Law, Morality and the Bible* (ed. B. N. Kaye and G. J. Wenham; Leicester/Downers Grove, IL: IVP, 1978), pp. 125–150.

J. Barr, *The Semantics of Biblical Language* (London/New York: OUP, 1961).

— 'Revelation through history in the Old Testament and in modern theology', *Int* 17 (1963), pp. 193–205.

*— *Old and New in Interpretation* (London/New York: SCM/Harper, 1966).

— 'Le Judaïsme postbiblique et la théologie de l'Ancien Testament', *RTP* III. 18 (1968), pp. 209–217.

— *Judaism – Its Continuity with the Bible* (Southampton: UP, 1968).

— *The Bible in the Modern World* (London/New York: SCM/Harper, 1973).

— *Reading the Bible as Literature* (Manchester: John Rylands Library, 1973) = *BJRL* 56 (1973–4), pp. 10–33.

— 'Some Old Testament aspects of Berkhof's 'Christelijk geloof', *Weerwoord: Reacties op Dr. H. Berkhof's 'Christelijk geloof'* (ed. E. Flesseman-van Leer and others; Nijkerk: Callenbach, 1974), pp. 9–19.

— 'Trends and prospects in biblical theology', *JTS* 25 (1974), pp. 265–282.

— 'Story and history in biblical theology', *JR* 56 (1976), pp. 1–17.

— 'Biblical theology' and 'Revelation in history', *IDBS* pp. 104–111 and 746–749.

— 'Some semantic notes on the covenant', *Beiträge zur alttestamentlichen Theologie* (W. Zimmerli volume, ed. H. Donner and others; Göttingen: Vandenhoeck, 1977), pp. 23–38.

C. K. Barrett, 'Ethelbert Stauffer's Theology of the New Testament', *ExpT* 72 (1960–1), pp. 356–360.

— *From First Adam to Last: A Study in Pauline Theology* (London/New York: Black/Scribner's, 1962).

— *A Commentary on the First Epistle to the Corinthians* (London/New York: Black/Harper, 1968).

— 'The interpretation of the Old Testament in the New', *CHB* 1, pp. 377–411.

C. Barth, 'Grundprobleme einer Theologie des Alten Testaments', *EvT* 23 (1963), pp. 342–372.

G. Barth, 'Matthew's understanding of the Law', in G. Bornkamm, G. Barth, and H. J. Held, *Tradition and Interpretation in Matthew* (ET London/Philadelphia: SCM/Westminster, 1963). pp. 58–164.

K. Barth, 'Gospel and Law', in *God, Grace and Gospel* (ET *SJT* Occasional Papers 8; Edinburgh: Oliver and Boyd, 1959), pp. 1–27.

*— *Church Dogmatics* (ET Edinburgh/New York: Clark/Scribner's, 1936–69).

M. Barth, 'The Old Testament in Hebrews', *Current Issues in New Testament Interpretation* (O. A. Piper volume, ed. W. Klassen and G. F. Snyder; New York/London: Harper/SCM, 1962), pp. 53–78, 263–273.

J. D. Barthélemy, 'Les tiqquné sopherim et la critique textuelle de l'Ancien Testament', in *Congress Volume: Bonn 1962* (*VTSupp* 9; 1963), pp. 285–304 = Barthélemy, *Études d'histoire du texte de l'Ancient Testament* (Freibourg/Göttingen: Éditions Universitaires/Vandenhoeck, 1978), pp. 91–110.

J. Barton, 'Judaism and Christianity: prophecy and fulfilment', *Theology* 79 (1976), pp. 260–266.

— 'Understanding Old Testament ethics', *JSOT* 9 (1978), pp. 44–64.

— 'Natural law and poetic justice in the Old Testament', *JTS* 30 (1979), pp. 1–14.

F. Baumgärtel, 'Erwägungen zur Darstellung der Theologie des Alten Testaments', *ThL* 76 (1951), columns 257–272.

*— *Verheissung: zur Frage des evangelischen Verständnisses des Alten Testaments* (Gütersloh: Bertelsmann, 1952).

— 'Der Dissensus im Verständnis des Alten Testaments', *EvT* 14 (1954), pp. 298–313.

— 'Gerhard von Rad's "Theologie des Alten Testaments" ', *ThL* 86 (1961), columns 801–816, 895–908.

— 'The hermeneutical problem of the Old Testament', ET in *Westermann, pp. 134–159.

R. Bavier, 'Judaism in New Testament times', in *The Study of Judaism: Bibliographical Essays* (J. Neusner and others; New York: Ktav, 1972), pp. 7–34.

P. Beauchamp, ' "Comprendre l'Ancien Testament": compte rendu d'un livre de A. H. J. Gunneweg', *Recherches de science religieuse* 67 (1979), pp. 45–57.

R. T. Beckwith, 'The Old Testament canon in the teaching and background of the New Testament' (unpublished paper, 1974).

P. Benoit, 'La plénitude de sens des Livres Saints', *RB* 67 (1960), pp. 161–196.

P. L. Berger, *A Rumour of Angels* (Garden City, NY: Doubleday, 1969/London: Allen Lane, 1970).

O. Betz, *Offenbarung und Schriftforschung in der Qumransekte* (Tübingen: Mohr, 1960).

*B. C. Birch and L. L. Rasmussen, *Bible and Ethics in the Christian Life* (Minneapolis: Augsburg, 1976).

M. Black, 'The Christological use of the Old Testament in the New Testament', *NTS* 18 (1971–2), pp. 1–14.

K. P. Bland, 'Interpretation, History of: early rabbinic', *IDBS*, pp. 446–448.

J. Blenkinsopp, 'Scope and depth of the exodus tradition in Deutero-Isaiah, 40–55', *Concilium* (New York) 20 (1967), pp. 41–50 = *Concilium* (London) Volume 10, Number 2 (1966), pp. 22–26.

*— *Prophecy and Canon* (Notre Dame/London: University of Notre Dame, 1977).

R. Bloch, 'Midrash' and 'Methodological note for the study of rabbinic literature', ET in *Approaches to Ancient Judaism* (ed. W. S. Green; Missoula: Scholars, 1978), pp. 29–50 and 51–75.

L. Blue, *To Heaven, with Scribes and Pharisees* (London: DLT, 1975/New York: OUP, 1976).

D. Bonhoeffer, *Letters and Papers from Prison* (ET New York/London: Macmillan/SCM, 1953, revised 1967, enlarged 1971; London: Collins Fontana, 1959).

— *Ethics* (ET London/New York: SCM/Macmillan, 1955).

— *No Rusty Swords: Letters, Lectures and Notes 1928–1936* (ET London/ New York: Collins/Harper, 1965; London: Collins Fontana, 1970).

— *Psalms* (ET Minneapolis: Augsburg, 1974).

P. Borgen, 'The place of the Old Testament in the formation of New Testament theology: response' [to Lindars: see below], *NTS* 23 (1976–7), pp. 67–75.

G. Bornkamm, 'End-expectation and church in Matthew', in G. Bornkamm, G. Barth, and H. J. Held, *Tradition and Interpretation in Matthew* (ET London/Philadelphia: SCM/Westminster, 1963), pp. 15–51.

H. Bornkamm, *Luther and the Old Testament* (ET Philadelphia: Fortress, 1969).

E. B. Borowitz, 'The problem of the form of a Jewish theology', *HUCA* 40–41 (1969–70), pp. 391–408.

J. W. Bowker, *The Targums and Rabbinic Literature: An Introduction to Jewish Interpretations of Scripture* (Cambridge/New York: CUP, 1969).

C. E. Braaten, *History and Hermeneutics* (Philadelphia: Westminster, 1966/ London: Lutterworth, 1968).

H. Braun, 'Das Alte Testament im Neuen Testament', *ZTK* 59 (1962), pp. 16–31.

C. Brekelmans (ed.), *Questions disputées d'Ancien Testament* (Gembloux/ Louvain: Duculot/Louvain UP, 1974).

*J. Bright, *The Authority of the Old Testament* (Nashville/London: Abingdon/SCM, 1967; reprinted Grand Rapids: Baker, 1975).

R. E. Brown, *The Sensus Plenior of Sacred Scripture* (Baltimore: St Mary's University, 1955).

— 'The *sensus plenior* in the last ten years', *CBQ* 25 (1963), pp. 262–285.

— 'Hermeneutics', *The Jerome Bible Commentary* (Englewood Cliffs, NJ: Prentice-Hall, 1968/London: Chapman, 1969), ch. 71.

W. H. Brownlee, 'Biblical interpretation among the sectaries of the Dead Sea Scrolls', *BA* 14 (1951), pp. 54–76.

F. F. Bruce, *Biblical Exegesis in the Qumran Texts* (Grand Rapids: Eerdmans, 1959/London: Tyndale, 1960).

— *This is That* (Exeter: Paternoster, 1968) = *The New Testament Development of Old Testament Themes* (Grand Rapids: Eerdmans, 1968).

— 'The earliest Old Testament interpretation', *The Witness of Tradition* (*OTS* 17; 1972), pp. 37–52.

— 'Salvation history in the New Testament', *Man and his Salvation* (S. G. F. Brandon volume, ed. E. J. Sharpe and J. R. Hinnells; Manchester: UP, 1973/Totawa, NJ: Rowman, 1974), pp. 75–90.

— *Paul and the Law of Moses* (Manchester: John Rylands Library, 1975) = *BJRL* 57 (1974–5), pp. 259–279 = *Paul*, pp. 188–202.

— *Paul: Apostle of the Free Spirit* (Exeter: Paternoster, 1977) = *Paul: Apostle of the Heart Set Free* (Grand Rapids: Eerdmans, 1977).

— 'Primary sense and plenary sense', *Epworth Review* 4.2 (1977), pp. 94–109.

— 'The theology and interpretation of the Old Testament', *Tradition and Interpretation* (ed. G. W. Anderson; Oxford: Clarendon/New York: OUP, 1979), pp. 385–416.

W. Brueggemann, *Tradition for Crisis: A Study in Hosea* (Richmond: John Knox, 1968).

— '*The Politics of God and the Politics of Man*, by Jacques Ellul', *JBL* 92 (1973), pp. 470–471.

— *The Land* (Philadelphia: Fortress, 1977/London: SPCK, 1978).

— 'Covenanting as human vocation', *Int* 33 (1979), pp. 115–129.

W. Brueggemann and H. W. Wolff, *The Vitality of Old Testament Traditions* (Atlanta: John Knox, 1975).

M. Buber, *Moses* (Oxford: Phaidon, 1946).

R. Bultmann, 'Ursprung und Sinn der Typologie als hermeneutischer Methode', *ThL* 75 (1950), columns 205–212 = *Exegetica* (Tübingen: Mohr, 1967), pp. 369–380.

— 'History and eschatology in the New Testament', *NTS* 1 (1954–5), pp. 5–16.

— 'The problem of hermeneutics', *Essays Philosophical and Theological* (ET New York/London: Macmillan/SCM, 1955), pp. 234–261.

— *History and Eschatology* (Edinburgh: UP, 1957) = *The Presence of Eternity* (New York: Harper, 1957).

— 'History of salvation and history' and 'Is exegesis without presuppositions possible?', ET in *Existence and Faith: Shorter Writings of Rudolf Bultmann* (New York: Meridian, 1960/London: Hodder, 1961), pp. 226–240 and 289–296, 314–315.

— *The History of the Synoptic Tradition* (ET Oxford/New York: Blackwell/Harper, 1963).

— 'The significance of the Old Testament for the Christian Faith', ET in *Anderson, pp. 8–35.

— 'Prophecy and fulfilment', *Essays*, pp. 182–208 = *Westermann, pp. 50–75.

M. J. Buss, 'The meaning of history', *Theology as History* (ed. J. M.

Robinson and J. B. Cobb; New York: Harper, 1967), pp. 135–154.

— (ed.), *Encounter with the Text: Form and History in the Hebrew Bible* (Philadelphia/Missoula: Fortress/Scholars, 1979).

J. Cairncross, *After Polygamy was Made a Sin* (London: Routledge, 1974).

J. Calvin, *Commentaries on the Four Last Books of Moses Arranged in the Form of a Harmony* (ET Edinburgh: Calvin Translation Society, 1852; reprinted Grand Rapids: Eerdmans, 1950).

— *Institutes of the Christian Religion* (ET by F. L. Battles; Philadelphia/London: Westminster/SCM, 1961).

*H. von Campenhausen, *The Formation of the Christian Bible* (ET London/Philadelphia: Black/Fortress, 1972).

C. M. Carmichael, 'On separating life and death: an explanation of some biblical laws', *HTR* 69 (1976), pp. 1–7.

R. P. Carroll: *When Prophecy Failed* (New York/London: Seabury/SCM, 1979).

R. H. Charles, *The Apocrypha and Pseudepigrapha of the Old Testament* (Oxford/New York: Clarendon/OUP, 1913).

B. S. Childs, 'Reflections on the modern study of the psalms', *Magnalia Dei* (G. E. Wright volume, ed. F. M. Cross and others; Garden City, NY: Doubleday, 1976), pp. 377–388.

— 'Interpretation in faith: the theological responsibility of an Old Testament commentary', *Int* 18 (1964), pp. 432–449.

*— *Biblical Theology in Crisis* (Philadelphia: Westminster, 1970).

— 'Psalm titles and midrashic exegesis', *JSS* 16 (1971), pp. 137–150.

— 'Midrash and the Old Testament', in *Understanding the Sacred Text* (M. S. Enslin volume, ed. J. Reumann; Valley Forge: Judson, 1972), pp. 45–59.

— *The Book of Exodus* (Philadelphia: Westminster, 1974) = *Exodus* (London: SCM, 1974).

— 'The sensus literalis of Scripture: an ancient and modern problem', *Beiträge zur alttestamentlichen Theologie* (W. Zimmerli volume, ed. H. Donner and others; Göttingen: Vandenhoeck, 1977), pp. 80–93.

— 'The canonical shape of the prophetic literature', *Int* 32 (1978), pp. 46–55.

— 'The exegetical significance of canon for the study of the Old Testament', in *Congress Volume: Göttingen 1977* (VTSupp 29; 1978), pp. 66–80.

— *Introduction to the Old Testament as Scripture* (Philadelphia/London: Fortress/SCM, 1979).

L. Clapham, 'Mythopoeic antecedents of the biblical world-view and their transformation in early Israelite thought', *Magnalia Dei* (G. E. Wright volume, ed. F. M. Cross and others; Garden City, NY: Doubleday, 1976), pp. 108–119.

H. Clavier, *Les variétés de la pensée biblique et le problème de son unité* (*NovT Suppl* 43; 1976).

R. E. Clements, 'The problem of Old Testament theology', *LQHR* 190 (1965), pp. 11–17.

— 'Covenant and canon in the Old Testament', in *Creation, Christ and Culture* (T. F. Torrance volume, ed. R. W. A. McKinney; Edinburgh: Clark, 1976), pp. 1–12.

*— *Old Testament Theology* (London/Atlanta: Marshall/John Knox, 1978).

— 'Patterns in the prophetic canon', in *Coats and Long, pp. 42–55.

R. E. Clements and C. S. Rodd, 'Talking points from books', *ExpT* 90 (1978–9), pp. 193–195.

D. J. A. Clines, *Social Responsibility in the Old Testament* (Nottingham: Shaftsbury Project, n.d.) = *Interchange* 20 (Sydney: AFES Graduates Fellowship, 1976), pp. 194–207.

G. W. Coats, 'The king's loyal opposition: obedience and authority in Exodus 32–34', in *Coats and Long, pp. 91–109.

— 'Moses versus Amalek', *Congress Volume: Edinburgh 1974* (*VTSupp* 28; 1975), pp. 29–41.

— 'Legendary motifs in the Moses death reports', *CBQ* 39 (1977), pp. 34–44.

*G. W. Coats and B. O. Long (ed.), *Canon and Authority: Essays in Old Testament Religion and Theology* (Philadelphia: Fortress, 1977).

R. J. Coggins, 'History and story in Old Testament study', *JSOT* 11 (1979), pp. 36–46.

R. G. Collingwood, *The Idea of History* (Oxford/New York: Clarendon/ OUP, 1946).

J. J. Collins, 'The "historical" character of the Old Testament in recent biblical theology', *CBQ* 41 (1979), pp. 185–204.

H. Conzelmann, *The Theology of St Luke* (ET New York/London: Harper/ Faber 1960).

— 'Fragen an Gerhard von Rad', *EvT* 24 (1964), pp. 113–125.

E. D. Cook, *Are Women People Too?* (Bramcote, Notts: Grove, 1978).

M. J. Cook, 'Judaism', *IDBS*, pp. 499–509.

J. Coppens, 'Levels of meaning in the Bible', *Concilium* (New York) 30 (1968) = *Concilium* (London) Volume 10, Number 3 (1967), pp. 62–69.

R. W. Cowley, 'The biblical canon of the Ethiopian Orthodox Church today', *Ostkirchliche Studien* 23 (1974), pp. 318–323.

C. E. B. Cranfield, 'St Paul and the law', *SJT* 17 (1964), pp. 43–68 = *New Testament Issues* (ed. R. Batey; New York/London: Harper/SCM, 1970), pp. 148–172 = *Romans* Vol. 2, pp. 845–862.

— *Romans* (Edinburgh: Clark, 1975 and 1979).

J. L. Crenshaw, *Samson: A Secret Betrayed, A Vow Ignored* (Atlanta: John Knox, 1978/London: SPCK, 1979).

O. Cullmann, *Christ and Time* (ET London: SCM, 1951, ³1962/Philadelphia: Westminster, 1950, ³1964).

— *Salvation in History* (ET London/New York: SCM/Harper, 1967).

D. Cupitt, *Christ and the Hiddenness of God* (London/Philadelphia: Lutterworth/Westminster, 1971).

N. A. Dahl, 'Promise and fulfillment', 'The future of Israel', and 'Contradictions in Scripture', ET in *Studies in Paul* (Minneapolis: Augsburg,

1977), pp. 121–136, 137–158, and 159–177.

H. Danby (ed.), *The Mishnah* (London/New York: OUP, 1933).

J. Daniélou, *From Shadows to Reality* (ET London/Westminster, MD: Burns and Oates/Newman, 1960).

D. Daube, 'Rabbinic methods of interpretation and Hellenistic rhetoric', *HUCA* 22 (1949), pp. 239–264.

— 'Alexandrian methods of interpretation and the rabbis', *Festschrift Hans Lewald* (Basel: Helbing, 1953), pp. 27–44 = *Essays in Greco-Roman and related Talmudic Literature* (ed. H. A. Fischel; New York: Ktav, 1977), pp. 165–182.

— *The Exodus Pattern in the Bible* (London: Faber, 1963).

R. Davidson, 'Some aspects of the Old Testament contribution to the pattern of Christian ethics', *SJT* 12 (1959), pp. 373–387.

— 'Orthodoxy and the prophetic word', *VT* 14 (1964), pp. 407–416.

— 'Some aspects of the theological significance of doubt in the Old Testament', *ASTI* 7 (1970), pp. 41–52.

— 'Faith and history in the Old Testament', *ExpT* 77 (1965–6), pp. 100–104.

G. H. Davies, 'Contemporary religious trends: the Old Testament', *ExpT* 67 (1955–6), pp. 3–7.

J. G. Davies, *Every Day God: Encountering the Holy in World and Worship* (London: SCM, 1973).

W. D. Davies, 'Apocalyptic and Pharisaism', *ExpT* 59 (1947–8), pp. 233–237 = *Christian Origins and Judaism* (London Westminster: DLT/Westminster, 1962), pp. 19–30.

— *Torah in the Messianic Age and/or the Age to Come* (Philadelphia: SBL, 1952).

— *Paul and Rabbinic Judaism* (London: SPCK, 1948, ²1955, ³1970/New York: Harper, 1967).

— 'Matthew, 5, 17–18, *Mélanges bibliques rédigés en l'honneur de André Robert* Paris: Bloud et Gay, 1957), pp. 428–456 = Davies, *Christian Origins and Judaism*, pp. 31–66.

— *The Setting of the Sermon on the Mount* (Cambridge/New York: CUP, 1964).

— 'The moral teaching of the early church', *The Use of the Old Testament in the New and other essays* (W. F. Stinespring volume, ed. J. M. Efird; Durham, NC: Duke UP, 1972), pp. 310–332.

— 'The significance of the law in Christianity', *Concilium* (New York) 98 (1974–5), pp. 24–32 = *Concilium* (London) Volumes 7/8, Number 10 (1974), pp. 118–126.

— *The Gospel and the Land* (Berkeley/London: University of California, 1974).

— 'Paul and the people of Israel', *NTS* 24 (1978), pp. 4–39.

S. T. Davies, 'Divine omniscience and human freedom', *RelS* 15 (1979) 303–316.

*A. Deissler, *Die Grundbotschaft des Alten Testaments* (Freiburg: Herder,

1972, ³1973).

Friedrich Delitzsch, *Die grosse Täuschung* 1 and 2 (Stuttgart: Deutsche Verlags-Anstalt, 1920 and 1922).

R. C. Dentan, *Preface to Old Testament Theology* (New Haven: Yale UP, 1950; revised New York: Seabury, 1963).

— (ed.), *The Idea of History in the Ancient Near East* (New Haven/London: Yale UP, 1955).

*J. W. Doeve, *Jewish Hermeneutics in the Synoptic Gospels and Acts* (Assen: van Gorcum, 1953).

M. Douglas, *Purity and Danger* (London/New York: Routledge/Praeger, 1966).

J. W. Drane, 'Tradition, law and ethics in Pauline theology', *NovT* 16 (1974), pp. 167–178.

— *Paul: Libertine or Legalist?* (London: SPCK, 1975).

— 'Typology', *EQ* 50 (1978), pp. 195–210.

A. Dulles, 'Response to Krister Stendahl's "Method in the study of biblical theology" ', *The Bible in Modern Scholarship* (ed. J. P. Hyatt; Nashville: Abingdon, 1965/London: Carey Kingsgate, 1966), pp. 210–216.

A. Dumas, *Political Theology and the Life of the Church* (ET London/Philadelphia: SCM/Westminster, 1978).

D. L. Dungan, 'The New Testament canon in recent study', *Int* 29 (1975), pp. 339–351.

G. Ebeling, 'The meaning of "Biblical theology" ', *JTS* 6 (1955), pp. 210–225 = *On the Authority of the Bible* (L. Hodgson and others; London: SPCK, 1960), pp. 49–67 = *Ebeling, *Word and Faith* (ET London/Philadelphia: SCM/Fortress, 1963), pp. 79–97.

— 'On the doctrine of the *triplex usus legis* in the theology of the Reformation', 'Reflexions on the doctrine of the Law', and 'Word of God and hermeneutics', *Word and Faith* pp. 62–78; 247–281, and 305–332.

— *The Study of Theology* (ET Philadelphia/London: Fortress/Collins, 1978).

W. Eichrodt, 'Hat die alttestamentliche Theologie noch selbständige Bedeutung innerhalb der alttestamentlichen Wissenschaft?', *ZAW* 47 (1929), pp. 83–91.

*— *Theology of the Old Testament* 1 and 2 (ET London/Philadelphia: SCM/Westminster, 1961 and 1967).

— 'Is typological exegesis an appropriate method?', in *Westermann, pp. 224–245.

— 'Vom Symbol zum Typos: ein Beitrag zur Sacharja-Exegese', *TZ* 13 (1957), pp. 509–522.

— 'Covenant and law: thoughts on recent discussion', *Int* 20 (1966), pp. 302–321.

— 'Darf man heute noch von einem Gottesbund mit Israel reden?', *TZ* 30 (1974), pp. 193–206.

O. Eissfeldt, 'Israelitisch-jüdische Religionsgeschichte und alttestamentliche Theologie', *ZAW* 44 (1926), pp. 1–12 = *Kleine Schriften* 1 (Tübingen:

Mohr, 1962), pp. 105–114.
— *The Old Testament: An Introduction* (ET Oxford/New York: Harper/ Blackwell, 1965).
K. Elliger, *Studien zum Habakuk-Kommentar von Toten Meer* (Tübingen: Mohr, 1953).
— *Deuterojesaja: 1 Teilband: Jesaja 40, 1 – 45*, (7 BKAT; 1978).
*E. E. Ellis, *Paul's Use of the Old Testament* (Edinburgh/Grand Rapids: Oliver and Boyd/Eerdmans, 1957).
— 'How the New Testament uses the Old', in *New Testament Interpretation* (ed. I. H. Marshall; Exeter/Grand Rapids: Paternoster/Eerdmans, 1977), pp. 199–219 = Ellis, *Prophecy and Hermeneutic*, pp. 147–172.
— *Prophecy and Hermeneutic in Early Christianity* (Tübingen/Grand Rapids: Mohr/Eerdmans, 1978).
H. L. Ellison, 'Typology', *EQ* 25 (1953), pp. 158–166.
J. Ellul, *To Will and to Do* (ET Philadelphia: Pilgrim, 1969).
— *Violence* (ET New York: Seabury, 1969/London: SCM, 1970).
— *The Meaning of the City* (ET Grand Rapids: Eerdmans, 1970).
— *The Judgment of Jonah* (ET Grand Rapids: Eerdmans, 1971).
— *The Politics of God and the Politics of Man* (ET Grand Rapids: Eerdmans, 1972).
— *Hope in Time of Abandonment* ET New York: Seabury, 1973).
I. Epstein, 'Talmud', *IDB* 4, pp. 511–515.
I. H. Eybers, 'Some light on the canon of the Qumran sect', *Die Ou Testamentiese Werkgemeenskap in Suid-Afrika* (Pretoria, 1962), pp. 1–14 = *Leiman, pp. 23–36.
P. Fairbairn, *The Typology of Scripture* 1 and 2 (Edinburgh: Clark, 1845 and 1847; ⁶1876; reprinted Grand Rapids: Zondervan, 1952/London: Oliphants, 1953).
A. M. Farrer, *The Glass of Vision* (London: Dacre, 1948).
F. C. Fensham, 'Covenant, promise, and expectation in the Bible', *TZ* 23 (1967), pp. 305–322.
— 'The covenant as giving expression to the relationship between the Old and New Testament', *TynB* 22 (1971), pp. 82–94.
D. Field, *The Homosexual Way – A Christian Option?* (Bramcote, Notts: Grove, 1976; Downers Grove, IL/Leicester: IVP, ²1979).
A. Finkel, 'The pesher of dreams and scriptures', *RQ* 4 (1963–4), pp. 357–370.
J. A. Fischer, 'Ethics and wisdom', *CBQ* 40 (1978), pp. 298–310.
M. Fishbane, 'Torah and tradition', in *D. A. Knight, pp. 275–300.
J. A. Fitzmyer, 'The use of explicit Old Testament quotations in Qumran literature and in the New Testament', *NTS* 7 (1960–1), pp. 297–333 = *Essays on the Semitic Background of the New Testament* (London: Chapman, 1971), pp. 3–58.
V. H. Fletcher, 'The shape of Old Testament ethics', *SJT* 24 (1971), pp. 47–73.
G. Fohrer, 'Die Struktur der alttestamentlichen Eschatologie', *ThL* 85

(1960), columns 401–420 = *Studien zur alttestamentlichen Prophetie (1949–1965)* (*BZAW* 99; Berlin: Töpelmann, 1967), pp. 32–58.

— 'Prophetie und Geschichte', *ThL* 89 (1964), columns 481–500 = *BZAW* 99 (see above), pp. 265–293.

— 'Altes Testament – "Amphiktyonie" und "Bund"?', *ThL* 91 (1966), columns 801–816, 893–904 = Fohrer, *Studien zur alttestamentlichen Theologie und Geschichte (1949–1966)* (*BZAW* 115; Berlin: De Gruyter, 1969), pp. 84–119.

— 'Der Mittelpunkt einer Theologie des Alten Testaments', *TZ* 24 (1968), pp. 161–172 = *Fohrer, ch. 4.

— 'Das Alte Testament und das Thema "Christologie" ', *EvT* 30 (1970), pp. 281–298 = *Fohrer, ch. 1.

*— *Theologische Grundstrukturen des Alten Testaments* (Berlin/New York: De Gruyter, 1972).

— *History of Israelite Religion* (ET Nashville: Abingdon, 1972/London: SPCK, 1973).

L. S. Ford, 'Biblical recital and process philosophy', *Int* 26 (1972), pp. 198–209.

H. E. Fosdick, *A Guide to Understanding the Bible* (London/New York: SCM/Harper, 1938).

F. Foulkes, *The Acts of God: A Study of the Basis of Typology in the Old Testament* (London: Tyndale, 1958).

R. T. France, ' "In all the scriptures" – A study of Jesus' typology', *TSFB* 56 (1970), pp. 13–16.

*— *Jesus and the Old Testament* (London/Downers Grove, IL: Tyndale/IVP, 1971).

D. N. Freedman, 'The Law and the Prophets', *Congress Volume: Bonn 1962* (*VTSupp* 9; 1963), pp. 250–265 = *Leiman, pp. 5–20.

— 'The Old Testament and Christian Faith: A Theological Discussion, edited by Bernhard W. Anderson', *Theology Today* 21 (1964–5), pp. 225–228.

— 'The biblical idea of history', *Int* 21 (1967), pp. 32–49.

— 'Canon of the OT', *IDBS* pp. 130–136.

H. W. Frei, *The Eclipse of Biblical Narrative* (New Haven/London: Yale UP, 1974).

C. T. Fritsch, *'to antitypon'*, *Studia Biblica et Semitica* (T. C. Vriezen volume, ed. W. C. van Unnik and A. S. van der Woude; Wageningen: Veenman, 1966), pp. 100–107.

H.-G. Fritzsche, 'Die Anfänge christlicher Ethik im Dekalog', *ThL* 98 (1973), columns 161–170.

R. M. Frye, 'A literary perspective for the criticism of the gospels', *Jesus and Man's Hope* 2 (ed. D. G. Miller and D. Y. Hadidian; Pittsburgh: Pittsburgh Theological Seminary, 1971), pp. 193–221.

E. Fuchs, 'Christus das Ende der Geschichte', *EvT* 8 (1948–9), pp. 447–461 = *Zur Frage nach dem historischen Jesus* (Tübingen: Mohr, 1960), pp. 79–99.

— 'The theology of the New Testament and the historical Jesus', *Studies of the Historical Jesus* (ET London/Naperville, IL: SCM/Allenson, 1964), pp. 167–190.

D. P. Fuller, 'The resurrection of Jesus and the historical method', *JBR* 34 (1966), pp. 18–24.

V. P. Furnish, *Theology and Ethics in Paul* (Nashville: Abingdon, 1968).

H. G. Gadamer, *Truth and Method* (ET London/New York: Sheed and Ward/Seabury, 1975).

B. Gärtner, 'The Habakkuk Commentary (DSH) and the Gospel of Matthew', *ST* 8 (1954), pp. 1–24.

M. Gertner, 'Midrashim in the New Testament', *JSS* 7 (1962), pp. 267–292.

— 'Terms of scriptural interpretation: a study in Hebrew semantics', *BSOAS* 25 (1962), pp. 1–27.

H. Gese, 'The idea of history in the ancient near east and the Old Testament', ET in *Journal for Theology and Church* 1 (1965), pp. 49–64.

— 'Psalm 22 und das Neue Testament', *ZTK* 65 (1968), pp. 1–22 = *Vom Sinai zum Zion: alttestamentliche Beiträge zur biblischen Theologie* (Munich: Kaiser, 1974), pp. 180–201.

— 'Erwägungen zur Einheit der biblischen Theologie', *ZTK* 67 (1970), pp. 417–436 = *Vom Sinai zum Zion*, pp. 11–30.

— 'Natus ex virgine', *Probleme biblischer Theologie* (G. von Rad volume, ed. H. W. Wolff; Munich: Kaiser, 1971), pp. 73–89 = *Vom Sinai zum Zion*, pp. 130–146.

— 'Anfang und Ende der Apokalyptik, dargestellt am Sacharjabuch', *ZTK* 70 (1973), pp. 20–49 = *Vom Sinai zum Zion*, pp. 202–230.

— *Zur biblischen Theologie: alttestamentliche Vorträge* (Munich: Kaiser, 1977).

— 'Tradition and biblical theology', ET in *D. A. Knight, pp. 301–326.

C. H. J. de Geus, *The Tribes of Israel* (Assen: van Gorcum, 1976).

H.-G. Geyer, 'Geschichte als theologisches Problem', *EvT* 22 (1962), pp. 92–104.

— 'Zur Frage der Notwendigkeit des Alten Testamentes', *EvT* 25 (1965), pp. 207–237.

L. B. Gilkey, 'Cosmology, ontology, and the travail of biblical language', *JR* 41 (1961), pp. 194–205.

— 'The concept of providence in contemporary theology', *JR* 43 (1963), pp. 171–192.

— *Naming the Whirlwind: The Renewal of God-Language* (Indianapolis: Bobbs-Merrill, 1969).

R. Gill, *Theology and Social Structure* (London: Mowbray, 1977).

J. Goldin, 'Josephus', *IDB* 2, pp. 987–988.

J. Goldingay, ' "That you may know that Yahweh is God": a study in the relationship betweeen theology and historical truth in the Old Testament', *TynB* 23 (1972), pp. 58–93.

— 'The Chronicler as a theologian', *BTB* 5 (1975), pp. 99–126.

— 'The study of Old Testament theology: its aims and purpose', *TynB* 26 (1975), pp. 34–52.

— 'History, culture, mission, and the people of God in the Old Testament', *Evangelical Fellowship for Missionary Studies Bulletin* 5 (1975), pp. 1–30.

— 'The man of war and the suffering servant: the Old Testament and the theology of liberation', *TynB* 27 (1976), pp. 79–113.

— 'The "salvation history" perspective and the "wisdom" perspective within the context of biblical theology', *EQ* 51 (1979), pp. 194–207.

— 'The patriarchs in scripture and history', *Essays on the Patriarchal Narratives* (ed. A. R. Millard and D. J. Wiseman; Leicester: IVP, 1980), pp. 11–42.

E. R. Goodenough, 'Philo Judeus', *IDB* 3, pp. 796–799.

*L. Goppelt, *Typos: die typologische Deutung des Alten Testaments im Neuen* (Gütersloh: Bertelsmann, 1939; reprinted Darmstadt: Wissenschaftliche Buchgesellschaft, 1973).

— 'Apokalyptik und Typologie bei Paulus', *ThL* 89 (1964), columns 321–344 = *Typos* (1973), pp. 259–299.

— 'Paul and Heilsgeschichte', ET in *Int* 21 (1967), pp. 315–326.

— '*Typos, antitypos, typikos, hypotypōsis*', *TDNT* 8, pp. 246–259.

N. K. Gottwald, 'Walther Eichrodt's "Theology of the Old Testament" ', *ExpT* 74 (1962–3), pp. 209–212.

— '*Theologische Grundstrukturen des Alten Testaments*, by Georg Fohrer', *JBL* 93 (1974), pp. 594–596.

M. D. Goulder, *Midrash and Lection in Matthew* (London: SPCK, 1974).

D. E. Gowan, *Bridge between the Testaments* (Pittsburgh/Edinburgh: Pickwick/Clark, 1976).

P. Grech, 'Interprophetic re-interpretation and Old Testament eschatology', *Augustinianum* 9 (1969), pp. 235–265.

— 'The "Testimonia" and modern hermeneutics', *NTS* 19 (1972–3), pp. 318–324.

— 'The Old Testament as a Christological source in the apostolic age', *BTB* 5 (1975), pp. 127–145.

M. Greenberg, 'On sharing the Scriptures', *Magnalia Dei* (G. E. Wright volume, ed. F. M. Cross and others; Garden City, NY: Doubleday, 1976), pp. 455–463.

A. J. Greig, 'Some formative aspects in the development of Gerhard von Rad's idea of history', *Andrews University Seminary Studies* 16 (1978), pp. 313–331.

*P. Grelot, *Sens chrétien de l'Ancien Testament* (Paris/New York: Desclée, 1962).

K. Grobel, 'Revelation and resurrection', *Theology as History* (ed. J. M. Robinson and J. B. Cobb; New York: Harper, 1967), pp. 155–175.

D. E. Groh, 'Hans von Campenhausen on canon', *Int* 28 (1974), pp. 331–343.

A. H. J. Gunneweg, 'Über die Prädikabilität alttestamentlicher Texte', *ZTK* 65 (1968), pp. 389–413.

*— *Understanding the Old Testament* (ET London/Philadelphia: SCM/Westminster, 1978).

J. M. Gustafson, 'Context versus principles: a misplaced debate in Christian ethics', *HTR* 58 (1965), pp. 171–202 = Gustafson, *Christian Ethics and the Community* (Philadelphia: Pilgrim, 1971), pp. 101–126.
— 'Christian ethics', in *Religion* (ed. P. Ramsey; Englewood Cliffs, NJ/ London: Prentice-Hall, 1965), pp. 285–354.
— 'The place of scripture in Christian ethics: a methodological study', *Int* 24 (1970), pp. 430–455 = Gustafson, *Theology and Christian Ethics* (Philadelphia: Pilgrim, 1974), pp. 121–145.
— 'The relation of the gospels to the moral life', *Jesus and Man's Hope* 2 (ed. D. G. Miller and D. Y. Hadidian; Pittsburgh: Pittsburgh Theological Seminary, 1971), pp. 103–117 = Gustafson, *Theology and Christian Ethics* (Philadelphia: Pilgrim, 1974), pp. 147–159, 290–291.
K. Haacker, P. Stuhlmacher, H.-J. Kraus, and H. H. Schmid, *Biblische Theologie heute* (Neukirchen: Neukirchener Verlag, 1977).
H. Haag, 'Typologisches Verständnis des Pentateuch?', *Studien zum Pentateuch* (W. Kornfeld volume, ed. G. Braulik; Vienna: Herder, 1977), pp. 243–257.
A. T. Hanson, *Jesus Christ in the Old Testament* (London: SPCK, 1965).
*— *Studies in Paul's Technique and Theology* (London/Grand Rapids: SPCK/Eerdmans, 1974).
P. D. Hanson, 'The theological significance of contradiction within the Book of the Covenant', in *Coats and Long, pp. 110–131.
R. P. C. Hanson, *Allegory and Event* (London: SCM, 1959).
M. Haran, 'Seething a kid in its mother's milk', ET *JJS* 30 (1979), pp. 23–35.
A. von Harnack, *Marcion: das Evangelium vom fremden Gott* (Leipzig: Hinrichs, 1921, ²1924; reprinted Darmstadt: Wissenschaftliche Buchgesellschaft, 1960).
— 'Das Alte Testament in den Paulinischen Briefen und in den Paulinischen Gemeinden', *Sitzungsberichte der Preussischen Akademie der Wissenschaften Jahrgang 1928: Philosophisch-historische Klasse* (Berlin: Akademie der Wissenschaften, 1928), pp. 124–141.
W. Harrelson, 'Life, faith, and the emergence of tradition', in *D. A. Knight, pp. 11–30.
*W. J. Harrington, *The Path of Biblical Theology* (Dublin/London: Gill and Macmillan/Macmillan: 1973).
*R. K. Harrison, *Introduction to the Old Testament* (Grand Rapids: Eerdmans, 1969/London: Tyndale, 1970).
J. Harvey, 'The new diachronic biblical theology of the Old Testament (1960–1970)', *BTB* 1 (1971), pp. 5–29.
V. A. Harvey, *The Historian and the Believer* (New York: Macmillan, 1966/London: SCM, 1967).
G. F. Hasel, 'The problem of history in Old Testament theology', *Andrews University Seminary Studies* 8 (1970), pp. 23–50.
– 'Methodology as a major problem in the current crisis of Old Testament theology', *BTB* 2 (1972), pp. 177–198; expanded in *Hasel, pp. 11–28,

169

81–95/²pp. 35–55, 129–143.

*— Old Testament Theology: Basic Issues in the Current Debate (Grand Rapids: Eerdmans, 1972, ²1975).

D. M. Hay, 'Interpretation, History of: NT interpretation of the OT', IDBS, pp. 443–446.

B. L. Hebblethwaite, 'Some reflections on predestination, providence and divine foreknowledge', RelS 15 (1979), pp. 433–448.

*P. Heinisch, Theology of the Old Testament (ET Collegeville, MN: Liturgical Press, 1950).

*W. Herberg, Faith Enacted as History: Essays in Biblical Theology (Philadelphia: Westminster, 1976).

S. Herrmann, 'Die konstruktive Restauration: das Deuteronomium als Mitte biblischer Theologie', Probleme biblischer Theologie (G. von Rad volume, ed. H. W. Wolff; Munich: Kaiser, 1971), pp. 155–170.

H. W. Hertzberg, 'Die Nachgeschichte alttestamentlicher Texte innerhalb des Alten Testaments', Werden und Wesen des Alten Testaments (ed. P. Volz and others; BZAW 66; Berlin: Töpelmann, 1936), pp. 110–121 = Hertzberg, Beiträge zur Traditionsgeschichte und Theologie des Alten Testaments (Göttingen: Vandenhoeck, 1962), pp. 69–80.

— 'Das Christusproblem im Alten Testament', Beiträge, pp. 148–161.

F. Hesse, 'Die Erforschung der Geschichte Israels als theologische Aufgabe', KD 4 (1958), pp. 1–19.

— 'Kerygma oder geschichtliche Wirklichkeit?', ZTK 57 (1960), pp. 17–26.

— 'The evaluation and authority of Old Testament texts', in *Westermann, pp. 285–313.

— 'Bewährt sich eine "Theologie der Heilstatsachen" im Alten Testament? Zum Verhältnis von Faktum und Deutung', ZAW 81 (1969), pp. 1–18.

*— Abschied von der Heilsgeschichte (Zürich: EVZ, 1971).

— 'Zur Profanität der Geschichte Israels', ZTK 71 (1974), pp. 262–290.

D. R. Hillers, Covenant: The History of a Biblical Idea (Baltimore: Johns Hopkins, 1969).

E. Hillman, Polygamy Reconsidered (Maryknoll, NY: Orbis, 1975).

E. D. Hirsch, Validity in Interpretation (New Haven/London: Yale UP, 1973).

— The Aims of Interpretation (Chicago/London: University of Chicago, 1976).

S. Holm-Nielsen, 'The book of Ecclesiastes and the interpretation of it in Jewish and Christian theology', ASTI 10 (1975–6), pp. 38–96.

T. Holtz, 'Zur Interpretation des Alten Testaments im Neuen Testament', ThL 99 (1974), columns 19–32.

S. H. Hooke, Alpha and Omega: A Study in the Pattern of Revelation (Welwyn: Nisbet, 1961).

J. L. Houlden, Ethics and the New Testament (Harmondsworth/Baltimore: Penguin, 1973).

H. Hübner, 'Das Gesetz als elementares Thema einer Biblischen Theologie?', KD 22 (1976), pp. 250–276.

D. Hume, *Philosophical Essays Concerning Human Understanding* (London: Millar, 1748) = 'An Enquiry Concerning Human Understanding', *Essays and Treatises on Several Subjects* (London: Millar, 1758, 1777); often reprinted.

H. D. Hummel, 'The Old Testament basis of typological interpretation, *Bib Res* 9 (1964), pp. 38–50.

*P. van Imschoot, *Theology of the Old Testament* 1: *God* (ET New York: Desclée, 1965).

V. T. Istavridis, *Orthodoxy and Anglicanism* (ET London: SPCK, 1966).

B. S. Jackson, 'Legalism', *JJS* 30 (1979), pp. 1–22.

— 'Reflections on biblical criminal law', *JJS* 24 (1973), pp. 8–38 = Jackson, *Essays on Jewish and Comparative Legal History* (Leiden: Brill, 1975), pp. 25–63.

E. Jacob, *Théologie de l'Ancien Testament* (Neuchâtel: Delachaux et Niestlé, 1955, ²1968).

*— *Theology of the Old Testament* (ET London/New York: Hodder/Harper, 1958).

— 'Les bases théologiques de l'éthique de l'Ancien Testament', *Congress Volume: Oxford 1959* (*VTSupp* 7; 1960), pp. 39–51.

— 'Possibilités et limites d'une théologie biblique', *RHPR* 46 (1966), pp. 116–130.

— 'La théologie de l'Ancien Testament: état présent et perspectives d'avenir', *De Mari à Qumrân* (J. Coppens volume, ed. H. Cazelles; Gembloux/Paris: Duculot/Lethielleux, 1969), pp. 259–271.

— *Grundfragen alttestamentlicher Theologie* (Stuttgart: Kohlhammer, 1970).

— 'Principe canonique et formation de l'Ancien Testament', *Congress Volume: Edinburgh 1974* (*VTSupp* 28; 1975), pp. 101–122.

L. Jacobs, *Jewish Biblical Exegesis* (New York: Behrman, 1973).

J. G. Janzen, 'The Old Testament in "Process" perspective', *Magnalia Dei* (G. E. Wright volume, ed. F. M. Cross and others; Garden City, NY: Doubleday, 1976), pp. 480–509.

— 'The Bible and our social institutions', *Int* 27 (1973), pp. 327–350.

F. N. Jasper, 'The relation of the Old Testament to the New', *ExpT* 78 (1966–7), pp. 228–232; 267–270.

J. Jensen, 'Does *porneia* mean fornication? A critique of Bruce Malina', *NovT* 20 (1978), pp. 161–184.

A Jepsen, 'The scientific study of the Old Testament', in *Westermann, pp. 246–284.

J. Jeremias, 'The present position in the controversy concerning the problem of the historical Jesus', *ExpT* 69 (1957–8), pp. 333–339.

P. K. Jewett, 'Concerning the allegorical interpretation of scripture', *WTJ* 17 (1954), pp. 1–20.

J. Jocz, *The Covenant: A Theology of Human Destiny* (Grand Rapids: Eerdmans, 1968).

W. Johnstone, 'The authority of the Old Testament', *SJT* 22 (1969),

pp. 197–209.

O. Kaiser, *Isaiah 1–12* (ET London/Philadelphia: SCM/Westminster, 1972).

W. C. Kaiser, 'The centre of Old Testament theology: the promise', *Themelios* 10 (1974), pp. 1–10.

*— *Toward an Old Testament Theology* (Grand Rapids: Zondervan, 1978).

E. Käsemann, 'Paul and early catholicism', *Journal for Theology and Church* 3 (1967), pp. 14–27 = *New Testament Questions of Today* (ET London/Philadelphia: SCM/Fortress, 1969), pp. 236–251.

— *Perspectives on Paul* (ET London/Philadelphia: SCM/Fortress, 1971).

— 'The problem of a New Testament theology', *NTS* 19 (1972–3), pp. 235–245.

P. Katz, 'The Old Testament canon in Palestine and Alexandria', *ZNW* 47 (1956), pp. 191–217 = *Leiman, pp. 72–98.

G. D. Kaufman, 'The *imago Dei* as man's historicity', *JR* 36 (1956), pp. 157–168.

— *Systematic Theology: A Historicist Perspective* (New York: Scribner's, 1968).

— 'On the meaning of "Act of God" ', *HTR* 61 (1968), pp. 175–201 = Kaufman, *God the Problem* (Cambridge, MA: Harvard UP, 1972), pp. 119–147.

— 'What shall we do with the Bible?', *Int* 25 (1971), pp. 95–112.

— *An Essay on Theological Method* (Missoula: Scholars, 1975, ²1979).

B. N. Kaye, *Using the Bible in Ethics* (Bramcote, Notts: Grove, 1976).

— and G. J. Wenham (ed.), *Law, Morality and the Bible* (Leicester/Downers Grove, IL: IVP, 1978).

S. Kealy, 'The canon: an African contribution', *BTB* 9 (1979), pp. 13–26.

L. E. Keck and J. L. Martyn (ed.), *Studies in Luke-Acts* (P. Schubert volume; Nashville: Abingdon, 1966/London: SPCK, 1968).

C. A. Keller, 'Gerhard von Rad, Theologie des Alten Testaments. 1', *TZ* 14 (1958), pp. 306–309.

D. Kidner, *Hard Sayings* (London: IVP, 1972).

J. A. Kirk, *The Origin of Accumulated Wealth: The Marxist Thesis and a Hermeneutical Reflection* (Nottingham: Shaftesbury Project, n.d.).

K. A. Kitchen, *The Bible in its World* (Exeter/Downers Grove, IL: Paternoster/IVP, 1977).

G. Klein, 'Römer 4 und die Idee der Heilsgeschichte', *EvT* 23 (1963), pp. 424–447 = Klein, *Rekonstruktion und Interpretation* (Munich: Kaiser, 1969), pp. 145–169.

— 'Heil und Geschichte nach Römer iv', *NTS* 13 (1966–7), pp. 43–47.

— 'Bibel und Heilsgeschichte: die Fragwurdigkeit einer Idee', *ZNW* 62 (1971), pp. 1–47.

— 'The biblical understanding of "The Kingdom of God" ', ET *Int* 26 (1972), pp. 387–418.

M. G. Kline, *The Structure of Biblical Authority* (Grand Rapids: Eerdmans, 1972); pp. 27–110 are substantially reprinted from articles in *WTJ* 32–33 (1969–70).

— 'The correlation of the concepts of canon and covenant', *New Perspectives on the Old Testament* (ed. J. B. Payne; Waco, TX: Word, 1970), pp. 265–279.

R. Knierim, 'Offenbarung im Alten Testament', in *Probleme biblischer Theologie* (G. von Rad volume, ed. H. W. Wolff; Munich: Kaiser, 1971), pp. 206–235.

*D. A. Knight (ed.), *Tradition and Theology in the Old Testament* (London/Philadelphia: SPCK/Fortress, 1977).

*G. A. F. Knight, *A Christian Theology of the Old Testament* (Richmond: John Knox, 1959/London: SCM, 1959, ²1964).

— *Law and Grace: Must a Christian Keep the Law of Moses?* (London: SCM, 1962).

K. Koch, *The Growth of the Biblical Tradition* (ET London/New York: Black/Scribner's, 1969).

*L. Köhler, *Old Testament Theology* (ET London/New York: Lutterworth/Harper, 1957).

J. Koenig, 'L'activité herméneutique des scribes dans la transmission du texte de l'Ancien Testament', *RHR* 161 (1962), pp. 141–174; 162 (1962), pp. 1–43.

J. L. Koole, 'Die Bibel des Ben-Sira', *OTS* 14 (1965), pp. 374–396.

*E. G. Kraeling, *The Old Testament Since the Reformation* (London/New York: Lutterworth/Harper, 1955; reprinted New York: Schocken, 1969).

H.-J. Kraus, 'Freude an Gottes Gesetz: ein Beitrag zur Auslegung der Psalmen 1; 19B und 119', *EvT* 10 (1950–1), pp. 337–351.

— 'Zur Geschichte des Überlieferungsbegriffs in der alttestamentlichen Wissenschaft', *EvT* 16 (1956), pp. 371–387 = *Biblisch-theologische Aufsätze* (Neukirchen: Neukirchener Verlag, 1972), pp. 278–295.

— *Psalmen* (*BKAT*; 1961, ³1966).

*— *Die biblische Theologie* (Neukirchen: Neukirchener Verlag, 1970).

— 'Theologie als Traditionsbildung?', *EvT* 36 (1976), pp. 498–507 = *Biblische Theologie heute* (K. Haacker and others; Neukirchen: Neukirchener Verlag, 1977), pp. 61–73.

J. K. Kuntz, *The Self-Revelation of God* (Philadelphia: Westminster, 1967).

E. Kutsch, *Verheissung und Gesetz: Untersuchungen zum sogenannten 'Bund' im Alten Testament* (*BZAW* 131; Berlin/New York: De Gruyter, 1973).

— 'Von der Aktualität alttestamentlicher Aussagen für das Verständnis des Neuen Testaments', *ZTK* 74 (1977), pp. 273–290.

W. G. Lambert, 'History and the Gods: a review article', *Orientalia* 39 (1970), pp. 170–177.

— 'Destiny and divine intervention in Babylon and Israel', *OTS* 17 (1972), pp. 65–72.

G. W. H. Lampe, 'Typological exegesis', *Theology* 56 (1953), pp. 201–208.

— 'Hermeneutics and typology', *LQHR* 190 (1965), pp. 17–25.

G. W. H. Lampe and K. J. Woollcombe, *Essays on Typology* (London/Naperville, IL: SCM/Allenson, 1957).

A. Lauha, *Kohelet* (*BKAT*; 1978).

R. B. Laurin, 'Tradition and canon', in *D. A. Knight, pp. 261–274.

J. C. H. Lebram, 'Aspekte der alttestamentlichen Kanonbildung', *VT* 18 (1968), pp. 173–189.

R. Le Déaut, *La Nuit Pascale: essai sur la signification de la Pâque juive à partir du Targum d'Exode XII 42* (Rome: PBI, 1963).

— 'Apropos a definition of midrash', ET in *Int* 25 (1971), pp. 259–282.

— 'La tradition juive ancienne et l'exégèse chrétienne primitive', *RHPR* 51 (1971), pp. 31–50.

— 'The current state of targumic studies', *BTB* 4 (1974), pp. 3–32.

F. J. Leenhardt, *Two Biblical Faiths: Protestant and Catholic* (ET London/ Philadelphia: Lutterworth/Westminster, 1964).

*S. Z. Leiman (ed.), *The Canon and Masorah of the Hebrew Bible* (New York: Ktav, 1974).

— *The Canonization of Hebrew Scripture: The Talmudic and Midrashic Evidence* (Hamden, CT: Archon, 1976).

E. B. Levine, 'Haggadah in Jewish Bible Study', *Concordia Theological Monthly* 40 (1969), pp. 92–96.

C. S. Lewis, *Reflections on the Psalms* (London/New York: Bles/Harcourt, Brace, 1958; reprinted London: Collins Fontana, 1961).

H. D. Lewis, *Freedom and History* (London/New York: George Allen/ Macmillan, 1962).

J. P. Lewis, 'What do we mean by Jabneh?', *JBR* 32 (1964), pp. 125–132 = *Leiman, pp. 254–261.

S. Lieberman, *Hellenism in Jewish Palestine* (New York: Jewish Theological Seminary, 1950).

J. N. Lightstone, 'The formation of the biblical canon in Judaism of late antiquity: prolegomenon to a general reassessment', *Studies in Religion* 8 (1979), pp. 135–142.

B. Lindars, 'The Bible and Christian ethics' and 'Imitation of God and imitation of Christ', *Theology* 76 (1973), pp. 180–189, 394–402.

B. Lindars and P. Borgen, 'The place of the Old Testament in the formation of New Testament theology', *NTS* 23 (1977), pp. 59–75.

H. Lindsey, *The Late Great Planet Earth* (Grand Rapids: Zondervan, 1970/ London: Marshall, 1971).

R. Loewe, 'The "plain" meaning of Scripture in early Jewish exegesis', *Papers of the Institute of Jewish Studies London*, 1 (ed. J. G. Weiss; Jerusalem: Hebrew University, 1964), pp. 140–185.

— 'Apologetic motifs in the targum to the Song of Songs', *Biblical Motifs: Origins and Transformations* (ed. A. Altmann; Cambridge, MA/London: Harvard UP/OUP, 1966), pp. 159–196.

— *The Targums and Rabbinic Literature: An Introduction to Jewish Interpretations of Scripture. By John Bowker*', *JTS* 21 (1970), pp. 459–464.

*N. Lohfink, *The Christian Meaning of the Old Testament* (ET Milwaukee: Bruce, 1968/London: Burns and Oates, 1969).

B. Lonergan, *Method in Theology* (ET London/New York: DLT/Herder,

1972).

E. L. Long, 'The use of the Bible in Christian ethics: a look at basic options', *Int* 19 (1965), pp. 149–162.

— *A Survey of Christian Ethics* (New York: OUP, 1967).

— 'Soteriological implications of norm and context', in *Norm and Context in Christian Ethics* (ed. G. H. Outka and P. Ramsey; New York: Scribner's, 1968/London: SCM, 1969), pp. 265–295.

R. N. Longenecker, *Paul: Apostle of Liberty* (New York/London: Harper, 1964; reprinted Grand Rapids: Baker, 1976).

— 'Can we reproduce the exegesis of the New Testament?', *TynB* 21 (1970), pp. 3–38.

*— *Biblical Exegesis in the Apostolic Period* (Grand Rapids: Eerdmans, 1975).

S. Lowy, 'Some aspects of normative and sectarian interpretation of the scriptures', *ALUOS* 6 (1969), pp. 98–163.

M. Luther, *Luther's Works* 1–30 (St Louis: Concordia, 1955–) and 31–55 (Philadelphia: Fortress/Muhlenberg, 1957–).

*D. Lys, *The Meaning of the Old Testament* (Nashville: Abingdon, 1967).

D. J. McCarthy, *Old Testament Covenant: A Survey of Current Opinions* (Oxford/Richmond: Blackwell/John Knox, 1972).

— 'Bᵉrit and covenant in the Deuteronomistic history', *Studies in the Religion of Ancient Israel* (*VTSupp* 23; 1972), pp. 65–85.

— 'bᵉrit in Old Testament history and theology', *Biblica* 53 (1972), pp. 110–121.

N. J. McEleney, 'The principles of the Sermon on the Mount', *CBQ* 41 (1979), pp. 552–570.

H. McKeating, 'Sanctions against adultery in ancient Israelite society, with some reflections on methodology in the study of Old Testament ethics', *JSOT* 11 (1979), pp. 57–72.

J. L. McKenzie, 'The significance of the Old Testament for Christian faith in Roman Catholicism', in *Anderson, pp. 102–114.

*— *A Theology of the Old Testament* (New York/London: Macmillan/Chapman, 1974).

M. McNamara, *The New Testament and the Palestinian Targum to the Pentateuch* (Rome: PBI, 1966, ²1978).

— *Targum and Testament: Aramaic Paraphrases of the Hebrew Bible: A Light on the New Testament* (Shannon: Irish UP, 1972).

— 'Targums', *IDBS*, pp. 856–861.

D. C. Maguire, 'Towards macromorality: a response to Philip Turner', *ATR* 61 (1979), pp. 54–59.

R. A. Markus, 'Presuppositions of the typological approach to scripture', *Church Quarterly Review* 158 (1957), pp. 442–451 = *The Communication of the Gospel in New Testament Times* (by A. Farrer and others; London/Greenwich, CN: SPCK/Seabury, 1961), pp. 75–85.

R. Martin-Achard, 'A propos de la théologie de l'Ancien Testament', *TZ* 35 (1979), pp. 63–71.

U. Mauser, 'Image of God and incarnation', *Int* 24 (1970), pp. 336–356.

— *Gottesbild und Menschwerdung: eine Untersuchung zur Einheit des Alten und Neuen Testaments* (Tübingen: Mohr, 1971).

A. D. H. Mayes, *Israel in the Period of the Judges* (London/Naperville, IL: SCM/Allenson, 1974).

J. Mays, 'Historical and canonical: recent discussion about the Old Testament and Christian faith', *Magnalia Dei* (G. E. Wright volume, ed. F. M. Cross and others; Garden City, NY: Doubleday, 1976), pp. 510–528.

J. P. Meier, *Law and History in Matthew's Gospel* (Rome: PBI, 1976).

— 'On the veiling of hermeneutics (1 Cor 11:2–16)', *CBQ* 40 (1978), pp. 212–226.

B. M. Metzger, 'The formulas introducing quotations of scripture in the NT and the Mishnah', *JBL* 70 (1951), pp. 297–307.

C. Michalson, 'Bultmann against Marcion', in *Anderson, pp. 49–63.

M. P. Miller, 'Targum, midrash and the use of the Old Testament in the New Testament', *JSJ* 2 (1971), pp. 29–82.

— 'Midrash', *IDBS*, pp. 593–597.

P. S. Minear, *Commands of Christ* (Nashville/Edinburgh: Abingdon/St. Andrew's Press, 1972).

J. P. Miranda, *Marx and the Bible: A Critique of the Philosophy of Oppression* (ET Maryknoll, NY: Orbis, 1974/London: SCM, 1977).

*K. H. Miskotte, *When the Gods are Silent* (ET New York/London: Harper/Collins, 1967).

J. Moltmann, *Theology of Hope* (ET London/New York: SCM/ Harper, 1967).

G. F. Moore, *Judaism* (Cambridge, MA: Harvard UP, 1927–30, reprinted 1946–1948).

R. Morgan, *The Nature of New Testament Theology* (London/Naperville, IL: SCM/Allenson, 1973).

W. G. Most, 'A biblical theology of redemption in a covenant framework', *CBQ* 29 (1967), pp. 1–19.

C. F. D. Moule, 'The New Testament and moral decisions', *ExpT* 74 (1962–3), pp. 370–373.

— 'Fulfilment-words in the New Testament', *NTS* 14 (1967–8), pp. 293–320.

S. Mowinckel, *He That Cometh* (ET Oxford: Blackwell, 1956).

— *The Old Testament as Word of God* (ET Nashville: Abingdon, 1959/ Oxford: Blackwell, 1960).

— *The Psalms in Israel's Worship* (ET Oxford: Blackwell, 1962/Nashville: Abingdon, 1963).

H. Müller, 'Der rabbinische Qal-Wachomer-Schluss in paulinischer Typologie: zur Adam-Christus-Typologie in Rm 5', *ZNW* 58 (1967), pp. 73–92.

J. Munck, *Paul and the Salvation of Mankind* (ET London/Richmond: SCM/John Knox, 1959).

R. E. Murphy, 'The interpretation of Old Testament wisdom literature', *Int*

23 (1969), pp. 289–301.

J. Murray, *Principles of Conduct* (Grand Rapids/London: Eerdmans/Tyndale, 1957).

J. Neusner, *Between Time and Eternity: The Essentials of Judaism* (Encino, CA: Dickenson, 1975).

— (ed.), *Understanding Jewish Theology* (New York: Ktav, 1973).

R. C. Newman, 'The Council of Jamnia and the Old Testament canon', *WTJ* 38 (1975–6), pp. 319–349.

D. Newton-De Molina (ed.), *On Literary Intention* (Edinburgh: UP, 1976).

H. R. Niebuhr, *Christ and Culture* (New York: Harper, 1951/London: Faber, 1952).

E. Nielsen, ' "Weil Jahwe unser Gott ein Jahwe ist" (Dtn 6, 4f.)', *Beiträge zur alttestamentlichen Theologie* (W. Zimmerli volume, ed. H. Donner and others; Göttingen: Vandenhoeck, 1977), pp. 288–301.

V. Nikiprowetzky, *Le commentaire de l'écriture chez Philon d'Alexandrie* (Leiden: Brill, 1977).

D. E. Nineham, 'Eye-witness testimony and the gospel tradition', *JTS* 9 (1958), pp. 13–25, 243–252, and 11 (1960), pp. 253–264 = Nineham, *Explorations in Theology* 1 (London: SCM, 1977), pp. 24–60, 189–194.

— *The Use of the Bible in Modern Theology* (Manchester: John Rylands Library, 1969) = *BJRL* 52 (1969–70), pp. 178–199 = Nineham, *Explorations in Theology* 1, pp. 92–111, 196–197.

*— *The Use and Abuse of the Bible* (London/New York: Macmillan/Barnes and Noble, 1976).

M. Noth, 'The "re-presentation" of the Old Testament in proclamation', in *Westermann, pp. 76–88 = *Int* 15 (1961), pp. 50–60.

*— 'The laws in the Pentateuch: their assumptions and meaning' and 'The understanding of history in Old Testament apocalyptic', in *The Laws in the Pentateuch and other studies* (ET Edinburgh/Philadelphia: Oliver and Boyd/Fortress, 1966), pp. 1–107 and 194–214.

— *A History of Pentateuchal Traditions* (ET Englewood Cliffs, NJ: Prentice-Hall, 1972).

O. M. T. O'Donovan, 'The possibility of a biblical ethic', *TSFB* 67 (1973), pp. 15–23.

— 'Old Testament ethics and moral change' (unpublished paper, 1974).

— *In Pursuit of a Christian View of War* (Bramcote, Notts: Grove, 1977).

— 'Towards an interpretation of biblical ethics', *TynB* 27 (1976), pp. 54–78.

S. M. Ogden, 'What sense does it make to say, "God acts in history"?', *JR* 43 (1963), pp. 1–19 = *The Reality of God and other essays* (New York: Harper, 1966/London: SCM, 1967), pp. 164–187.

T. W. Ogletree, *Christian Faith and History* (Nashville: Abingdon, 1965).

Orthodox Church Interorthodox Commission, *Towards the Great Council* (ET London: SPCK, 1972).

E. Osswald, 'Zur Hermeneutik des Habakuk-Kommentars', *ZAW* 68 (1956), pp. 243–256.

177

— 'Theologie des Alten Testaments – eine bleibende Aufgabe alttestamentlicher Wissenschaft', *ThL* 99 (1974), columns 641–658.

E. Otto, 'Erwägungen zu den Prolegomena einer Theologie des Alten Testaments', *Kairos* 19 (1977), pp. 53–72.

T. W. Overholt, 'Jeremiah and the nature of the prophetic process', in *Scripture in History and Theology* (J. C. Rylaarsdam volume, ed. A. L. Merrill and T. W. Overholt; Pittsburgh: Pickwick, 1977), pp. 129–150.

H. P. Owen, 'Some philosophical problems in Christian ethics', *Theology* 76 (1973), pp. 15–21.

J. I. Packer, *Our Lord's Understanding of the Law of God* (London: Westminster Chapel, 1962).

W. Pannenberg, 'The revelation of God in Jesus of Nazareth', and 'Response to the discussion' in *Theology as History* (ed. J. M. Robinson and J. B. Cobb; New York: Harper, 1967), pp. 101–133 and 221–276.

*— *Basic Questions in Theology* 1 and 2 (ET London/Philadelphia: SCM/Fortress, 1970 and 1971); 3 (ET London: SCM, 1973) = *The Idea of God and Human Freedom* (ET Philadelphia: Fortress, 1973).

— 'Glaube und Wirklichkeit im Denken Gerhard von Rads', in *Gerhard von Rad: seine Bedeutung für die Theologie* (by H. W. Wolff and others; Munich: Kaiser, 1973), pp. 37–54, 57–58.

— *Theology and the Philosophy of Science* (ET London/Philadelphia: DLT/Westminster, 1976).

— (ed.) *Revelation as History* (ET New York/London: Macmillan/Collier-Macmillan, 1968; London: Sheed and Ward, 1969).

S. Paradise, 'Visions of the good society and the energy debate', *ATR* 61 (1979), pp. 106–117.

*D. Patte, *Early Jewish Hermeneutic in Palestine* (Missoula: SBL/Scholars, 1975).

J. B. Payne, *The Theology of the Older Testament* (Grand Rapids: Zondervan, 1962).

— 'The b'rith of Yahweh', *New Perspectives on the Old Testament* (ed. Payne; Waco, TX: Word, 1970), pp. 240–264.

L. Perlitt, *Bundestheologie im Alten Testament* (Neukirchen: Neukirchener Verlag, 1969).

N. Perrin, *Jesus and the Language of the Kingdom* (Philadelphia/London: Fortress/SCM, 1976).

T. Peters, 'The use of analogy in historical method', *CBQ* 35 (1973), pp. 475–482.

R. H. Pfeiffer, 'Canon of the OT', *IDB* 1, pp. 498–520.

A. C. J. Phillips, *Ancient Israel's Criminal Law* (Oxford: Blackwell, 1970).

J. P. M. van der Ploeg, 'Slavery in the Old Testament', *Congress Volume: Uppsala 1971* (*VTSupp* 22; 1972), pp. 72–87.

N. W. Porteous, 'Old Testament theology', in *The Old Testament and Modern Study* (ed. H. H. Rowley; Oxford/New York: Clarendon/OUP, 1951), pp. 311–345.

— 'The present state of Old Testament theology', *ExpT* 75 (1963–4), pp. 70–74.

*— *Living the Mystery* (Oxford: Blackwell, 1967).

— 'Old Testament and history', *ASTI* 8 (1970–1), pp. 21–77.

— 'Magnalia Dei', *Probleme biblischer Theologie* (G. von Rad volume, ed. H. W. Wolff; Munich: Kaiser, 1971), pp. 417–427.

R. H. Preston, 'Middle axioms in Christian social ethics', *Crucible* [10] (January 1971), pp. 9–15.

— *From the Bible to the Modern World: A Problem for Ecumenical Ethics* Manchester: John Rylands Library, 1976) = *BJRL* 59 (1976–7), pp. 164–187.

H. D. Preuss, *Jahweglaube und Zukunftserwartung* (Stuttgart: Kohlhammer, 1968).

*O. Procksch, *Theologie des Alten Testaments* (Gütersloh: Bertelsmann, 1950).

F. C. Prussner, 'The covenant of David and the problem of unity in Old Testament theology', *Transitions in Biblical Scholarship* (ed. J. C. Rylaarsdam; Chicago/London: Chicago UP, 1968), pp. 17–41.

G. von Rad, *Studies in Deuteronomy* (ET London/Chicago: SCM/Regnery, 1953).

— *Genesis* (ET London/Philadelphia: SCM/Westminster, 1961, ³1972).

— 'Typological interpretation of the Old Testament', in *Westermann, pp. 17–39 = *Int* 15 (1961), pp. 174–192.

*— *Old Testament Theology* (ET Edinburgh/New York: Oliver and Boyd/Harper, 1962 and 1965; reprinted London: SCM, 1975).

— 'Antwort auf Conzelmanns Fragen', *EvT* 24 (1964), pp. 388–394.

— *Wisdom in Israel* (ET London/Nashville: SCM/Abingdon, 1972).

— *Biblical Interpretations in Preaching* (Nashville: Abingdon, 1977).

K. Rahner, 'The Old Testament and Christian dogmatic theology', *Theological Investigations* 16 (ET London/New York: DLT/Seabury, 1979), pp. 177–190.

P. Ramsey, *Deeds and Rules in Christian Ethics* (*SJT* Occasional Papers 11, 1965, 1967/New York: Scribner's, 1967).

W. E. Rast, *Tradition History and the Old Testament* (Philadelphia: Fortress, 1972).

R. Rendtorff, 'Hermeneutik des Alten Testaments als Frage nach der Geschichte', *ZTK* 57 (1960), pp. 27–40 = Rendtorff, *Gesammelte Studien zum Alten Testament* (Munich: Kaiser, 1975), pp. 11–24.

— 'Geschichte und Überlieferung', *Studien zur Theologie des alttestamentlichen Überlieferungen* (G. von Rad volume, ed. R. Rendtorff and K. Koch; Neukirchen: Neukirchener Verlag 1961), pp. 81–94 = Rendtorff, *Gesammelte Studien*, pp. 25–38.

— 'The concept of revelation in ancient Israel', *Revelation as History* (ed. W. Pannenberg; ET New York/London: Macmillan/Collier-Macmillan 1968; London: Sheed and Ward, 1969), pp. 23–53.

J. Reumann, '*Oikonomia*-terms in Paul in comparison with Lucan *Heils-*

geschichte', *NTS* 13 (1966–7), pp. 147–167.

H. Graf Reventlow, 'Grundfragen der alttestamentlichen Theologie im Lichte der neueren deutschen Forschung', *TZ* 17 (1961), pp. 81–98.

— 'Die Eigenart des Jahweglaubens als geschichtliches und theologisches Problem' *KD* 20 (1974), pp. 199–217.

—'Basic problems in Old Testament theology', *JSOT* 11 (1979), pp. 2–22.

A. Richardson, 'Is the Old Testament the propaedeutic to Christian faith?', in *Anderson, pp. 36–48.

— *History: Sacred and Profane* (London/Philadelphia: SCM/Westminster, 1964).

P. Richardson, 'Spirit and letter: a foundation for hermeneutics', *EQ* 45 (1973), pp. 208–218.

P. Ricoeur, 'The narrative function', *Semeia* 13 (A. N. Wilder volume, Part 2, ed. W. A. Beardslee; Missoula: SBL, 1978), pp. 177–202.

H. Ridderbos, *Paul: An Outline of his Theology* (ET Grand Rapids: Eerdmans, 1975/London: SPCK, 1977).

A. Robert, 'Littéraires (Genres)' *DBS* 5 (1957), columns 405–421.

B. J. Roberts, *The Dead Sea Scrolls and the Old Testament scriptures* (Manchester: John Rylands Library, 1953) = *BJRL* 36 (1953–4), pp. 75–96.

J. J. M. Roberts, 'A Christian perspective on prophetic prediction', *Int* 33 (1979), pp. 240–253.

*H. W. Robinson, *Inspiration and Revelation in the Old Testament* (Oxford/New York: Clarendon/OUP, 1946).

J. M. Robinson, 'The historicality of biblical language', in *Anderson, pp. 124–158.

— 'Scripture and theological method: a protestant study in *sensus plenior*', *CBQ* 27 (1965), pp. 6–27.

J. M. Robinson and J. B. Cobb (ed.), *Theology as History* (New York: Harper, 1967).

C. S. Rodd, 'Shall not the judge of all the earth do what is just? (Gen. 18^{25})', *ExpT* 83 (1971–2), pp. 137–139.

J. Rogerson, *The Supernatural in the Old Testament* (Guildford: Lutterworth, 1976) = part one of B. Kaye and J. Rogerson, *Miracles and Mysteries in the Bible* (Philadelphia; Westminster, 1978).

J. M. Ross, 'The status of the apocrypha', *Theology* 82 (1979), pp. 183–191.

D. Rössler, *Gesetz und Geschichte* (Neukirchen: Neukirchener Verlag, 1966).

— 'Die Predigt über alttestamentliche Texte', in *Studien zur Theologie der alttestamentlichen Überlieferungen* (G. von Rad volume, ed. R. Rendtorff and K. Koch; Neukirchen: Neukirchener Verlag, 1961), pp. 153–162.

W. M. W. Roth, 'The wooing of Rebekah: a tradition-critical study of Genesis 24', *CBQ* 34 (1972), pp. 177–187.

H. H. Rowley, *The Re-discovery of the Old Testament* (London/Philadelphia: Clarke/Westminster, 1946).

*A. A. van Ruler, The Christian Church and the Old Testament (ET Grand Rapids: Eerdmans, 1971).

K. Runia, 'The interpretation of the Old Testament by the New Testament', TSFB 49 (1967), pp. 9–18.

J. C. Rylaarsdam, 'Jewish-Christian relationship: the two covenants and the dilemmas of Christology', Journal of Ecumenical Studies 9 (1972), pp. 249–270.

— 'The Song of Songs and biblical faith', Bib Res 10 (1965), pp. 7–18.

H. W. F. Saggs, The Encounter with the Divine in Mesopotamia and Israel (London: Athlone, 1978).

A. J. Saldarini, 'Apocalyptic and rabbinic literature', CBQ 37 (1975), pp. 348–358.

— 'The uses of apocalyptic in the Mishna and Tosepta', CBQ 39 (1977), pp. 396–409.

*E. P. Sanders, Paul and Palestinian Judaism (Philadelphia/London: Fortress/SCM, 1977).

J. A. Sanders, 'Habakkuk in Qumran, Paul, and the Old Testament', JR 39 (1959), pp. 232–244.

*— Torah and Canon (Philadelphia: Fortress, 1972).

— 'The ethic of election in Luke's Great Banquet Parable', Essays in Old Testament Ethics (J. P. Hyatt volume, ed. J. L. Crenshaw and J. T. Willis; New York: Ktav, 1974), pp. 245–271.

— 'From Isaiah 61 to Luke 4', Christianity, Judaism and other Greco-Roman Cults (M. Smith volume, ed. J. Neusner; Leiden: Brill, 1975), Part 3, pp. 75–106.

— 'Torah and Christ' Int 29 (1975), pp. 372–390.

— 'Adaptable for life: the nature and function of canon', Magnalia Dei (G. E. Wright volume, ed. F. M. Cross and others; Garden City, NY: Doubleday, 1976), pp. 531–560.

— 'Text and canon: concepts and method', JBL 98 (1979), pp. 5–29.

— 'Hermeneutics in true and false prophecy', in *Coats and Long, pp. 21–41.

— 'Hermeneutics', IDBS pp. 402–407.

J. T. Sanders, Ethics in the New Testament (Philadelphia/London: Fortress/SCM, 1975).

S. Sandmel, 'The haggada within scripture', JBL 80 (1961), pp. 105–122 = Sandmel (ed.), Old Testament Issues (New York/London: Harper/SCM, 1969), pp. 94–118 = Sandmel, Two Living Traditions (Detroit: Wayne State UP, 1972), pp. 316–334.

J. F. A. Sawyer, From Moses to Patmos (London: SPCK, 1977).

P. Schäfer, 'Die sogenannte Synode von Jabne: zur Trennung von Juden und Christen im ersten/zweiten Jh. n. Chr.', Judaica 31 (1975), pp. 54–64, 116–124 = Schäfer, Studien zur Geschichte und Theologie des Rabbinischen Judentums (Leiden: Brill, 1978), pp. 45–64.

H. H. Schmid, 'Schöpfung, Gerechtigkeit und Heil: "Schöpfungstheologie" als Gesamthorizont biblischer Theologie', ZTK 70 (1973), pp. 1–19.

181

L. Schmidt, 'Die Einheit zwischen Altem und Neuem Testament in Streit zwischen Friedrich Baumgärtel und Gerhard von Rad', *EvT* 35 (1975), pp. 119–139.

W. H. Schmidt, *Das erste Gebot: seine Bedeutung für das Alte Testament* (Munich: Kaiser, 1969).

G. Scholem, 'Revelation and tradition as religious categories in Judaism', ET in *The Messianic Idea in Judaism and other essays on Jewish Spirituality* (New York: Schocken, 1971), pp. 282–303, 363.

K. Schwarzwäller, 'Das Verhältnis Altes Testament – Neues Testament im Lichte der gegenwärtigen Bestimmungen', *EvT* 29 (1969), pp. 281–307.

H. Seebass, 'Der Beitrag des Alten Testaments zum Entwurf einer biblischen Theologie', *WD* 8 (1965), pp. 20–49.

— 'Zur Ermöglichung biblischer Theologie', *EvT* 37 (1977), pp. 591–600.

I. L. Seeligmann, 'Voraussetzungen der Midraschexegese', *Congress Volume Copenhagen 1953* (*VTSupp* 1, 1953), pp. 150–181.

— 'Menschliches Heldentum und göttliche Hilfe', *TZ* 19 (1963), pp. 385–411.

M. Sekine, 'Vom Verstehen der Heilsgeschichte: das Grundproblem der alttestament lichen Theologie', *ZAW* 75 (1963), pp. 145–154.

*E. Sellin, *Alttestamentliche Theologie auf religionsgeschichtlicher Grundlage* (Leipzig: Quelle und Meyer, 1933).

H. M. Shires, *Finding the Old Testament in the New* (Philadelphia: Westminster, 1974).

G. Siegwalt, 'Biblische Theologie als Begriff und Vollzug', *KD* 25 (1979), pp. 254–272.

L. H. Silberman, 'Unriddling the riddle: a study in the structure and language of the Habakkuk pesher (1 Q p Hab.)', *RQ* 3 (1961–2), pp. 323–364.

C. F. Sleeper, 'Language and ethics in biblical interpretation', *JR* 48 (1968), pp. 288–310.

— 'Ethics as a context for biblical interpretation', *Int* 22 (1968), pp. 443–460.

E. Slomovic, 'Toward an understanding of the exegesis in the Dead Sea Scrolls', *RQ* 7 (1969–71), pp. 3–15.

*J. D. Smart, *The Strange Silence of the Bible in the Church* (Philadelphia/London: Westminster/SCM, 1970).

R. Smend, *Elemente alttestamentlichen Geschichtsdenkens* (Zürich: EVZ, 1968).

— *Die Mitte des Alten Testaments* (Zürich: EVZ, 1970).

— 'Zur Frage der altisraelitischen Amphiktyonie', *EvT* 31 (1971), pp. 623–630.

— 'Tradition and history: a complex relation', in *D. A. Knight, pp. 49–68.

D. M. Smith, 'The use of the Old Testament in the New', *The Use of the Old Testament in the New and other essays* (W. F. Stinespring volume, ed. J. M. Efird; Durham, NC: Duke UP, 1972), pp. 3–65.

N. H. Søe, 'The three "uses" of the law', in *Norm and Context in Christian Ethics* (ed. G. H. Outka and P. Ramsey; New York: Scribner's, 1968/London: SCM, 1969), pp. 297–322.

J. A. Soggin, 'Alttestamentliche Glaubenszeugnisse und geschichtliche Wirklichkeit', *TZ* 17 (1961), pp. 385–398.

— 'Geschichte, Histoire, und Heilsgeschichte im Alten Testament', *ThL* 89 (1964), columns 721–736.

F. Sontag, 'Is God really in history?', *RelS* 15 (1979), pp. 379–390.

S. G. Sowers, *The Hermeneutics of Philo and Hebrews* (Richmond/Zürich: John Knox/EVZ, 1965).

*D. G. Spriggs, *Two Old Testament Theologies* (London/Naperville, IL: SCM/Allenson, 1971).

J. J. Stamm and M. E. Andrew, *The Ten Commandments in Recent Research* (ET London/Naperville, IL: SCM/Allenson, 1967).

E. Stauffer, *New Testament Theology* (ET London/New York: SCM/Macmillan, 1955).

O. H. Steck, 'Alttestamentliche Impulse für eine Theologie der Natur', *TZ* 34 (1978), pp. 202–211.

G. Steiner, *After Babel: Aspects of Language and Translation* (London/New York: OUP, 1975).

J. H. Stek, 'Biblical typology yesterday and today', *CTJ* 5 (1970), pp. 133–162.

G. Stemberger, 'Die sogenannte "Synode von Jabne" und das frühe Christentum', *Kairos* 19 (1977), pp. 14–21.

K. Stendahl, 'Biblical theology, Contemporary', *IDB* 1, pp. 418–432.

— *The School of St. Matthew and its Use of the Old Testament* (Uppsala: Gleerup, 1954; Lund/Philadelphia: Gleerup/Fortress, ²1968).

— 'The apostle Paul and the introspective conscience of the west', ET *HTR* 56 (1963), pp. 199–215.

— 'Method in the study of biblical theology', *The Bible in Modern Scholarship* (ed. J. P. Hyatt; Nashville: Abingdon, 1965/London: Carey Kingsgate, 1966), pp. 196–209.

H. J. Stoebe, 'Überlegungen zur Theologie des Alten Testaments', *Gottes Wort und Gottes Land* (H. W. Hertzberg volume, ed. H. Graf Reventlow; Göttingen: Vandenhoeck, 1965), pp. 200–220.

M. E. Stone, 'Pseudepigrapha', *IDBS*, pp. 710–712.

J. R. W. Stott, *Christian Mission in the Modern World* (London/Downers Grove, IL: CPAS/IVP, 1975).

P. Stuhlmacher, 'Das Bekenntnis zur Auferwerkung Jesu von den Toten und die biblische Theologie', *ZTK* 70 (1973), pp. 365–403 = Stuhlmacher, *Schriftauslegung auf dem Wege zur biblischen Theologie* (Göttingen: Vandenhoeck, 1975), pp. 128–166.

— 'Das Gesetz als Thema biblischer Theologie', *ZTK* 75 (1978), pp. 251–280.

A. C. Sundberg, 'The Old Testament of the early church', *HTR* 51 (1958), pp. 205–226.

*— The Old Testament of the Early Church (Cambridge, MA/London: Harvard UP/OUP, 1964).

— 'The Protestant Old Testament canon: should it be re-examined?', CBQ 28 (1966), pp. 194–203 = Old Testament Issues (ed. S. Sandmel; New York/London: Harper/SCM, 1969), pp. 252–265.

— 'The "Old Testament": a Christian canon', CBQ 30 (1968), pp. 143–155 = *Leiman, pp. 99–111.

— 'The Bible canon and the Christian doctrine of inspiration', Int 29 (1975), pp. 352–371.

S. Talmon, 'DSIa as a witness to ancient exegesis of the Book of Isaiah', ASTI 1 (1962), pp. 62–72 = Qumran and the History of the Biblical Text (ed. F. M. Cross and S. Talmon; Cambridge, MA/London: Harvard UP, 1975), pp. 116–126.

*S. Terrien, The Elusive Presence: Toward a New Biblical Theology (San Francisco: Harper, 1978).

H. Thielicke, Theological Ethics 1 and 2 (ET Philadelphia: Fortress, 1966– /London: Black, 1968–   ; reprinted Grand Rapids: Eerdmans, 1979).

Thomas Aquinas, Summa Theologiae (ET London/New York: Eyre & Spottiswoode/McGraw-Hill, 1964–   ).

R. J. Thompson, Moses and the Law in a Century of Criticism since Graf (VTSupp 19; 1970).

T. L. Thompson, The Historicity of the Patriarchal Narratives (BZAW 133; Berlin/New York: De Gruyter, 1974).

E. Tov, 'Septuagint: Contribution to OT scholarship', IDBS, pp. 807–811.

J. T. Townsend, 'Rabbinic sources', in The Study of Judaism: Bibliographical Essays (J. Neusner and others; New York: Ktav, 1972), pp. 35–80.

G. M. Tucker, 'Prophetic superscriptions and the growth of a canon', in *Coats and Long, pp. 56–70.

E. F. Tupper, The Theology of Wolfhart Pannenberg (Philadelphia: Westminster, 1973/London: SCM, 1974).

P. W. Turner, 'Human nature and goodness', ATR 61 (1979), pp. 38–53.

R. de Vaux, 'A propos de la théologie biblique', ZAW 68 (1956), pp. 225–227.

— 'Is it possible to write a "Theology of the Old Testament"?', The Bible and the Ancient Near East (ET Garden City, NY: Doubleday, 1971/ London: DLT, 1972), pp. 49–62.

B. Vawter, 'The fuller sense: some considerations', CBQ 26 (1964), pp. 85–96.

— 'Intimations of immortality and the Old Testament', JBL 91 (1972), pp. 158–171.

— 'Prophecy and redaction', No Famine in the Land (J. L. McKenzie volume, ed. J. W. Flanagan and A. W. Robinson; Missoula: Scholars, 1975), pp. 127–139.

A. Verhey, 'The use of Scripture in ethics', Religious Studies Review 4 (1978), pp. 28–39.

P. A. Verhoef, 'The relationship between the Old and the New Testaments',

New Perspectives on the Old Testament (ed. J. B. Payne; Waco, TX: Word, 1970), pp. 280–303.

G. Vermes, *Scripture and Tradition in Judaism: Haggadic Studies* (Leiden: Brill, 1961, ²1973).

— 'The Qumran interpretation of scripture in its historical setting', *ALUOS* 6 (1969), pp. 85–97 = Vermes, *Post-Biblical Jewish Studies* (Leiden: Brill, 1975), pp. 37–49.

— 'Bible and midrash: early Old Testament exegesis', *CHB* 1, pp. 199–231, 592 = Vermes, *Post-Biblical Jewish Studies*, pp. 59–91.

— 'Dead Sea Scrolls' and 'Interpretation, History of: At Qumran and in the Targums', *IDBS*, pp. 210–219 and 438–443.

D. O. Via, *The Parables* (Philadelphia: Fortress, 1967).

— *Kerygma and Comedy in the New Testament* (Philadelphia: Fortress, 1975).

W. Vischer, *Das Christuszeugnis des Alten Testaments*, I: *Das Gesetz* (Munich: Kaiser, 1934) and II, 1 *Die früheren Propheten* (Zollikon-Zürich: Evangelischer Verlag, 1942).

— 'The book of Esther', ET *EQ* 11 (1939), pp. 3–21.

*— *The Witness of the Old Testament to Christ*, 1: *The Pentateuch* (ET London: Lutterworth, 1949).

— 'La méthode de l'exégèse biblique', *RTP* III. 10 (1960), pp. 109–123.

— 'Everywhere the Scripture is about Christ alone', in *Anderson, pp. 90–101.

*E. Voegelin, *Order and History*, 1: *Israel and Revelation* (Baton Rouge: Louisiana State UP, 1956).

— 'History and gnosis', in *Anderson, pp. 64–89.

J. Vollmer, *Geschichtliche Rückblicke und Motive in der Prophetie des Amos, Hosea und Jesaja* (*BZAW* 119; Berlin: De Gruyter, 1971).

G. Vos, *Biblical Theology* (Grand Rapids: Eerdmans, 1948; reprinted Edinburgh: Banner of Truth, 1975).

*T. C. Vriezen, *An Outline of Old Testament Theology* (ET Oxford/Newton, MA: Blackwell/Branford, 1958, ²1970).

S. Wagner, ' "Biblische Theologien" und "Biblische Theologie" ', *ThL* 103 (1978), columns 785–798.

G. Wallis, 'Psalm 8 und die ethische Fragestellung der modernen Naturwissenschaft', *TZ* 34 (1978), pp. 193–201.

P. S. Watson, 'The nature and function of biblical theology', *ExpT* 73 (1961–2), pp. 195–200.

M. Weinfeld, '*Bᶜrît* – covenant vs. obligation', *Biblica* 56 (1975), pp. 120–128.

— '*bᶜrîth*', *TDOT* 2, pp. 253–279.

J. Weingreen, *From Bible to Mishna* (Manchester: UP, 1976).

— 'Interpretation, History of: Within the OT', *IDBS*, pp. 436–438.

M. Weippert, *The Settlement of the Israelite Tribes in Palestine* (ET London/ Naperville, IL: SCM/Allenson, 1971).

— 'Fragen des israelitischen Geschichtsbewusstseins', *VT* 23 (1973),

pp. 415–442.

D. Wenham, 'Jesus and the law: an exegesis on Matthew 5:17–20', *Themelios* 4 (1979), pp. 92–96.

G. J. Wenham, 'The ordination of women: Why is it so divisive?', *Churchman* 92 (1978), pp. 310–319.

J. W. Wenham, *Christ and the Bible* (London/Downers Grove, IL: Tyndale/IVP, 1972).

P. Wernberg-Møller, 'Some reflections on the biblical material in the Manual of Discipline', *ST* 9 (1955), pp. 40–66.

— 'Is there an Old Testament theology?', *HJ* 59 (1960–1), pp. 21–29.

S. Westerholm, *Jesus and Scribal Authority* (Lund: Gleerup, 1978).

C. Westermann, *A Thousand Years and a Day* (ET Philadelphia/London: Fortress/SCM, 1962).

*— (ed.), *Essays on Old Testament Hermeneutics* (ET Richmond: John Knox, 1963) =*Essays on Old Testament Interpretation* (ET London: SCM, 1963).

— 'Remarks on the theses of Bultmann and Baumgärtel', in *Westermann, pp. 123–133.

— *Handbook to the Old Testament* (ET Minneapolis: Augsburg, 1967/ London: SPCK, 1969).

— *The Old Testament and Jesus Christ* (ET Minneapolis: Augsburg, 1970).

— 'Zu zwei Theologien des Alten Testaments', *EvT* 34 (1974), pp. 96–112.

— *Genesis: I. Teilband: Genesis 1–11* (*BKAT*; 1974).

— *Blessing in the Bible and in the Life of the Church* (ET Philadelphia: Fortress, 1978).

— *What Does the Old Testament Say about God?* (ET London/Atlanta: SPCK/John Knox, 1979).

H. Wildberger, 'Auf dem Wege zu einer biblischen Theologie', *EvT* 19 (1959), pp. 70–90.

M. Wiles, 'In what sense is Christianity a "historical" religion?', *Theology* 81 (1978), pp. 4–14 = Wiles, *Explorations in Theology* 4 (London: SCM, 1979), pp. 53–65, 107.

T. Willi, *Die Chronik als Auslegung* (Göttingen: Vandenhoeck, 1972).

R. Williamson, *Philo and the Epistle to the Hebrews* (Leiden: Brill, 1970).

I. Willi-Plein, *Verformen der Schriftexegese innerhalb des Alten Testaments* (*BZAW* 123; Berlin/New York: De Gruyter, 1971).

— 'Das Geheimnis der Apokalyptik', *VT* 27 (1977), pp. 62–81.

W. K. Wimsatt and M. C. Beardsley, 'The intentional fallacy', *Sewanee Review* 54 (1946), pp. 468–488 = Wimsatt and Beardsley, *The Verbal Icon* (Lexington, KY: University of Kentucky, 1954), pp. 3–18 = D. Newton-De Molina (ed.), *On Literary Intention* (Edinburgh: UP, 1976), pp. 1–13.

H. W. Wolff, 'Der grosse Jesreeltag', *EvT* 12 (1952–3), pp. 78–104.

— 'The hermeneutics of the Old Testament', in *Westermann, pp. 160–199 = *Int* 15 (1961) pp. 439–472.

— and others, *Gerhard von Rad: seine Bedeutung für die Theologie* (Mun-

ich: Kaiser, 1973).
— *The Old Testament: A Guide to its Writings* (ET Philadelphia: Fortress, 1973/London: SPCK, 1974).
— *Anthropology of the Old Testament* (ET London/Philadelphia: SCM/Fortress, 1974).
— *Hosea* (ET Philadelphia: Fortress, 1974).
— *Joel and Amos* (ET Philadelphia: Fortress, 1977).
A. S. van der Woude, 'Micah in dispute with the pseudo-prophets', *VT* 19 (1969), pp. 244–260.
W. Wrede, 'The task and methods of "New Testament theology" ', *The Nature of New Testament Theology* (ET ed. R. Morgan; London/Naperville, IL: SCM/Allenson, 1973), pp. 68–116, 182–193.
A. G. Wright, *The Literary Genre Midrash* (Staten Island: Alba House, 1967) = *CBQ* 28 (1966), pp. 105–138, 417–457.
C. J. H. Wright, 'Ethics and the Old Testament', *Third Way* 1.9–11 (1977) = *What Does the Lord Require: Reflections on the Old Testament Contribution to Christian Ethics* (Nottingham: Shaftesbury Project, 1978).
D. F. Wright, 'The fulfilment of the law', *Christian Graduate* 29 (1976), pp. 99–105.
G. E. Wright, *God Who Acts: Biblical Theology as Recital* (London/Chicago: SCM/Regnery, 1952).
— 'History and reality', in *Anderson, pp. 176–199.
— 'Reflections concerning Old Testament theology', *Studia Biblica et Semitica* (T. C. Vriezen volume, ed. W. C. van Unnik and A. S. van der Woude; Wageningen: Veenman, 1966), pp. 376–388.
*— *The Old Testament and Theology* (New York: Harper, 1969).
— 'Historical knowledge and revelation', *Translating and Understanding the Old Testament* (H. G. May volume, ed. H. T. Frank and W. L. Reed; Nashville: Abingdon, 1970), pp. 279–303.
— and R. H. Fuller, *The Book of the Acts of God* (Garden City, NY: Doubleday, 1957, revised 1960/London: Duckworth, 1960).
E. Würthwein, 'Zur Theologie des Alten Testaments', *TR* 36 (1971), pp. 185–208.
N. Wyatt, 'The Old Testament historiography of the exilic period', *ST* 33 (1979), pp. 45–67.
— 'The development of the tradition in Exodus 3', *ZAW* 91 (1979), pp. 437–442.
A. D. York, 'The dating of targumic literature', *JSJ* 5 (1974), pp. 49–62.
W. Zimmerli, 'Das Gesetz im Alten Testament', *ThL* 85 (1960), columns 481–498 = *Gottes Offenbarung* (see below), pp. 249–276.
— 'Le nouvel "exode" dans le message des deux grands prophètes de l'exil', *Maqqēl Shâqēdh: La branche d'amandier* (W. Vischer volume, ed. D. Lys; Montpellier: Causse, Graille, Castelnau, 1960), pp. 216–227.
— ' "Offenbarung" im Alten Testament', *EvT* 22 (1962), pp. 15–31.
— *Gottes Offenbarung: Gesammelte Aufsätze* (Munich: Kaiser, 1963).
— 'Gerhard von Rad, *Theologie des Alten Testaments*', *VT* 13 (1963),

pp. 100–111.
— 'The place and limit of the wisdom in the framework of the Old Testament theology', ET *SJT* 17 (1964), pp. 146–158.
— 'Promise and fulfillment', in *Westermann, pp. 89–122 = *Int* 15 (1961), pp. 310–338.
— *The Law and the Prophets* (ET Oxford: Blackwell, 1965/New York: Harper, 1967).
— *Man and His Hope in the Old Testament* (ET London/Naperville, IL: SCM/Allenson, 1971).
— 'Alttestamentliche Traditionsgeschichte und Theologie', *Probleme biblischer Theologie* (G. von Rad volume, ed. H. W. Wolff; Munich: Kaiser, 1971), pp. 632–647 = Zimmerli, *Studien zur alttestamentlichen Theologie und Prophetie: Gesammelte Aufsätze* II (Munich: Kaiser, 1974), pp. 9–26.
— 'Erwägungen zur Gestalt einer alttestamentlichen Theologie', *ThL* 98 (1973), columns 81–98 = Zimmerli, *Studien zur alttestamentlichen Theologie und Prophetie*, pp. 27–54.
— 'Zum Problem der "Mitte des Alten Testamentes" ', *EvT* 35 (1975), pp. 97–118.
— *The Old Testament and the World* (ET London/Atlanta: SPCK/John Knox, 1976).
— 'Prophetic proclamation and reinterpretation', in *D. A. Knight, pp. 69–100.
— 'Wahrheit und Geschichte in der alttestamentlichen Schriftprophetie', *Congress Volume: Göttingen 1977* (*VTSupp* 29; 1978), pp. 1–15.
*— *Old Testament Theology in Outline* (ET Atlanta/Edinburgh; John Knox/Clark, 1978).

1989 Postscript

The decade since the first edition of this survey was completed has seen the publication of a vast number of further books on its themes, many of which continue lines of thought familiar from the 1970s; with regard to each chapter, I have noted in this Postscript some of these more recent works which continue discussion along lines already marked out. The 1970s were also a period in which fundamental questions were raised about the historical–critical paradigm which had governed OT study for a century, and it was asked what discipline might replace history as handmaid for theology, rather as history once replaced philosophy.[1] The 1980s have seen three such handmaids courted. One is sociology, noted in section 2 below. Another is literary study, a major trend considered at greater length in section 3. A third is study of the canonical form of the OT itself, noted in section 5 though also perhaps underlying the recurrent theme in recent OT theology described in section 1.[2]

In this Postscript, the works marked † appear in the supplementary bibliography on pages 200 to 204; other works referred to appear in the main bibliography on pages 156–188 above.

1. The Old Testament as a faith

A recurring theme in a number of theologies and other recent works is the study of polarities within OT faith. Taken together these polarities comprise a complex series of overlapping antitheses which

---

[1] Cf. Nineham, 'A partner for Cinderella', What About the New Testament? (C. F. Evans Festschrift, ed. M. Hooker and C. Hickling; London: SCM, 1975), pp. 143–154; = Explorations in Theology 1, pp. 134–144.

[2] For further survey see †Hasel; †Reventlow; and on OT theology in particular, †Birch and others; †Hayes/Prussner; †Oeming; †Terrien.

189

might form a focus, or even *the* focus, of OT faith, such as the visionary and the pragmatic, form and reform, the teleological and the cosmic, deliverance and blessing, creation and redemption, wisdom and salvation history, praise and lament, structure legitimation and the embrace of pain.[3] Of the recent theologies, *Terrien and †Westermann reflect this development, as does †Martens' remarkable synthesis based on the themes of deliverance, community, knowledge of God, and life or land.[4] Investigation of these polarities has been accompanied by renewed interest in whichever of the poles seems to have been lost sight of; many of these studies concern themselves with aspects of the theological significance of creation, a theme neglected under the influence of the Eichrodt/von Rad axis.[5]

One of the underlying concerns of these works is a desire to do greater justice to the complexity of thought represented in the OT itself, and to lessen the extent to which Christian study of the OT gives excessive or exclusive attention to those themes which are prominent in the NT, or slants the OT so as to make it lead into the NT. In this connection it is also significant that †Levenson's *Sinai and Judah* is the first Jewish theology of the Hebrew Bible (see also †Tsevat). A related stimulus to Christian concern to do justice to the OT itself is development in Jewish-Christian dialogue.[6]

2. The Old Testament as a way of life

On the broad way in which narrative, wisdom, and psalmic material, as well as legal and prophetic, can shape the moral life and speak to ethical issues, see †Aukerman and †Tambasco (in relation to the nuclear threat); †Bauckham (in relation to politics); and

---

[3] *E.g.* *Terrien; †Brueggemann; †Goldingay, pp. 191–239 (also pp. 122–127 on the 'canon within the canon'); †P. D. Hanson; †Knierim; †Levenson; †Westermann.

[4] For other theologies, see †Childs, †De Vries, and the substantial OT section in †Kraus; also studies of OT themes by †Dumbrell and †McComiskey (on the covenant) and by †Dyrness; and books on preaching the OT by †Gowan and †Wolff. †Hesse maintains the stress on discontinuity between the Testaments.

[5] See †Reventlow, *Problems of OT Theology*, pp. 134–186; †Steck; and the *Themes* studied by †Lohfink. Note also †Fretheim on the nature of God, and †Seebass.

[6] See †Fuchs-Kreimer; also †Blenkinsopp; †Schmid; †Reventlow's excursus on 'Israel and the Church', *Problems of Biblical Theology*, pp. 64–132; and †Sanders' desire to replace 'Old Testament' by 'First Testament'.

†McEvenue. For further studies of law and related topics see †Patrick (on the characteristics of the lawcodes and their significance for Christians); †C. J. H. Wright (on their significance for social ethics); †Swartley (reflecting on the way scriptural material has been used on various sides of debates over the centuries); †Kaiser (surveying other aspects of scholarly study); †Countryman (a study of sex ethics which illustrates one form of looking for principles behind biblical prescriptions so that these can be translated for today); †Levenson (putting sharp questions to Christian emphasis on seeing law in the context of covenant).

In an important survey of modern study of the covenant, †Nicholson suggests that the significance of this notion is that it demystified or desacralized or relativized the human social order in the name of God's righteousness. Such a sociological account of the matter illustrates the way sociology is becoming an important ancillary discipline to OT interpretation, with particularly clear implications for the OT as a way of life.[7] More reductionistically Gottwald describes Yahwism as 'the function of communal egalitarianism', as 'a servomechanism to reinforce the social system', and as 'the symbolic expression of the Israelite socioeconomic revolution'.[8]

3. The Old Testament as the story of salvation

It is in connection with this approach to the OT that clearest developments are evident in the 1980s. In the critique of the notion of salvation history, one aspect related to the gap between the story which the OT tells and the history of Israel as scholars reconstructed it. The 1980s saw the flowering of an interest (already beginning to blossom in the 1970s) in the story itself, for its own sake, independently of its relationship to history.

Hans Frei's book *The Eclipse of Biblical Narrative* played an important role in the development of interest in the OT as story.[9] Frei argued that we are the heirs or victims of a change in ways of reading Scripture which began to come about in the eighteenth

[7] Cf. †Brueggemann's *Hope within History*, pp. 7–48, for a parallel approach to Exodus and Isaiah.
[8] †*Tribes of Yahweh*, pp. 692, 693, 700.
[9] See now the Frei Festschrift, ed. †G. Green.

century. Before then, as the writings of the Fathers and the Reformers reveal, people assumed that the narrative they were reading corresponded to events that we would have been able to witness if we had been present, and that the history through which we ourselves live is one with that history. Beginning two hundred years ago, scholars began to look for the *actual* events behind the narrated events, to see our world as essentially discontinuous from that world, and to incline to judge the narrative's presentation of its world by ours rather than the other way round. Frei's study pointed scholars once more towards the actual text of the OT, the story Israel told, as the proper subject for interpretation, rather than the events which lay behind the story. It is the story which is life-giving.

The past decade has thus seen a flourishing of interest in the nature of the OT story and in methods of interpretation appropriate to it. 'The literary approach' is too deceptively simple a phrase to describe these; the OT has already been the beneficiary or the prey of a sequence of literary approaches, following developments in literary studies itself. Since †M. H. Abrams it has become common to distinguish approaches to interpretation according to their focus: is it on the realities (*e.g.* historical or theological) which lie behind the text and which the text refers to, or on its authors and their 'intentions', or on the actual text itself, or on the reader? These foci are distinguished diagrammatically:

(2) external realities to which the work refers
(*e.g.* historical, theological)
|
(1) the work itself
/   \
(3) the author   (4) the reader

Traditional OT interpretation has focused on (2) and (3). The easiest and most clearly fruitful literary approach moves the focus to (1). It aims at a careful, 'close' reading of the story in its own right, one which seeks to follow its intrinsic concerns in terms of structure, plot, and character, as these are suggested by the patterns, images, and actual words present objectively in the form of the text itself. Such *formalism* has provided a suggestive way into books

192

such as Genesis, Judges, Ruth, 1 and 2 Samuel, Esther, and Jonah.[10]
Studying the stories in themselves rather than in the light of their
intention in some (purported) historical context can make for a
perceptible enriching of their interpretation. Our understanding of
Ruth and Jonah, for instance, is narrowed down when they are read
in the light of questions arising in the post-exilic period, when they
are supposed to have been written. When they are released from this
historical constraint, it is easier to perceive a broader range of
themes in them.

Formalist study includes among its concerns the text's structure.
In a more technical sense *structuralist* study is a distinguishable
formalist approach which concerns itself with structures or patterns
that lie underneath the surface of the text more than with the distinctive meaning of particular texts.[11] With this and with the further
approaches we shall consider, an approach to texts and a philosophy
or ideology are bound up together; they also have in common the
fact that discussion has focused more on the *theory* of interpretation
that they suggest than on its application to specific texts, and that
this discussion is commonly difficult to follow. I shall confine comment to the practical application of these theories.

Deconstructionist and *reader-response* approaches to interpretation
concern themselves in different ways with what the text leaves
unsaid, with ambiguities it leaves unresolved, or opennesses it manifests, or questions it raises. Traditional interpretation has difficulty
tolerating ambiguity; it assumes that the author aimed at clarity, and
it brings all the resources of historical and linguistic scholarship to
bear on the elucidating of the text's clear meaning. Deconstructionist and reader-response approaches presuppose that ambiguity may
be inherent in texts.

The story of Abraham, for instance, is much more sparing of
information on Abraham's own attitudes, feelings, and thinking

---

[10] For introduction focusing more on methods, see †Alter; †Bar-Efrat; †Barton,
Reading the OT; †Berlin; †Greidanus, pp. 188–227; †Licht; †Ryken; †T. R. Wright;
more on worked-out examples, see †Alter/Kermode; †Gros Louis; †Good; †Gunn;
†Long; †Webb. The term 'new criticism' is often used to describe this approach,
but it has ceased to be novel or to be the latest thing, and the more descriptive term
'formalism' (though it can be used more broadly) seems a better one.

[11] For introductions see †Armerding; †Barton, *Reading the* OT (esp. pp. 116–133
for OT examples); †Greenwood; †Jobling, vol. 1; †Longman; †McKnight, *Meaning in
Texts*.

than we usually notice (we assume attitudes of trust, for instance, even where these are unstated). A reader-response approach (moving the focus to (4) in the diagram) asks what this does to readers, or what they do with it, noting that precisely in its ambiguity at such points it can challenge readers regarding their own attitude – they have to 'fill in the blanks' in the story.[12] It is possible to allow that there are texts to which a reader-response approach is appropriate, because of their own nature, without implying that the sense of all texts is in principle indeterminate.[13]

But 'ambiguity is not always a result of insufficient evidence or material; in many instances it can be the result of too much evidence'.[14] Deconstructionism seeks to look beneath the surface of the construction the text may put on matters, or the construction interpreters put on the text, to the more complex questions and uncertainties which may lie beneath it and which it may be concealing. It notes the irresolvable ambiguities in the portraits of characters such as Saul or David (or God[15]) and prohibits simple readings of their stories. Deconstruction 'permits me to read [the Bible] on its own terms without having to force it into modes of meaning and interpretation that gloss over, harmonize, or remove its repetitions, contradictions, details, gaps, etc.'[16]

The application of formalist methods to the OT raises a number of questions. One arises from the paradox of the fact that a method of interpretation that claims to be objective and analytical can be so fruitful in enabling modern readers to be drawn into the text itself and addressed by it. Admittedly this is not always so; formalist study can seem to be a matter of dry word-count. And in having these two capacities, it parallels other methods of exegesis, and illustrates how exegetical method and hermeneutics are not always as separate in practice as they are in theory. Nor is this a development confined to the application of formalism to *biblical* material. Literary criticism

---

[12] See †Miscall, *Workings of OT Narrative.*

[13] See †Gunn, *JSOT* 39; *cf.* †McKnight's repeated aphorism 'readers make sense' (*e.g. The Bible and the Reader,* p. 133). For introduction to reader-response approaches, see †Detweiler, Semeia 31; Thiselton, in †Lundin; †Lategan/Vorster.

[14] †Miscall, *1 Samuel,* p. ix.

[15] See †T. R. Wright, *Theology and Literature,* pp. 62–66.

[16] †Miscall, *1 Samuel,* p. xxiv. For other examples of deconstructionist OT interpretation, see †Bal; †Elata-Alster and Salmon; †Fewell; †Jobling, vol. 2; and for the background, †Detweiler, Semeia 23.

itself is both a would-be objective, scientific affair, *and* an enterprise which hopes to discover and unveil truth about the world and about what it means to be human. A story creates a world before people's eyes and ears and invites them to recognize that they do or can live in that world. It is perhaps this concern which literature has in common with Scripture that in part makes methods of interpretation that are appropriate to the former also fruitful with regard to the latter.

At least we may note that when formalist critics say they are not concerned with truth in the world outside the text (objective truth) but only with truth in the terms of the text's own world, they only half mean it. Formalism in itself focuses on the meaning of texts rather than on their reference, though both the friends and the enemies of this approach are mistaken when they infer that this focus is incompatible with a concern that 'there is reality out there' to which the text refers. One reason for disquiet at the idea of treating the Bible in particular as literature is the conviction that it was not brought into existence merely (if at all) through an act of artistic creation or the desire to entertain. It was designed to convey information to people. But the same is often true of literature itself.[17]

In particular, to seek to understand OT stories in their own right leaves quite open the possibility that they need to have some historical reference in order to 'work' as stories. 'Transformative power is found not only in the Exodus event but also in the Exodus narrative.'[18] But would we be entitled to surrender to the power of the narrative if there is no event behind it? †Ramsey, asking 'If Jericho was not razed, is our faith in vain?', criticizes writers such as †Schaeffer who imply that historical study can and does verify faith in Yahweh. His own view is that the validity of the biblical story stems from its ability to make sense of our lives *rather than* its connection with historical events.[19] This seems to raise difficulties at

---

[17] For the disquiet, see *e.g.* †Barton and †Reed, *LT* 1 (1987), pp. 135–166. But contrast *e.g.* †T. R. Wright, pp. 20–40; †Green, pp. 79–96; Walhout in †Lundin; also †Patrick, *Rendering of God*, for the suggestion that precisely the literary approach, envisaging God as a character portrayed as taking a part in the OT drama, enables us to see how the reality of that God and of the events in which God is involved are compellingly presented so that we are drawn into believing in them.

[18] Brueggemann, †*Hope within History*, p. 8.

[19] Page 124; Ramsey follows V. Harvey (see chapter 3 above).

least as great as those he finds in Schaeffer, though there is force in his observation that the assertion of the essential significance of history may seem to die the death of a thousand qualifications when we consider how little we can certainly affirm *on purely historical grounds* about an event such as the fall of Jericho.[20]

Although OT narratives have literary features, most OT narratives also have historical concerns. They are not novels or short stories.[21] That makes historical approaches to interpretation also appropriate to them. The literary approaches themselves suggest no answer to the question of their relationship with historical study; it is only by systematically bracketing this question that they can concentrate on the one that is their particular concern, the actual meaning of the texts. Their focusing on this does not exclude their texts from referring to realities outside themselves; the study of that is simply not the particular aim of these approaches.

Another difficulty about a strictly formalist approach has been pressed by two powerful exponents of the 'close reading' of texts, †Kugel and †Sternberg. As the words used in any text derive part of their meaning from their historical context, so the form of the text gains part of its meaning from the conventions of the author's day; texts cannot be reckoned to contain within themselves everything that is necessary to their understanding. Apparent ambiguity in texts may often derive from our not sharing the conventions and assumptions that author and first readers shared. Interpreters need to be wary of imposing alien literary categories on ancient Near Eastern religious texts[22] – though in principle that is no more of a problem with literary approaches than with historical or theological ones, and †Miscall argues that a deconstructionist approach helps one to avoid reading the Bible as a modern Western text.[23]

---

[20] *Cf.* †Clements' comments on the submerging of historical concerns beneath religious ones in a way that makes it difficult for us to gain access to them.

[21] See †Sternberg's assertion (pp. 1–57) that OT narrative combines ideology, historiography, and aesthetics – it aims to inculcate a worldview and to relate history but uses the conventions of art to do so. *Cf.* †T. R. Wright, pp. 41–42; †Prickett; also †Barr, *Scope and Authority of the Bible*, p. vi, on the OT as story yet as still having a concern with history. †Oeming (*EvT* 44 [1984]) and †Green (pp. 79–96) discuss the way in which, paradoxically, fiction can sometimes be a particularly effective way of presenting historical truth about the past. On Israelite historiography, see now †Van Seters.

[22] The issue is illustrated well in *Tragedy and Comedy in the Bible* (†Exum).

[23] *The Workings of* OT *Narrative*, p. 143.

The most recent literary approach to interpretation, *speech act theory*,[24] thus asks again what was the author trying to do in writing this text? – 'trying to *do*' in that speech is not just a matter of propositional content but of 'illocutionary force'; it is designed to effect something. But *what* the text was designed to do may not be overt in the text itself. We are back at (3) in the diagram.

Another observation we might make on the paradoxical fact that literary study often manages to be fruitful in engaging the readers' own horizons, even when engaged in a quite objectivist or positivist approach to texts, is that literary study, while sophisticated in its exegetical method, is unreflective over the hermeneutical questions involved in the move between text and today (†Poland). How is it that texts in their foreignness are to be grasped by people and are to grasp people? Literary approaches need to be more consciously combined with hermeneutical ones.

Liberation hermeneutics, and feminist hermeneutics in particular, attempt this (both can be seen as instances of reader-response approaches to the OT), using their particular initial horizons or pre-understandings as their ways in to the text's concerns. The past decade has been particularly fruitful in feminist interpretation, especially with regard to narrative.[25] Feminist and political liberationist interpretation (in its variety: there is not just one form[26]) illustrates the way in which readers with particular backgrounds are able to perceive, articulate, and respond to aspects of texts which readers with other backgrounds may miss and be missed by, even though they also illustrate how the same readers (like all readers) are also by virtue of their background liable to misread the text in other respects.

[24] For introduction, see †H. C. White (esp. the article on Gn. 2 – 3 by Lanser); also Thiselton and Walhout in †Lundin.

[25] See *e.g.* (mainly for discussion) †Fewell; †Russell; †Schüssler Fiorenza; †Trible (ed.); †Yarbro Collins; (for worked-out examples) †Bal; †Tolbert; †Trible. See †Gottwald (ed.); †van Iersel and Weiler for examples of liberationist interpretation (also †Gutiérrez, *On Job*, though not a narrative work; and †Goldingay, *HBT* 4/2, on liberationist hermeneutic).

[26] Thus in the light of deconstructionism †Fewell critiques the more formalist approaches to Ruth by Trible (in †*God and the Rhetoric of Sexuality*) and E. Fuchs (in †Yarbro Collins, pp. 117–136), while in the light of speech act theory †Lanser critiques both Trible's formalist approach to Gn. 2 – 3 (in the same volume) and †Bal's deconstructionist approach to Gn. 2 – 3, though †Lanser comes to a deconstructionist conclusion. †Jobling (2:17–43) includes a deconstructionist feminist study of Gn. 2 – 3 by a man.

4. The Old Testament as witness to Christ

On the 'fuller sense' (*sensus plenior*) see D. J. Moo in †Carson and Woodbridge, *Hermeneutics, Authority and Canon*, pages 175–211. For the English translation of *Goppelt on typology, see †Goppelt; on allegory, see †Whitman; on the way prophecy came to be read as essentially foreknowledge of the interpreter's own day, see †Barton, *Oracles of God*, especially pages 179–213; on 'Israel in the plan of God', see †Motyer.

5. The Old Testament as Scripture

For systematic critique of Childs' *Introduction to the Old Testament as Scripture*, see †Barr, *Holy Scripture*, and †Barton, *Reading the Old Testament*; also †Birch and others; †Kittel and others; †McEvenue. Childs illuminatingly draws attention to the shaping of individual OT books so as to enable them to 'function canonically', but does not quite prove his view that this is *uniquely* the stage at which they must be viewed theologically. He also seems to underestimate the significance of the historical context in which God's word and creative human insights emerged, of the tradition process, and of the actual historical events which are fundamental to the story of salvation. Admittedly it may be that such an assessment presupposes the traditional historical-critical paradigm, and takes insufficient account of the novelty of the new paradigm which Childs offers to Christian OT study.[27] Nevertheless, in my view it remains regrettable that his concern for a biblical theology which takes the whole canon seriously[28] became focused first on the use of the OT in the NT (see also Childs, *Exodus*) and then on a questionable preoccupation with the canonical shaping of individual books. See †Sanders for a different approach to canonical criticism.

†Westermann's *Theology* takes further his own attempt to work theologically with the shape of the canon, while †Brueggemann's *The Creative Word* attempts a canonical exposition which sees

[27] See †Fowl's illuminating comparison of Childs and Gadamer.

[28] See *Childs and section 1c above, pp. 29–37; Childs' †*Theology* does not seem to me a very satisfying working-out of this concern, since it tends to ignore key themes of the OT canon (*e.g.* the land) and stress ones not prominent in the canon (*e.g.* revelation).

Torah, Prophets and Writings as serving complementary functions in the education of Israel.

On 'The earliest OT interpretation', †Fishbane is a monumental and definitive survey of legal, haggadic, and prophetic (re)interpretation within the OT; while on 'The defining of the OT canon', †Beckwith is a monumental and definitive defence of the view that the Hebrew canon was settled by the mid-second century BC. On 'The interpretation of the OT as Scripture in NT times', †A. T. Hanson is a systematic account of NT use of the OT, with some consideration of what we make of it today.[29] More briefly and systematically on these topics, see †Mulder.

[29] See also M. Silva in †Carson and Woodbridge, *Scripture and Truth*, pp. 147–165; also †Neusner on midrash.

Supplementary bibliography

M. H. Abrams, *The Mirror and the Lamp* (New York: OUP, 1953).

R. Alter, *The Art of Biblical Narrative* (New York/London: Basic/Allen and Unwin, 1981).

R. Alter and F. Kermode, *The Literary Guide to the Bible* (Cambridge, MA/London: Harvard UP/Collins, 1987).

C. E. Armerding, *The Old Testament and Criticism* (Grand Rapids: Eerdmans, 1983).

D. Aukerman, *Darkening Valley* (New York: Seabury, 1981).

M. Bal, *Lethal Love* (Bloomington: Indiana UP, 1987).

S. Bar-Efrat, *Narrative Art in the Bible* (ET Sheffield: Sheffield Academic Press, 1989).

J. Barr, *The Scope and Authority of the Bible* (Explorations in Theology 7; London/Philadelphia: SCM/Westminster, 1980).

— *Holy Scripture: Canon, Authority, Criticism* (Philadelphia/Oxford: Westminster/OUP, 1983).

J. Barton, *Reading the Old Testament* (London/Philadelphia: DLT/Westminster, 1984.

— *Oracles of God* (London/Philadelphia: DLT/Westminster, 1986).

— 'Reading the Bible as literature', *LT* 1 (1987), pp. 135–153.

R. Bauckham, *The Bible in Politics* (London: SPCK, 1989).

R. Beckwith, *The Old Testament Canon of the New Testament Church and its Background in Early Judaism* (London: SPCK, 1985/Grand Rapids: Eerdmans, 1986).

A. Berlin, *Poetics and Interpretation of Biblical Narrative* (Sheffield: Almond, 1983).

B. C. Birch and others, reviews of Childs, *Introduction to the* OT *as Scripture* [with response by Childs], *HBT* 2 (1980), pp. 113–211.

— 'Old Testament theology: its task and future', *HBT* 6/1 (1984), pp. iii–ix, 1–80.

J. Blenkinsopp, 'Old Testament theology and the Jewish-Christian connection', JSOT 28 (1984), pp. 3–15.

W. Brueggemann, 'A convergence in recent Old Testament theologies', *JSOT* 18 (1980), pp. 2–18.

— *The Creative Word* (Philadelphia: Fortress, 1982).

— *The Message of the Psalms* (Minneapolis: Augsburg, 1984).

— *David's Truth in Israel's Imagination and Memory* (Philadelphia: Fortress, 1985).

— 'A shape for Old Testament theology', *CBQ* 47 (1985), pp. 28–46, 395–415.

— *Hope within History* (Atlanta: Knox, 1987).

D. A. Carson and J. D. Woodbridge (ed.), *Scripture and Truth* (Grand Rapids/Leicester: Zondervan/IVP, 1983).

— *Hermeneutics, Authority and Canon* (Grand Rapids/Leicester: Zondervan/IVP, 1986).

B. S. Childs, *Old Testament Theology in a Canonical Context* (London: SCM, 1985/Philadelphia: Fortress, 1986).

R. E. Clements, 'History and theology in biblical narrative', *HBT* 4/2 (1982), pp. 45–60.

L. W. Countryman, *Dirt, Greed and Sex* (Philadelphia: Fortress, 1988/London: SCM, 1989).

R. Detweiler (ed.), *Derrida and Biblical Studies* (Semeia 23; Chico, CA: Scholars, 1982).

— *Reader Response Approaches to Biblical and Secular Texts* (Semeia 31; Decatur, GA: Scholars, 1985).

S. J. De Vries, *The Achievements of Biblical Religion* (Lanham, MD/London: University Press of America, 1983).

W. J. Dumbrell, *Covenant and Creation* (Exeter: Paternoster, 1984/New York: Nelson, 1985).

W. Dyrness, *Themes in Old Testament Theology* (Exeter/Downers Grove, IL: Paternoster/IVP, 1979).

G. Elata-Alster and R. Salmon, 'The deconstruction of genre in the Book of Jonah', *LT* 3 (1989), pp. 40–60.

J. C. Exum (ed.), *Tragedy and Comedy in the Bible* (Semeia 32; Decatur, GA: Scholars, 1985).

D. N. Fewell, 'Feminist reading of the Hebrew Bible', *JSOT* 39 (1987), pp. 77–87.

M. Fishbane, *Biblical Interpretation in Ancient Israel* (Oxford/New York: OUP, 1985).

S. Fowl, 'The canonical approach of Brevard Childs', *ExpT* 96 (1984–85), pp. 173–175.

T. E. Fretheim, *The Suffering of God* (OBT 14; 1984).

N. Fuchs-Kreimer, 'Christian Old Testament theology: a time for new beginnings', *Journal of Ecumenical Studies* 18 (1981), pp. 76–92.

H. Gese, *Essays on Biblical Theology* (Minneapolis: Augsburg, 1981). [ET of *Zur biblischen Theologie*: see main bibliography.]

J. Goldingay, 'The hermeneutics of liberation theology', *HBT* 4/2 (1982), pp. 133–161.

— *Theological Diversity and the Authority of the Old Testament* (Grand Rapids: Eerdmans, 1987).

E. M. Good, *Irony in the Old Testament* (Philadelphia/London: Westminster/SPCK, 1965; ²Sheffield: Almond, 1981).

L. Goppelt, *Typos: The Typological Interpretation of the Old Testament in the New* (Grand Rapids: Eerdmans, 1982). [ET from German: see main bibliography.]

N. K. Gottwald, *The Tribes of Yahweh* (Maryknoll, NY: Orbis, 1979/ London: SCM, 1980).

— (ed.), *The Bible and Liberation* (Maryknoll, NY: Orbis, ²1983).

D. E. Gowan, *Reclaiming the Old Testament for the Christian Pulpit* (Atlanta: Knox, 1980/Edinburgh: Clark, 1981).

G. Green (ed.), *Scriptural Authority and Narrative Interpretation* (Hans Frei Festschrift; Philadelphia: Fortress, 1987).

D. C. Greenwood, *Structuralism and the Biblical Text* (Berlin/New York: Mouton, 1985).

S. Greidanus, *The Modern Preacher and the Ancient Text* (Grand Rapids/ Leicester: Eerdmans/IVP, 1988).

K. R. R. Gros Louis and others (eds.), *Literary Interpretations of Biblical Narratives* (2 vols.; Nashville: Abingdon, 1974 and 1982).

D. M. Gunn, *The Story of King David* (Sheffield: JSOT, 1978).

— *The Fate of King Saul* (Sheffield: JSOT, 1980).

— 'New directions in the study of biblical Hebrew narrative', *JSOT* 39 (1987), pp. 65–75.

G. Gutiérrez, *On Job* (ET Maryknoll, NY: Orbis, 1987).

A. T. Hanson, *The Living Utterances of God* (London: DLT, 1983).

P. D. Hanson, *The Diversity of Scripture* (OBT 11; 1982).

G. F. Hasel, 'A decade of Old Testament theology', *ZAW* 93 (1981), pp. 165–183.

— 'Biblical theology', *HBT* 4/1 (1982), pp. 61–93.

— 'Major recent issues in Old Testament theology 1978–1983', *JSOT* 31 (1985), pp. 31–53.

J. H. Hayes and F. C. Prussner, *Old Testament Theology: Its History and Development* (Atlanta/London: Knox/SCM, 1985).

F. Hesse, 'Die Israelfrage in neuren Entwürfen Biblischer Theologie', *KD* 27 (1981), pp. 180–197.

B. van Iersel and A. Weiler, *Exodus: A Lasting Paradigm* (Concilium 189; 1987).

D. Jobling, *The Sense of Biblical Narrative* (2 vols.; Sheffield: JSOT, 1978 [²1986] and 1986).

W. C. Kaiser, *Towards Old Testament Ethics* (Grand Rapids: Zondervan, 1983).

B. Kittel and others, reviews of Childs, *Introduction to the* OT *as Scripture* [with response by Childs], *JSOT* 16 (1980), pp. 2–60.

R. Knierim, 'Cosmos and history in Israel's theology', *HBT* 3 (1981), pp. 59–123.

H.-J. Kraus, *Systematische Theologie im Kontext biblischer Geschichte und Eschatologie* (Neukirchen: Neukirchener, 1983).

J. Kugel [with response by A. Berlin], 'On the Bible and literary criticism', *Prooftexts* 1 (1981), pp. 217–236; 2 (1982), pp. 323–332.

S. S. Lanser, '(Feminist) criticism in the garden: inferring Genesis 2 – 3', in †H. C. White, pp. 67–84.

B. C. Lategan and W. S. Vorster, *Text and Reality* (Philadelphia: Fortress, 1985).

J. D. Levenson, 'The theologies of commandment in biblical Israel', *HTR* 73 (1980), pp. 17–33.

— *Sinai and Zion* (Minneapolis: Winston, 1985).

J. Licht, *Storytelling in the Bible* (Jerusalem: Magnes, 1978).

N. Lohfink, *Great Themes from the Old Testament* (ET Chicago: Franciscan Herald, 1981/Edinburgh: Clark, 1982).

B. O. Long (ed.), *Images of Man and God* (Sheffield: Almond, 1981).

T. Longman III, *Literary Approaches to Biblical Interpretation* (Grand Rapids: Zondervan, 1987/Leicester: IVP, 1989).

R. Lundin, A. C. Thiselton, and C. Walhout, *The Responsibility of Hermeneutics* (Grand Rapids/Exeter: Eerdmans/Paternoster, 1985).

T. E. McComiskey, *The Covenants of Promise* (Grand Rapids: Baker, 1985/Leicester: IVP, 1987).

S. E. McEvenue, 'The Old Testament, scripture or theology?', *Interpretation* 35 (1981), pp. 229–242.

E. V. McKnight, *Meaning in Texts* (Philadephia: Fortress, 1978).

— *The Bible and the Reader* (Philadelphia: Fortress, 1985).

E. A. Martens, *Plot and Purpose in the Old Testament* (Leicester: IVP, 1981) = *God's Design* (Grand Rapids: Baker, 1981).

P. D. Miscall, *The Workings of Old Testament Narrative* (Philadelphia: Fortress, 1983).

— *1 Samuel* (Bloomington: Indiana UP, 1986).

S. Motyer, *Israel in the Plan of God* (Leicester: IVP, 1989).

M. J. Mulder (ed.), *Mikra* (Philadelphia: Fortress, 1988).

J. Neusner, *What is Midrash?* (Philadelphia: Fortress, 1987).

E. W. Nicholson, *God and his People: Covenant and Theology in the Old Testament* (Oxford/New York: OUP, 1986).

M. Oeming, 'Bedeutung und Funktionen von "Fiktionen" in der alttestamentlichen Geschichtsschreibung', *EvT* 44 (1984), pp. 254–266.

— *Gesamtbiblische Theologien der Gegenwart: Das Verhältnis von AT und NT in der hermeneutischen Diskussion seit Gerhard von Rad* (Stuttgart: Kohlhammer, 1985; ²1987).

D. Patrick, *The Rendering of God in the Old Testament* (OBT 10; 1981).

— *Old Testament Law* (Atlanta: Knox, 1985/London: SCM, 1986).

L. M. Poland, *Literary Criticism and Biblical Hermeneutics* (Chico, CA: Scholars, 1985).

S. Prickett, *Words and The Word* (Cambridge/New York: CUP, 1986).

G. W. Ramsey, *The Quest for the Historical Israel* (Atlanta: Knox, 1981/London: SCM, 1982).

W. L. Reed, 'A poetics of the Bible', *LT* 1 (1987), pp. 154–166.

H. Graf Reventlow, *Problems of Old Testament Theology in the Twentieth Century* (ET London/Philadelphia: SCM/Fortress, 1985).

— *Problems of Biblical Theology in the Twentieth Century* (ET London/Philadelphia: SCM/Fortress, 1986).

— 'Zur Theologie des Alten Testaments', *TR* 52 (1987), pp. 221–267.

L. M. Russell (ed.), *Feminist Interpretation of the Bible* (Philadelphia/ Oxford: Westminster/Blackwell, 1985).

L. Ryken, *How to Read the Bible as Literature* (Grand Rapids: Zondervan, 1984).

J. A. Sanders, *Canon and Community* (Philadelphia: Fortress, 1984).

— *From Sacred Story to Sacred Text* (Philadelphia: Fortress, 1987). [Mostly reprints articles listed in main bibliography.]

— 'First Testament and Second', *BTB* 17 (1987), pp. 47–49.

F. A. Schaeffer, *The God Who is There* (Chicago/London: IVP/Hodder, 1968).

H. Schmid, 'Erwägungen zur christlichen Hermeneutik des Alten Testament unter Beachtung der "bleibenden Erwählung Israels"', *Judaica* 37 (1981), pp. 16–30.

E. Schüssler Fiorenza, *Bread not Stone* (Boston: Beacon, 1984).

H. Seebass, *Der Gott der ganzen Bibel* (Freiburg: Herder, 1982).

O. H. Steck, *World and Environment* (ET Nashville: Abingdon, 1980).

M. Sternberg, *The Poetics of Biblical Narrative* (Bloomington: Indiana UP, 1985).

W. M. Swartley, *Slavery, Sabbath, War, and Women* (Scottdale, PA: Herald, 1983).

J. G. Tambasco, 'The Bible and nuclear war', *BTB* 13 (1983), pp. 75–81.

S. Terrien, 'Biblical theology: the Old Testament (1970–1984)', *BTB* 15 (1985), pp. 127–135.

M. A. Tolbert (ed.), *The Bible and Feminist Hermeneutics* (Semeia 28; Chico, CA: Scholars, 1983).

P. Trible, *God and the Rhetoric of Sexuality* (OBT 2; 1978).

— *Texts of Terror* (OBT 13, 1984).

— (ed.) 'The effects of women's studies on biblical studies', *JSOT* 22 (1982), pp. 3–71.

M. Tsevat, 'Theology of the Old Testament – a Jewish view' [with a response by B. W. Anderson], *HBT* 8/2 (1986), pp. 33–59.

J. Van Seters, *In Search of History* (New Haven/London: Yale UP, 1983).

B. G. Webb, *The Book of the Judges* (Sheffield: JSOT, 1987).

C. Westermann, *Elements of Old Testament Theology* (ET Atlanta: Knox, 1982).

H. C. White (ed.), *Speech Act Theory and Biblical Criticism* (Semeia 41; Decatur, GA: Scholars, 1988).

J. Whitman, *Allegory* (Oxford/New York: OUP, 1987).

H. W. Wolff, *Old Testament and Christian Preaching* (ET Philadelphia: Fortress, 1986).

C. J. H. Wright, *Living as the People of God* (Leicester: IVP, 1983) = *An Eye for an Eye* (Downers Grove, IL: IVP, 1983).

T. R. Wright, *Theology and Literature* (Oxford/New York: Blackwell, 1988).

A. Yarbro Collins (ed.), *Feminist Perspectives on Biblical Scholarship* (Chico, CA: Scholars, 1985).

Index